Both THOMAS D. YAWKEY, Ph.D., and KENNETH C. JONES, Ph.D., teach courses on early childhood education at Pennsylvania State University. In addition, Mr. Yawkey is also a researcher of pretend play among young children and the author of several books. Mr. Jones is involved in parental training and family therapy.

Caring

ACTIVITIES TO TEACH THE YOUNG CHILD TO CARE FOR OTHERS

Thomas D. Yawkey

Kenneth C. Jones

The Pennsylvania State University

A SPECTRUM BOOK

Prentice-Hall, Inc., Englewood Cliffs, New Jersey 07632

Library of Congress Cataloging in Publication Data

Yawkey, Thomas D.
    Caring: activities to teach the young child to
care for others.

    "A Spectrum Book."
    Bibliography: p.
    Includes index.
    1. Child rearing.   2. Moral education.   3. Al-
truism.   I. Jones, Kenneth C.   II. Title
HQ769.Y38   649'.7   82-3760
                                   AACR2

This Spectrum Book is available to businesses and organizations at a special discount when ordered in large quantities. For information contact Prentice-Hall, Inc., General Publishing Division, Special Sales, Englewood Cliffs, N.J. 07632

10   9   8   7   6   5   4   3   2   1

Printed in the United States of America

ISBN 0-13-114827-3

ISBN 0-13-114835-4 {PBK.}

Prentice-Hall International, Inc., *London*
Prentice-Hall of Australia Pty. Limited, *Sydney*
Prentice-Hall Canada, Inc., *Toronto*
Prentice-Hall of India Private Limited, *New Delhi*
Prentice-Hall of Japan, Inc., *Tokyo*
Prentice-Hall of Southeast Asia Pte. Ltd., *Singapore*
Whitehall Books Limited, Wellington, *New Zealand*

Dedicated in memoriam to:

Katherine Yawkey

who, by example, taught us—
her sons, Tom and Dan—
CARING.

Contents

Foreword

"Education is the art/science of teaching people how to become warm, loving human beings," said noted anthropologist Ashley Montagu.*

Yawkey and Jones show us how. Moreover, as is Montagu, Yawkey and Jones are fully cognizant that the process of becoming warm, loving human beings is not limited to either the classroom or the family. Most volumes on care-giving for young children are written exclusively for either parents or extra-familial care-givers or teachers, suggesting that the process must be substantively different in different settings. This volume cracks through the environmental and superficial differences that exist among these different caregiving situations, recognizing in concrete ways that teaching is done by parents and that much nurturing must be provided by educators. Yawkey and Jones deal with the generic business of communicating caring for children in any type of relationship—even those of children with other children.

What is most exciting about this comprehensive work is the emphasis on concrete methods of self-esteem promotion. The desire to stimulate cognitive growth and competencies is so important to all of us that books for teachers and parents tend to concentrate on narrow

*Ashley Montagu, *Becoming Human in the Social World of Tomorrow*, Address to the conference on "Becoming Truly Human" (Institute for Child Study, University of Maryland, October 1980).

areas of skill building in children, and deal with self-esteem as a separate, strictly affective concern. Yawkey and Jones manage to attend to this important area, along with others, to go far beyond mere cognitive stimulation.

Methods of promoting all of these worthy goals are clearly spelled out. All of the approaches described are based on sound knowledge of children's development of self-esteem, peer, and adult relationships. But readers are not expected to follow merely a list of procedures. Sound rationales for the methods are included so that readers have the principles behind the procedures right in the same volume, thus enriching their ability to put them into practice.

This volume should move care-givers toward the much idealized but rarely realized goal of active consideration of the "whole child." In their articulation of methods sensitive to the personal and inter-personal contexts in which developmental tasks must be accomplished, Yawkey and Jones have managed to provide us with a means of moving closer to a holistic education of the person, not merely of the mind.

Louise F. Guerney
The Pennsylvania State University
University Park, Pennsylvania

Preface

Caring is for teachers, for parents, and for anyone involved in raising and teaching youngsters. The book:

- shows by numerous examples and activities that caring for children means nurturing, role-taking, considering, expectations, an awareness of self, and self-esteem.
- explains in clear ways how to use and develop caring actions and activities in the classroom and in the home.
- describes a model for developing caring and gives ways of using and modifying it in the home, the classroom, the supermarket, friends' homes, and other situations.
- illustrates adults' caring-in-action for their youngsters in single-parent families and for those who are handicapped or who have other special problems.
- moves the reader through its pages in a meaningful and easy way, using words, phrases, and activities that are easily put into thought and action.
- provides an extensive set of suggestions for additional readings in each of the aspects of caring covered in the text.

Overall, two organizational techniques are used. One is the "movement" from the general to the specific. The other is the format or structure in each of the chapters (except the last one on "Caring: Useful Resources").

In the "movement" from general to specific, the early sections of the book acquaint the parent and professional educator with caring and its importance. Various aspects of caring, such as nurturing and considering, are then introduced. Toward the latter portion of the text, the focus is on caring-in-action, particularly on such special situations as those of the handicapped and single-parent families. This progression from general to specific makes it easy for readers to absorb, understand, and apply the activities in the book.

The format or structure of the chapters is also key to helping readers understand and use the activities. Each chapter begins with a succinct introduction that points out the importance of the components of caring processes that follow. Then, sample activities offer meaningful ways to apply caring ideas with youngsters. Each activity contains sections on materials, procedures, and variations. Following the activities, the chapter ends with a section called "Tips." This section gives meaningful and easy-to-read strategies for guiding youngsters through the activities. It may also suggest techniques to modify them to fit younger and older children. The layout of the activities chapters has been specially designed to make this format self-evident.

As they read and use the ideas in the book, teachers and parents will come to realize that caring and interacting are primary components of sound and healthful growth for both children *and* adults. To that successful end . . . "Best wishes!"

THOMAS D. YAWKEY
KENNETH C. JONES

The Pennsylvania State University
University Park, Pennsylvania

Caring

LEARNING AND COMMUNICATING

Our child rearing and educational goals have changed with the changing needs of our society. At its more primitive level society was concerned with transmitting the basic skills required for physical survival. Gradually society has shifted its focus to cognitive and academic development.

Yet these narrow traditional emphases on first the physical and then the academic disciplines are inadequate by themselves, and they cannot be separated from the socio-emotional, affective development of young children. Their obvious inadequacy is reflected in the statistics on unemployment, suicide, crime, mental illness, family disorganization, drug use, and school and social dropouts.

If we are to be effective in our childrearing and teaching practices, we must be capable of living lives of caring, of humaneness, and of meaning. To do so, parents and teachers must be concerned with the socio-emotional, affective development of children. The most effective learning processes are cues that enable children to acquire or to develop skills and abilities needed to solve their *own* motor, cognitive, and affective problems. Hence total human development must be the goal of childrearing and teaching.

A very important part of the child's total development is caring. Young children are basically egocentric. So the natural caring they exhibit is caring about themselves. It is difficult for them to understand why they can't have what they want when they want it. Being in a very

egocentric stage of development, young children are also unable to see things from the perspective of another. Yet the ability to do so is necessary to develop empathy and sympathy for others, which are both essential in showing that they do care.

Although many factors influence the growth and development during a child's early years, the foremost, many agree, is the family. Our complex society has brought about many changes in our child-rearing practices, which have made it necessary for parents and teachers to stress the interrelationship of local and worldwide communication at a much earlier age than in the past. These changes have also given rise to the growing need for coordination between home childrearing practices and the teaching techniques used in nurseries, kindergartens, and primary schools. Perhaps most important, for our children to develop caring attitudes and skills in communication, our responsibility is not only to discuss, to clarify, and to communicate our own attitudes, but also to model behaviors that communicate caring to children.

Caring in general—defined by the dictionary as, "To have a strong feeling or opinion; be concerned or interested"—encompasses the total environment of our world. People, objects, and nature are all aspects of our world that deserve to be cared for. From the perspective of this chapter, caring is an internal, cognitive activity involving a mental process that centers around the relationships children have with other people and with the objects in their world. The main focus of this chapter is the role played by these interpersonal relationships during the early years. In sum, the following activities have been designed to facilitate children's understanding of themselves and of others, as well as to develop skills for the communication of their understanding.

While doing these activities, keep in mind that they are for you and the child to share. Take the role of friend or participant rather than that of teacher.

[1] The communication of caring is a skill that must be developed. Try some of the following activities to refine your own and your children's effectiveness in communication.

ACTIVITY TITLE **Feelings in Favorite Stories**

MATERIALS The only materials needed to complete this activity on the sensitivity of feelings is a copy of one of the child's favorite stories.

PROCEDURES Begin this activity by reading the story to the child. After reading the story, discuss how the characters felt or how the child thinks he or she would have felt in that situation.

Explain that you are going to read the story over and change some of the things that happen in it. While reading the story this time, stop after the changed parts and ask the child how the characters felt or how he or she would have felt in that situation. Then ask the child what was different in the story that made a difference in how he or she felt.

Examples:

1. When Goldilocks is lost in the forest, she never finds anything to eat.
2. When Little Red Riding Hood reaches Grandmother's, the wolf jumps out of the bed and bites her arm off. She runs from the house and has to spend three weeks in the hospital.
3. When Prince Charming comes to Cinderella's house, no one is home. So he goes back to his castle and is never able to find the girl who lost the shoe.

VARIATION Use pictures of people in different situations to discuss how they must be feeling. Then ask the child to describe the same situation with a change that would cause very different feelings.

Examples:

1. A picture of a boy with a fishing pole and a big fish in his hand. Change the situation to show the boy with the pole and the fish swimming away.
2. Show a farmer looking out over a very green garden and smiling. Change the picture to show a barren field or dried-out plants in the garden.

You may need to suggest a few changes before the child "gets the hang of it." Discuss the difference in feelings and how the differences are caused.

ACTIVITY TITLE Mad and Angry

MATERIALS To complete this activity on anger, you need paper plates, markers, scissors, and string.

PROCEDURES Anger is an emotion that, as adults, we usually have difficulty in letting a child express. So this activity is most appropriate soon after an incident where the child has confronted a situation that has made him very angry. After the child has "gotten over" the anger, talk to him about how it felt.

Then, since anger is as difficult for the child to deal with as it is for us, invite him to make a mask of the most angry face he can think of. After the mask is completed, role play the same situation that recently occurred with the child wearing the mask. This way the child can try out new ways to deal with the situation without being himself.

After you and the child are satisfied with the extent of the role play, discuss with him the actual physical feelings of the anger. Often people get red in the face, or their faces feel hot. They may also get a tightness in the chest and/or a feeling of distress in the stomach. Talk about how you can feel these sensations coming on, and discuss ways to prevent the feelings from becoming overpowering.

VARIATION In the classroom provide commercial masks or the time to make masks to represent different feelings. Set up an area where children can take part in role play activities to express these emotions. Let them share what feelings the masks represent.

ACTIVITY TITLE	"Me" Badge

MATERIALS To complete this very personal "me" badge, the child will need a piece of thin cardboard, markers, glue, and a toy catalog.

PROCEDURES This activity helps to sensitize children to their own feelings and preferences. First, explain to the child that everyone is different and feels differently about many things. Then cut a distinctive shape out of the cardboard and divide it into four areas. Tell the child that each area is for a special like or feeling that she has. You may make suggestions as to the kind of things to include. For instance, one area could be for her favorite food, color, toy, or whatever. Another could be for her favorite pastime—fishing, painting, playing with toys or tools, and so on. Another could be for an expression of how she feels right now or how she feels when she's outside.

The idea is for her to come to the understanding that we are all different, that we feel different, and that we have our own personal preferences. A good idea is to do this activity along with the child, but take care to pace yourself so that you do not "coach" her into what she *should* put on her badge.

VARIATION When working with groups, it's better to assign topics for each area rather than leave it to personal choice. This allows everyone to "read" them.

ACTIVITY TITLE International Road Signs

MATERIALS To complete this activity, which is designed to stress the use of symbols for communication, you will need several squares (6 x 8") of cardboard or a similar material, a red and black marker, a straightedge, and scissors. It is useful also to have a copy of the international road signs, which are available at local police or highway patrol stations.

PROCEDURES Either draw the international signs, or cut and paste the ones from the highway patrol station on the cardboard. The pictures are clear and self-explanatory, but let the child explain the signs while you clarify them.

Discuss the need for international signs, that is, clarity, non-English-speaking readers, quick reference.

After discussing these uses, you and the youngster together then design some useful signs for your home or neighborhood. These might be reminders to flush the toilet, turn off the light, put dirty clothes in a basket or hamper, watch for children, and so on.

VARIATION Take a drive with the youngster. Locate all of the international signs you can. Be sure to drive on the highway as well as in a downtown area. Lead the discussion to bring out all the reasons for having these signs, and discuss why they are located where they are (such as no passing, no parking, pass on left only).

5

ACTIVITY TITLE   Family Role Plays

MATERIALS   To complete this activity on understanding the roles of various family members, you need either a family photograph album containing a variety of family members or pictures of families cut from magazines.

PROCEDURES   Look through the pictures with the child identifying each person (such as Mother, Father, Grandmother, Uncle Bert, and so on). After a brief discussion of what is happening in the pictures, let the child know the persons' relationships to him and what other roles they have in life: their jobs, hobbies, avocations, and the like. Extend the discussion to include things that those persons do within the family structure like sending birthday cards, helping with illnesses, lending money, or being a listener and advisor. If necessary, fall back on the stereotyped roles for each family member.

Now have the child select a family member and a role that he is interested in. Together you and the child design a role play to act out. As many family members as possible should participate. The role play could involve all members of the family displaying excitement over the forthcoming visit and making all the preparations.

For example, the child may choose to be the Grandmother, playing the role of Grandmother coming to visit. Have the child exit and make an entrance as Grandmother. Everyone makes a fuss over how happy they are to see "her" and how much they have missed "her." Lots of hugs and kisses and excitement over the visit! Now end this part of the role play and have everyone discuss the feelings they experienced.

Then have everyone re-enter their roles. When the child enters this time, as Grandmother, he will face unsmiling faces, a passing hug, and problems from each family member. The Mother could be concerned over money problems, and the other children could be sad over losing a friend. They all want Grandmother to solve their problems or at least be a listener. Now discuss everyone's feelings, especially the difference in Grandmother's feelings during the two role plays.

A good culmination of this activity is to send a card or letter to the chosen family members.

VARIATION   Using paper and markers, make a "family tree" of the family members that the child knows and provide listings of the variety of roles each member fills.

Discuss the way each member could feel in each role. How does the child feel about them?

ACTIVITY TITLE   Facial Communication

MATERIALS   No materials are needed for this activity.

PROCEDURES   Begin by making faces (funny, sad, angry, happy, and so on) and talking about each of them. Talk with your child about how the way we look often communicates as much as what we say. Practice some sincere
6   statements with appropriate facial expressions. For example, say, "I

sure missed you today," accompanied by a soft expression. Then, with a stern and angry expression, say, "I told you not to do that again!" Now have the child try some very expressive statements with the correct facial expressions.

To emphasize the effect of facial expressions on communication, the next step is to practice statements while showing incongruous expressions. With a very stern, angry expression try saying, "I love you very much." Or with a very soft look, be very critical.

VARIATION

Do the same activity using contrasting tones of voice as well as expressions. The idea is to show clearly that how you say something, the way you look while saying something, and the things you are saying all affect the way you communicate.

ACTIVITY TITLE

I Messages

MATERIALS

All that is needed to complete this introspective communication activity is paper and pen. A tape recorder is useful but not necessary.

PROCEDURES

Often, when we speak to a child, we intend to teach appropriate behaviors based on health or accepted societal norms. Examples are: "Don't run in the street . . . Use correct table manners . . . Nice young people don't use words like that." These statements imply a judgment of right and wrong or of the appropriateness of the actions in the situation.

Other times when we speak to children, especially in a reprimand or in a directive manner, we address the child from the viewpoint of our own personal orientation or of our preference of behavior. These could be exemplified by "Don't make so much noise," "Be sure to keep your toothbrush in the holder," or any other direction you must give the child based on your own personal preferences.

These are opportunities to use *I-Messages*. The I-Message communicates to the child that you are not passing judgment or telling her what is right and wrong, but rather that you are letting her know how *you* feel about something. Common forms of I-Messages are:

I feel _____. When you do _____, I feel. I like it when you _____. I don't like it when _____. It makes me feel _____ when _____.

This very personalized form of communication affects the outcome of the interaction with children. It communicates very differently from: "It's bad to _____." "Don't do that!" "It's not nice to _____."

Think through or listen to a recording of a day or of a particular incident, and list all the judgment-laden statements explicit or implied that you have made. Write down these statements in an I-Message format, and say them out loud. Do you feel different? Do they communicate your feelings more effectively? Practice this with children and note the difference in their reaction. This approach not only shows consideration for them but fosters consideration in them for you and your feelings.

Use the tape recorder or list to initiate a discussion of I-Messages with the children. Pair off the participants and practice I-Messages. Throughout the day, take note of I-Messages and discuss the effect.

ACTIVITY TITLE ## People of Many Hats

MATERIALS To do this activity on the many roles that people fill, you need a collection of hats (firefighter, nurse, sailor, businessperson, baseball player, hard hat, fancy ladies' hats, and so on). If a variety of actual hats are not available, a single hat (even a newspaper hat) and pictures of other hats will do for pretending.

PROCEDURES Begin the activity by looking at, discussing, and playing with the hats or pictures. Most of the hats will identify the roles of the wearers, and some will allow several descriptions of roles. After the child is familiar with the hats, help him develop a role play that will involve wearing several of the hats.

Many role plays can involve several roles. For example, he could be a *baseball* player who is also a volunteer *firefighter* and a *business manager* in the off season. As you and the child act out these roles, you would change hats for the appropriate roles. Another example could be a *nurse* who joined the *navy*. This way the child would wear the nurse cap at the hospital, the sailor cap at official navy functions, and a dress hat for a date.

VARIATION The hats or pictures can be displayed at a table or along a bulletin board, and the children can use them for stimulation in a creative writing activity.

ACTIVITY TITLE ## Look at Me!

MATERIALS No materials are needed for this parental awareness activity. However, you might like to have pencil and paper handy.

PROCEDURES "Look at me!" is a common cry on the playground and in the home. Children want attention and recognition paid to what they do. Behavioral learning theory tells us that when an action is positively rewarded (that is, when it gets attention), the action will be repeated. Conversely if the action is not rewarded, then it will not be repeated. From a common sense point of view, this theory seems true.

As parents and teachers, one of our goals is to foster appropriate behaviors and to get rid of inappropriate ones. This activity helps to sensitize you to the effects you have just by giving attention.

Take note of the kinds of things the child does during a day that draw your attention. Your "attention" might take the form of asking for help, giving help unasked, giving direction and information, and correcting inappropriate behaviors (such as playing with electric plugs, ash trays, playing in the streets, noisy activities, and so on).

Try to see how many negative behaviors draw your attention, as compared to positive ones. Your goal is to make the attention you pay to positive behavior far outweigh the attention you give to negative behaviors.

Think about this in terms of adults as well!

VARIATION   Using the paper and pencil, keep a tally for a week of the number of times that you interact with the child during a day about positive and negative behaviors. At the end of the week, chart these frequencies of interaction. Is there a day that shows extremely low or high interaction? Was this due to you, the child or the day?

ACTIVITY TITLE   Reflecting Action and Intent

MATERIALS   No materials are needed to complete this activity on communication.

PROCEDURES   For children to share their caring, feelings, and ideas, they must feel accepted. For a child to extend or to elaborate feelings, it is important that we "feed back" an understanding of what she is saying or doing. It is frustrating to continue telling someone something if you can't tell whether they understand or are even listening. Like I-Messages, this activity helps parents and teachers to establish that climate of acceptance that is necessary.

Reflecting actions and intents represent two levels of communication. Both convey an understanding of the child. Reflecting action is a lower-level skill and easy to master. Basically it is just a verbal statement of what the child is doing. Reflecting interest is a much higher level of communication, and practice is necessary to perfect this technique.

The following are two situations with examples of reflecting actions and intent.

The child is looking very intently at a candy dish, then traces the outside of the dish with a finger. To reflect the action, you could say, "You're looking at the candy bowl." The reflection of interest might be, "Ah, you would like to have some candy."

In this instance you could feel relatively confident of the intent. But the following situation is not as easy to interpret.

You are putting the child down for a nap. She points to the clock and says, "That clock is tic, tic, ticking. It takes over my mind!"

A reflection of the action or statement might be, "That ticking is so loud that it's all you can think about." This would show understanding. A reflection of intent could be, "That clock is so loud that you wish I would take it away." Although this is very much a statement of intent, it may or may not be correct: She may like the ticking. If the child is comfortable with you, she will correct you when you are wrong. If the child is not secure with you, she will not correct you and feel that you do not understand. It is important not to infer intent if it isn't clear. By using reflection you allow the child to become secure with you and to express herself more fully.

Try these reflections with adults for practice. Adults generally have much more refined skills of communication, thus making it easier. The reactions you get from adults are always interesting.

9

Try this activity in dealing with questions. When a child asks a question, don't give an answer. Instead, respond with, "You would like to know _____." When she asks again, say something like, "You *really* want to know _____." Continue this as long as possible without frustrating or angering the child. Often she knows the answer or doesn't really care. This response also leads the child to discover the answers for herself.

[2] Learning to care is important for both children and adults. The following activities center around learning to care for self, for others, for material objects, and for the community.

ACTIVITY TITLE **Small Spaces**

MATERIALS This activity, which is designed to establish a secure place for the child to share feelings and ideas, requires a large box (such as a stove or refrigerator box) or a sheet. You will also need paper scraps, markers, tape, and scissors.

PROCEDURES Children feel very safe in a closed, secure environment. You often find they have a favorite place under a bed or desk, behind a curtain, or in a hollow between some bushes. Most of us had special places like these as we grew up. We don't want to take away the child's private space, but we can help to establish a special place to share with him.

Choose a place where the child enjoys playing in a normal way. Either the bedroom, backyard, playroom, or any place where the child spends lots of time playing. Bring out the box or sheet, and tell the child you would like to make a special place to share with him. (The sheet works well because it can be taken out and put away easily.) You and the child decorate the special place any way you wish, making sure that both of you contribute to the decor. If using the box you need to cut a door and maybe a window. The sheet can be draped over the back of a couch, over the bed, or over chairs.

Initiate this special place by sitting quietly with the child for a few minutes. Let the child set the tone of the special place and let the space be for him.

Later you can invite the child to share the space and lead a discussion of how it feels to have that private space, that security, and that control.

VARIATION Group situations often preclude any sense of privacy for children. In your class, provide a decorated box or hide-away. Use an old throw rug or carpet scraps and possibly a pillow to add that touch of comfort and home-like quality.

To introduce this new addition to the class, lead a group discussion on privacy and how we all need to be alone sometimes. Also clearly state ground rules. Depending on the situation, your ground rules could include, only one person at a time, a limit of fifteen minutes, keeping it a quiet place, using it only during "free time," and so on. Another approach to ground rules is to say, "Use the special

10

space any way you like, being careful to consider all our needs. If there is any question, I'll help."

You can change the ground rules as you feel necessary. After many children have had a chance to use this space, discuss the experiences and elicit new ideas for its use.

ACTIVITY TITLE **Silent TV**

MATERIALS   To complete this activity on reading people's feelings, you will need a television, paper, pencils, and a TV program guide.

PROCEDURES   Have your child choose a television program that she enjoys. Make sure it is not an animated show.

After watching the first part of the show, suggest that you play a game together. Turn the sound completely off. Now choose either one character for each of you or the same character for both of you. As you watch the silent show, describe the feeling the character may be having by talking about the character's behaviors. Write the essential words to describe that character's feelings and the role in the show: angry, happy, sad . . . brother, father, daughter, good guy, bad guy, victim, villain, and so on. Then use these few words as an accuracy check when you turn the sound back on to listen to the second part. If you've really enjoyed this game, try watching only the first third of a show silently. Then check your perceptions for the characters by listening for a while, and again turn the sound off. Now predicting the ending of the show can be fun.

VARIATION   For younger children, the time periods must be short. Watch TV with sound for the first fifteen minutes, then alternately change from silent to sound two or three times for five minutes each.

It is also useful to provide puppets for younger children to use in acting out their character's role.

ACTIVITY TITLE   **Stroking**

MATERIALS   To do this very physical activity, all you need is body powder or oil.

PROCEDURES   Young children are very physical creatures. Often touching is a primary means of communication for them.

Choose a quiet time, a nap period, the period right before bed, or TV time. Suggest that the two of you take turns making each other feel good.

Begin by using a little powder to rub the child's arms and hands. As you work your way up her arms, talk about what the skin feels like and how it feels to be stroking her. If you and the child are not body conscious, continue to lightly stroke the entire body with very soothing motions. If body shyness prohibits doing so, then concentrate on the arms, legs, and neck.

When you are finished, change positions and ask the child to describe the same feelings and sensations.

VARIATION	To do this in the classroom or with groups, pair the children off and limit the stroking to hands and feet. For closure, have a group discussion of how it felt to stroke and to be stroked.

ACTIVITY TITLE	A Web of Significant Others
MATERIALS	This activity on the recognition of important adults in the child's life requires that you have a set of magic markers of different colors, large sheets of paper or cardboard, scissors, and glue or tape.
PROCEDURES	Elicit from the child or children the names of all the adults that they feel are important to them. These people are usually mothers, fathers, teachers, aunts and uncles, siblings, and other close ones. You might want to use just these, or you may increase the list by you adding other adults that you feel are important to the child. When you have a list that you and the child are satisfied with, cut a number of shapes to represent the important persons and put their names on the shapes.
	Paste the shapes on the large sheet of paper and draw lines to interconnect them to show the relationship between each of them and the child. You might place a picture of the child or a shape with his name on it in the center and space the other pictures around it. Connect each picture to the child's picture with lines of different colors to form a Web of Significant Others.
VARIATION	Rather than spacing the pictures around the child, let the child make a collage placing the adults with the most importance to him in prominent positions close to his own name or picture. Provide a time and audience for the child to explain the arrangement and to share how the adults pictured are important to him.

ACTIVITY TITLE	Walking in Trust
MATERALS	To complete this activity on trusting others, you need blindfolds and a safe place to walk. Your neighborhood or local park—even in your own backyard—may provide a good place.
PROCEDURES	Begin this activity by talking about the people in your life that you can really trust. Have the children share the people they feel they can trust, too. Explain that sometimes it's difficult to trust someone until you have given them a chance to be trustworthy. Tell them that this game is to let them feel what it's like to be trusting and to be trusted.
	Pair the children off or pair a child with an adult. Either by drawing a card or by choice, have one of the pair put on the blindfold. Instruct the pair that the person without the blindfold is the leader, and the blindfolded person must follow the directions of the leader.
	Allow about fifteen minutes for the pairs to move around the designated area talking about what they are sensing, feeling objects in the environment, and judging where they are. Announce that the fifteen minutes are up, and let the participants change roles.
	End this activity with a discussion of how it felt to be in both roles

and how you feel now about the person that was paired with you. Have you gained or lost any trust for that person?

VARIATION
In a limited space, you can do this same activity as a "falling" activity. Using pairs or trios, blindfold one participant and ask her to relax and slowly fall into the arms of the other two participants. You will find that many children are not trusting enough to actually let themselves fall into the arms of another person. This really opens up the discussion on whom you do trust and why you trust them.

ACTIVITY TITLE
The Sunday Newspaper

MATERIALS
To do this traditional family activity, you will need a Sunday newspaper with cartoons, white paper, a black ink pen, scissors, and tape.

PROCEDURES
This activity can actually be done with any newspaper comic, but the Sunday funnies are usually in color and Sundays are usually good for finding a quiet time to do things.

Sit very close to your child and read the comics together. If the child can read, you can take turns reading. If the child is a pre-reader, allow him to "read" the pictures and then you may read the words aloud.

Find some comic strips that concern families doing things, some school happenings, or any topical area you would like to discuss. While looking at the comics and reading them, talk about how they are similar to your family or experience. A good way is to say something like, "That reminds me of _____." Or, "Do you remember that time _____?"

Take out the other materials and cut some cartoon word balloon shapes out of the paper. Using the pen, write some dialog, based on the incident you remembered in the balloons. These are taped over the cartoon balloons.

During this process, lead the discussion toward the feelings of the recalled experience and how it feels to be talking about it now. This shared time together is important to the "belonging" feeling of families.

If the child doesn't recall experiences, use the comics to discuss the possible feelings of the characters in the strips. Then lead the discussion to the feelings you are currently sharing.

VARIATION
For use in classrooms or for kids to use alone, select some comic strips suggestive of decisions or problems. Using either paper or typing white-out paint, block out the balloons and allow children to fill in the dialog for creative writing and expression activities. (Large balloons must be provided for younger children.)

Clear-cut art paper, lamination, or a stack of balloons will allow the repeated use of the comics.

ACTIVITY TITLE
Sell Yourself Commercial

MATERIALS
To complete this activity on caring for self, you need large pieces of paper, colored markers, something the child has made, a large cardboard box, and tape. A tape recorder would be a great addition.

PROCEDURES   Many youngsters enjoy watching TV commercials as much as watching TV shows. After talking about commercials—which ones they like and why—suggest that you try to make a commercial together.

First cut the bottom out of the box to make your own TV. Using a large piece of paper, write the child's full name and tape it on the inside of the box so it can be seen from outside. Now you have the beginning scene of the commercial.

Let the child tell you what positive characteristics, traits, skills, talents, and the like that she has. You may add to them after she has finished. Put these on sheets of paper to be "flashed" on the screen.

You can now introduce the objects the child has made as "proof" of the claims.

Let the child get behind the box (the "screen") and pretend that she is doing the commercial for you as the audience. If you tape record it, the child can see what it sounds like.

VARIATION   To simplify this activity, make it a radio commercial. This entails only a verbal description, which can be written by the child or dictated to an adult. A tape recording of the advertisement is an excellent addition.

ACTIVITY TITLE   ## The Family Shoes

MATERIALS   Pairs of dress shoes, shoe polish, and rags are needed for this activity about caring for personal possessions.

PROCEDURES   This activity is a hands-on experience in taking care of your things.

Shoes are an example of things that need regular care if they are to be usable for a long period.

Invite the child or family to join in a shoe polishing session. Everyone can bring his or her shoes and polish them. The polishing

activity itself can be inspiring: The smells and textures of the shoes and of the polish lend themselves well to discussion.

It is important to explain to the child that the polish not only removes the scuffs and scratches but that, if the leather is not protected, it will dry out and crack. Lead the discussion to other things that need constant care to function properly, such as all parts of the car, machines, the floor or carpet, plants, animals, wood, bicycles, toys, and so on.

This activity can provide new tasks for the Home Free Game, Task Jar, or other activities in this book.

VARIATION

Rather than using the shoes, buy a bottle of "Armor All" or other protectant spray. Read the label with the child and search the house for all the places it could be used—rubber, vinyl, leather, plastic . . . tires, seats, luggage, tables, shoes, sporting goods, and so on. Lead the discussion to cover the need for the care of all these and other objects.

ACTIVITY TITLE

The Rainy Day Box

MATERIALS

This activity on caring about your things requires a cardboard box and an assortment of the child's toys and books.

PROCEDURES

The intent of this activity is to help the child become sensitive to the number of toys he has and to the value that they have for him.

Sit with the child in his room or play room, and talk about the toys. Point out which toys are used the most, and let him tell you about his favorite ones. Usually a few receive lots of attention, and a larger number are not played with much.

Make the suggestion that when a toy is new it gets lots of use, but that often, as it becomes familiar, it is moved to the back of the shelf. Help the child choose several toys and books that he likes but hasn't been using much. Place these in the box and put them away.

On the next rainy day, pull out the box. The child will remember the toys, but they will now seem new to him. Discuss how it feels to "make the toys new" again. (You don't really have to wait for a rainy day.)

VARIATION

Rather than choosing toys that the child likes but hasn't played with lately, help him choose toys that he doesn't play with or that he either doesn't like, has outgrown, or just doesn't want anymore. Place these in a box to be given to the Good Will, a friend, or day care center. Or sell them at a yard sale. This will stress the value he has for the toys and how values change.

ACTIVITY TITLE

Who Lives in Our Community?

MATERIALS

This activity on your community requires transportation, a note pad, a pencil, large sheets of paper, glue, magazines, and marker.

PROCEDURES

In our society many young children never get out of their neighborhoods. This activity expands their concepts causing the make-up and functions of their community.

Begin this activity by taking a tour of the community. Be sure to include the businesses, residential, rental, and industrial sections, as well as the upper-, middle-, and lower-income housing areas. Use the note pad to record the children's reactions to the different scenes.

Return home and, using pictures from the magazines, make a collage that depicts the community, the different people of the community, and the positive as well as the negative aspects of the community.

VARIATION   Using the large paper, make a map of the community. List the child's reactions and recall of what the different sections looked like and what she thought about them. This can be done in a listing of the positive and negative aspects of each section you visited.

[3]   Learning to care and accepting responsibility go hand-in-hand. The following activities help to develop a sense of responsibility for self, for others, and for the community.

ACTIVITY TITLE   Lost and Found

MATERIALS   To complete this activity on consideration for other people's property, you need paper, a pen, and access to a telephone.

PROCEDURES   Children are always finding things. Bottles, money, watches, wallets, and the like are common fare for kids six and up.

It's often difficult for parents to judge the best procedure based on the situation and the object found. This activity can help to ease that dilemma and provide an opportunity to stress the consideration necessary for others' property. It is probably best to wait for the situation to arise, but the idea can be suggested if you feel the time is right.

When an object is found, discuss how it feels to lose some of your own things. This feeling varies depending on the monetary value or sentimental value of the object. Continue the discussion, brainstorming alternative solutions to the situation. The usual ideas include keeping it, finding the owner, putting an ad in the paper, or calling the police.

This last option, if warranted, provides a good occasion to stress the role of the police as community helpers. The next step is to call the police station. Depending on the situation, the police will either take a description of the found object (a dog, cat, or wallet) and call you if it is reported missing. Or they will send an officer out to file a report.

Whichever way the situation is handled, you and the child will make a step-by-step listing of the proper procedures. This activity can help kids feel good about themselves and a part of a larger community.

VARIATION   A trip to the police station including a tour, a discussion of bike safety, what all the police do for us, and a listing of procedures to follow when objects are lost or found is a good experience too.

ACTIVITY TITLE	**Spying**
MATERIALS	Binoculars are needed to complete this activity. If real ones are not available, a pretend pair can be made from two toilet paper rolls taped together.
PROCEDURES	Take the child to a park or other public place. Using the binoculars, watch people at a distance and talk about how they look and what they are doing.

Children often get into spying on each other and even on adults in the neighborhood. While watching people in this public place, you will be pointing out that in public people expect to be watched. In contrast, people's privacy is a right that we all have. There are even laws against the invasion of privacy.

Bring the discussion around to talk about the consideration necessary when they are thinking about spying on friends or neighbors. Provide opportunities for watching others rather than spying.

VARIATION	Discuss how it feels to be planning a big surprise and to have someone give the surprise away. This is usually a familiar feeling to children. Relate this feeling to the helplessness you feel when someone has broken into your house, stolen something from you, or spied on you. Stress that privacy is important and should not be "stolen away."

ACTIVITY TITLE	**Moving Day**
MATERIALS	To complete this activity on sensitivity to feelings, you will need a map, markers, and paper. Toy house furniture, a doll family, shoe boxes, and a toy truck would be great but not absolutely necessary.
PROCEDURES	Moving, especially a long distance, is frightening to children and often to adults as well. This activity helps your child to be sensitive to the loss of friends and security. It may also help to prepare the child for a move in your own future.

Use the map to pinpoint a place your "family" will be moving to. On the chart paper, make a quick list of tasks for each member of the family to do in preparation for the move. If the actual toys are not available, you can make packing lists for each person, box, or room of the house. The idea is to set the imaginary tone of actually moving.

Now that you are "all packed," it's time to discuss the feelings involved. Make comments like, "Gee, I sure will miss the old place . . . I wonder who will take care of the neighbors' lawn, when they go on vacation? . . . I hope my new job is good . . . It sure is exciting to be going to a new place." Also elicit and discuss responses from the kids to questions like, "What will you miss? . . . Who will you write to? . . . What do you think it will be like in the new place? . . How do you feel about moving?"

Although all this is pretend, the children may become very in-
17   volved and emotional.

VARIATION	When a child is actually moving, the teacher or parent can help to clarify his feelings by making a positive–negative chart with the child.

List all the positive feelings for him and his family on one side of a page and the negative on the other. This provides a clear picture of the feelings and a chance to talk about them.

ACTIVITY TITLE	Where Is _____?

MATERIALS	To complete this activity, you need materials to build shelves—concrete blocks or bricks, 1 x 8″ boards, cardboard, markers, and tape. If the building materials are not available, several shoeboxes will do.

PROCEDURES	The idea of this activity is to demonstrate that there is a place for everything and to show that, if everything is in its place, you will know where it is.

The next time you hear, "Where is my _____?" try this activity. First help the child find the article. Then discuss why she was unable to find it herself. (She didn't know where it was.) From this discussion turn the conversation into a planning session on how organization can help us keep track of things. If you have your kitchen, workroom, or desk organized, take her in and explain how you have done it for your things. Then help to develop a plan for her things. Together you can build the shelves (or organize the shoeboxes), and label a place for individual articles and types of articles. This is also a good time to label the storage areas of the room, closets, drawers, and other areas with descriptions of the articles that go in each.

VARIATION	With very young children it would be best to use pictures of the items that go into each place. The adult can label each area and help the child put all the things in the appropriate places.

ACTIVITY TITLE	Things About Me

MATERIALS	This activity requires paper and pencils for both the adult and the child. You will also need a collection of magazines, some glue, and scissors.

PROCEDURES	The outcome of this activity will be a collage of all the things the child must do to care for himself.

Begin the activity by talking about all the things we have to do every day. A good way to begin this listing is to pretend you are just waking up and "walk" through the whole day helping the child identify those things he must do to care for himself. A sample list might look like this:

Brush teeth
Get dressed
Eat breakfast
Pick up room
Decide what to do (play)
Make school decisions

Do school tasks
Eat lunch
Decide who to play with
Talk with people
Go to bathroom
Take bath
Eat dinner
Go to sleep

The list should contain anything the child feels he does to care for himself, as well as the things you feel he should do to take care of himself.

When you both feel you have a complete list, use the magazines to find pictures that represent these activities. You may have to cut portions of several pictures to represent the actions. Glue these in a random fashion to a piece of cardboard to make the collage. Find a family member or friend to share this with, pointing out all the things the child does to care for himself.

VARIATION   With older children or in the classroom, use the same idea to generate a daily routine or schedule for the group or the individual child. The collage is still appropriate but not absolutely necessary.

ACTIVITY TITLE   ## Home Free—A Board Game of Household Problems

MATERIALS   To make up this game of household problems, you need the board of a discarded game or a piece of cardboard about the size of a board game, small squares of paper, pens, glue, scissors, dice, and markers (such as buttons or beans as tokens for each player).

PROCEDURES   This game can be made by the adult and taught to the child for future play. Or the making of the game itself can be a growth experience for the adult and the child to do together.

Using a commercial game board or the cardboard marked off in a trail of squares as the base plan, you need to think of the household problem or tasks you would like to deal with. Make a small square of paper to glue into some of the squares. You might choose chores like "Take out the trash . . . Clean the bathroom . . . Pick up dirty clothes . . . Clean the bedroom . . . Take a shower . . . Mow the lawn." The number you choose depends on the length of the board and on how much time you would like the game to take to play. Label the last square "Home Free." Two spaces should be labeled "Move ahead 5 squares," and one should read "Move back 4 squares." These squares provide a sense of luck to the game.

After so labeling these squares, label approximately one-third of the remaining squares with "Draw a card." Be sure that a blank square is left on either side of the "card" square. Players who land on these spots must draw a card from the pile in the middle of the table. The stack of cards should be household problems that must be solved: how to distribute chores, keeping your room neat, who chooses which TV show tonight, getting home on time, as well as some "Free Pass Cards" (about one-third of the cards). These "Free Passes" allow the holders to

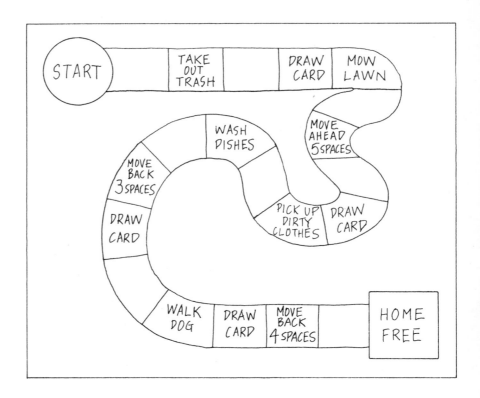

move past the task square or problem card without performing that task or solving that problem.

To play the game, have each player choose a token and decide who goes first. Rolling the dice and letting the high roller begin, and then moving clockwise around the board, is a good way. As players move around the board, any task square means they must lose a turn. This delay reflects the idea that doing the task takes up some time. As players land on the "Draw a card" squares, they must come up with a satisfactory solution to the problem. If the solution is not appropriate from all players' point of view, then it must be discussed until some agreement is reached. If no solution can be reached, then all players must lose one turn. (In reality this means that no one will lose a turn on account of the other players, but it points out that, when no agreement can be reached, everyone loses.) When an appropriate solution is reached, then the player gets to move ahead a free square. Any player who has collected "Free Pass" cards may choose to turn one of these in and move the free square without discussion or without losing a turn.

Continue this pattern until someone has reached the "Home Free" square and is declared the winner.

VARIATION Reverse the cards and task squares: make the squares on the board represent the household problems that you wish to discuss, and let the cards reflect the daily tasks that must be done. This way the players can

20 see the problems that may be discussed and formulate their solutions

throughout the game. Also, you allow several players the opportunity to come up with a new solution to the problem.

Be flexible with the rules. As new ideas occur for tasks or problems, add them to the game and allow rules to be changed when all players can agree on the change. This could even be another square on the board—"The New Game Square."

ACTIVITY TITLE | **Moderation for Your Body**

MATERIALS | This activity requires a sunny day or a sun lamp and suntan oil. A medicine bottle and a sweet food treat are optional.

PROCEDURES | The obvious popularity of suntanning in our society provides a good opportunity to point out that many things feel good and are good for you—but only in moderation. The sun is a good example because it does feel good, but there is some debate over the health aspects of tanning, and a sunburn is obviously damaging to your body. Your skin actually peels off, and your body must produce new skin to replace it. While outside on a sunny day, or when under a sun lamp, discuss this bad aspect of tanning with the child. Be sure to explain the qualities of the suntan oil while you are putting it on. (This might be a good time to do the Stroking activity.) Ask the child if she can think of other things that are good for your body but that can be harmful. The medicine bottle is one example, and the sweet treat is another.

VARIATION | Make a list of all the things you like to do and eat. Star each item that can be damaging or painful in excess. Which ones have you done to the point of "paying the price"?

ACTIVITY TITLE | **Citizenship**

MATERIALS | For this activity on understanding what it means to be a good citizen, you will need pictures of the community, politicians, people in the community, the flag, paper, pencils, and a dictionary.

PROCEDURES | Begin this activity by asking the child what a good citizen is and what a good citizen does. After talking about good citizenship, use the dictionary to find the definition. Write this definition at the top of the page. Under this definition draw three columns labeling one "Duties," one "Rights," and the third "Privileges."

Using the pictures as stimulation, list under each heading as many activities as you and the child can think of. Now ask the child to circle the ones that even children have as Duties, Rights, and Privileges. Extend the discussion to cover when he will be able to participate in the others.

VARIATION | Using a large piece of paper, draw a picture of the American flag. Have the child color the stars and stripes. In each of the white stripes, list a responsibility we have to be good citizens. Display and discuss the "Flag of Good Citizenship."

ACTIVITY TITLE	Our World Community

MATERIALS	This activity sensitizes children to our relationship, as a community, to the nation and to the world. It calls for a globe, a world map, a map of the United States, a state map, and a map of the local community (available at the Chamber of Commerce).

PROCEDURES	Spread all the maps out on the floor. Ask the children to point out which may represent the largest area, next largest, and so on. This task may be difficult for them, and you will need to clarify the size order. Arrange the maps in descending order of how much area they cover. You should have from left to right, the world, the United States, the state, and the local community.

Help the children find and mark their community on each map. Through discussion, the children will realize that states are made up of communities, that countries are made up of states, and that the world is an interrelated array of countries.

VARIATION	Make a series of puzzles from the maps. Cut each map into pieces that represent communities, states, and countries. Allow the children time to work with and to discuss the puzzles.

ACTIVITY TITLE	I'd Rather Do It Myself!

MATERIALS	This activity on responsibility requires paper and pencil, a box with two compartments, scissors, and a marking pen.

PROCEDURES	Children can do many activities alone, but many require an adult's assistance.

Cut the paper into squares that fit into the compartments. With the child, write things that she can do alone and things that she needs help with. Which is which depends on her age and developmental level. Some samples for either pile are tying shoes, dressing, cleaning her room, setting the table, fixing a broken toy, washing the car, choosing TV shows, doing yard work, sweeping floors, planning parties, and so on.

Label each compartment as "I'd Rather Do It Myself" and "Help!" Place the slips in appropriate compartments discussing each as you go.

VARIATION	Do the activity as a chart and stick the slips on. As children acquire new skills, add them to the "I'd Rather Do It Myself" list and as they learn the "Help" activities move them into the other side.

[4] TIPS

1. To teach caring you must *show caring*.
2. Use simple and direct statements to communicate a sense of caring.

3. Pretending is vital to the socio-emotional development of the child.

4. There are times to protect children from their fears and times to help them face those fears.

5. Accepting feelings, both positive and negative, is the first step in clarifying and dealing with emotions.

6. Children's pace of sharing feelings is much slower than adults. Be *patient!*

7. Help children learn to generate their own solutions to problems.

8. Be sensitive to the intent of children's behavior, not just to their actions.

9. Provide many opportunities for children to participate in dramatic play.

10. Caring is for *everyone* and *everything!*

Nurturing

BEING THERE, LISTENING, MAKING DECISIONS, REFLECTING

Young children, three to eight, must feel loved, cared for, and wanted. They must see themselves as worthwhile. Only then can they reach out and care for others. Loving, caring for, and showing children that they are wanted and worthwhile all define nurturing.

In working to develop nurturing in young children, remember that nurturing requires three elements:

1. nurturing itself,
2. acts, not words, and,
3. opportunities.

Nurturing First, youngsters who are nurtured show nuturing actions in turn with peers, objects, people, and situations. In this respect, the teacher and parent play an extremely vital role in facilitating nurturing in young children by being nurturing. When youngsters are cared for, when they see themselves as worthwhile, and when they are enjoyed and given loving physical contact, they show the potential for nurturing.

Words, Not Actions

In relation to this idea, nurturing requires acts, not words. Nurturing is not developed simply by telling youngsters that, "I love or care for you!" They learn nurturing and how to nurture through your actions and not from your words. You can demonstrate and show nurturing through actions in the following ways:

By being there with youngsters. By being there, adults who work with young children can observe them, while recognizing and supporting their efforts. "Being there" does not imply or mean that the more time you spend with children, the more they are nurtured or will show nurturing. Nurturing by being there rests on the *quality* of your interactions with the child—with the kinds and types of things you do and not on how much time you spend with them.

By listening to them. Listening implies becoming aware of messages the children convey through their activities. Listening gives youngsters a picture of an adult who is unhurried, who acknowledges and understands them as individuals, and who genuinely believes they can offer and make sound contributions to themselves and others.

By facilitating decision-making. Encourage children to make decisions and to learn of their consequences (which excludes letting them to be physically harmed as a direct result of their actions). In permitting youngsters to do so, you allow them the freedom to accept risk, to try things, and to experiment with their environments. For example, ask whether the child would like eggs or pancakes, and have the

children decide to put away either the celery stalks or milk containers after you shop. If they refuse to eat the eggs, the consequences mean going hungry, not as a form of punishment but as a result of choosing not to eat the eggs.

By reflecting. In mopping up the milky mess, you show and demonstrate nurturing through actions by reflecting. You show that you are aware of the children's emotions and mirror them back to them. Reflecting leads to nurturing because it helps youngsters to think about their emotions and to learn about them in genuine and constructive ways. For example, children might hear you say, "I am angry because the door is stuck and I can't open it!" Or you might comment, "Tell John you were upset when he took your doll!" In such cases, you are mirroring feelings and showing children how to handle their emotions and hurts before they turn into fears and frustrations.

By being there, by listening to them, by facilitating decision-making, and by reflecting, you demonstrate and show nurturing through actions.

Opportunities

Provide youngsters with opportunities for nurturing. Providing such opportunities is vital for the development of youngsters in three ways. First, it not only encourages and develops nurturing, but it also enhances the growth of the child's social self by fostering independence, decision-making, responsibility, courtesy, and a willingness to accept. All of these attributes contribute to youngsters' ability to see themselves as individuals and as constructive members of groups.

Second, since movement is a crucial part of every individual's life, providing nurturing opportunities for the youngster's physical self is also important. Movement is basic to the development of nurturing, because it assists children's ability to cope with the world. Such opportunities for movement should focus on:

1. selecting reference points,
2. finding a center of balance in space,
3. discovering shapes,
4. using small and large muscles, and
5. moving to determine height.

Third, providing nurturing opportunities focuses on solving problems, on resourcefulness, on happiness, on confidence, on competence, and on initiative. When you encourage the growth of nurturing in the effecting self, youngsters develop trust in themselves and in others, as well as a positive view of themselves as valued contributors. No matter how hard teachers and parents try, nurturing of the social, physical, and effecting self is developed and encouraged by activities and not by pressure from you.

The activities in this chapter focus on providing the events, ideas, and situations that encourage nurturing the youngster's social, physical, and effecting self. These opportunities, which encourage and develop nurturing, can be used either in school or in home settings.

[1] Opportunities for encouraging nurturing of the social self include activities focusing on:

1. decision-making
2. courteousness,
3. responsibility,
4. independence, and
5. acceptance of self and others.

ACTIVITY TITLE **Deciding and Playing**

MATERIALS The materials consist of two play objects that the child equally enjoys. For example, and depending on the child, the decision could be between playing with a toy truck or a stuffed giraffe, or between a puzzle and a pot or pan, or between a piece of wood and toy telephone. The decision between the two alternatives in toys should be left up to the youngster to make. In addition, either choice should be acceptable to you.

PROCEDURES In determining the two equally viable alternatives, you need to observe the youngster to determine which of the toys he enjoys playing with more. Then, at an opportune time, ask him to decide by asking, "Do you want to play with this . . . or that . . . ?" Since both toys are equally desired, entirely within the child's ability, and just as acceptable to you, he learns and practices decision-making as a part of developing his social self.

VARIATION As the youngster practices and learns to decide between two objects, increase the number of play objects from two to three, and change from objects to play activities. In determining the type of activities to use, you should again make sure that they are entirely within the child's capacity and that you are comfortable with either of the choices you offer.
Examples:

1. "Do you want to play ball or watch TV?"
2. "Do you want to go to the movies or visit Uncle Frank and Aunt Sue?"

Here too, the number of choices can be increased from two to three after the child practices and learns decision-making between two activities. Finally, numerous play activities can be used, such as choices between books the child wants you to read and between restaurants at which the child wants to eat.

ACTIVITY TITLE **Deciding Between Positives**

MATERIALS This activity has the child make decisions between positive alternatives of her behavior. No specific materials are required.

PROCEDURES   There are plenty of times in working with young children when their behaviors warrant possible negative reprimands. These instances can be turned into learning experiences for nurturing the child's social self using decision-making. When children leave their toys, clothes, or other possessions scattered over the floor, your immediate response to the child is most likely a negative reprimand, such as, "Don't leave your toys on the floor!" When these situations occur, try offering positive alternatives in building decision-making. For instance, "Do you want to pick up the toys by yourself or do you want me to help you?" The youngster, in turn, decides which of these two positive alternatives she would prefer to do; the choices she has are also meaningful to you.

VARIATION   This deciding activity has a number of variations. After the youngster has learned and practiced with two choices, increasing the meaningful choices to three is again possible. In addition, this procedure can be used with any set of actions the child makes that can be followed by negative reprimands. In lieu of, "Don't put that picture on the chair!" say "Do you want to throw that torn picture away, or do you want to tape it up!" As another example, you might comment, "Do you want to use a paper towel or mop to clean up the spill!" instead of, "Don't spill milk!" Third, you can also use the youngster's own suggestions about behavioral alternatives when these choices are meaningful and acceptable to you. Youngsters who practice and learn decision-making about self should be able to offer alternatives to a situation, decide on one, and let the adult follow through if that choice is acceptable.

ACTIVITY TITLE   ## Courtesy Begins at School and Home

MATERIALS   In having the youngster develop nurturing of the social self by showing courtesy, no materials are needed for this activity.

PROCEDURES   Children learn to say genuinely "thank you . . . please . . . have a nice day . . . I'm sorry" and other similar phrases of courtesy by watching and listening to what teachers and parents say and do, as well as how adults relate to one another in everyday situations. In helping the youngsters to develop nurturing of the social self through courtesy, you should show and demonstrate courteous actions between yourself and other adults and between yourself and children. For example, genuinely use the "courtesy words"—"thank you . . . please . . . how are you?"—as people hand you an object, pick something up for you, or hold a door open for you when your arms are filled. When children show helpful actions, you should genuinely use the expressions of courtesy that are appropriate. When youngsters are immersed in courtesy and see such actions by adults and others, they will mirror those actions.

VARIATION   Instead of waiting for the situations to occur to model courteous actions, you can plan them. For example, hand objects to a spouse, relative, or other adult and also the children, making sure the courtesy actions and words are used in these situations. Or ask for help when unloading

28   packages, and then show courtesy actions and use courtesy words as

the youngsters respond. In addition, planning for situations involves the purposeful use of courtesy actions and words when buying ice cream, going to a restaurant, and visiting the relatives, visiting the park or zoo, and many others. You can genuinely model courtesy behaviors in response to any number of planned situations.

As another variation, think back over the past day or week, and recall the situations in which you and the youngsters have both used courtesy actions and words. Thus you can clarify in your own mind the ways in which you have used courtesy acts and situations and in which the youngsters have seen you use them. In turn, you can use these situations again as you plan for them or as they spontaneously arise.

ACTIVITY TITLE ## Courtesy at Birthday Parties and Other Socials

MATERIALS No actual materials are used in nurturing the child's social self by demonstrating courtesy actions.

PROCEDURES Having the children show courtesy actions in a genuine way is meaningful and facilitative for nurturing the social self. Yet forcing or directing children to use courtesy words, such as "Thank you . . . I had a nice time at a party! . . . Good-bye," is meaningless in teaching courtesy. So is saying to them, "Tell Johnny (or Mrs. Knoll) that you enjoyed your visit!" In addition, prompting them to show courtesy even when the youngsters didn't enjoy the social activity is even more meaningless because they are taught to be deceitful. On the other hand, teachers and parents have found it useful to talk with the children about the amount of time and planning it takes for social events at school or home. As youngsters understand the large amounts of time, planning, and caring that go into these social activities, they should respond in courteous ways to show their appreciation.

VARIATION Instead of asking the youngster to show courtesy actions that are not meaningful or helpful, you can simply wait for him to demonstrate his appreciation. If the child doesn't respond, the teacher or parent could suggest that he show appreciation that is appropriate and aimed at him rather than the adult host or hostess. Examples of this type of suggestion include: "You may thank _____ for the ice cream! . . . You may thank _____ for asking you to come to the party! . . . You may say good-bye to _____ !"

Even in situations in which children do not have good times, they can still show genuine courtesy actions. Talk with the youngsters and say that it is normal and okay to enjoy some but not other social activities. This shows them the importance of being genuine, that these types of feelings and reactions are normal in all individuals, and that they serve to reduce feelings of guilt when they didn't have a good time. In addition, brainstorm ideas about what you can say to show courtesy even when you didn't enjoy the social activity; these suggestions must be truthful and genuine. Understanding the time and effort that goes into planning and carrying out social activities, for example, helps the youngsters focus on showing courtesy for a particular food served or for a special thing that happened at the gathering that they truly enjoyed. Their action may be only something like "good-bye" or "I liked the soda pop . . . or . . . I'm glad Johnny was here!" But the courtesy actions and words are still genuine and truthful.

ACTIVITY TITLE

Showing Responsibility, Not Duty

MATERIALS

This activity, focusing on nurturing the social self by showing responsibility, can be completed without materials.

PROCEDURES

In the classroom or the home, *a responsibility*, which is something, you want to do, should not be confused with a *duty*, which is something you have to do. Developing responsibility means volunteering, because the child wants to do a task rather than being told to do it. Children should be allowed to be responsible for tasks and chores that they want to do.

Gathering the youngsters together, explain that tasks and chores need to be completed to help maintain and care for the classroom or home. Instead of listing the tasks and chores that need to be completed, asked the youngsters to identify what needs to be done. After the listing is complete, ask them how they would do them and who would like to volunteer to complete them. In turn, and as the youngsters begin, show the children by your own actions that you expect them to complete their tasks. In this instance, and as the youngsters see you volunteer, begin and complete the assignments you have chosen, they too will model your actions and those of their peers. As the youngsters suggest tasks and comment about how they would complete them, make sure you think about and carry through the safety procedures.

As a variation, add an evaluation period and focus on whether the task is completed and not on the youngster who has done it. As another variation, depending on the actions and reactions of the youngsters in completing the needs for which they volunteered, you might wish to add supportive statements. For example, "When you complete washing the table, then you may play with the blocks (or another favorite activity they want to do)." Such statements, accompanied immediately by pleasurable actions, take the place of punishing statements, such as, "If you don't finish washing the table, you can't play with your blocks." Also, as another variation, make sure that you guide them to rotate their chores so that they do not feel stuck in completing the same ones all the time. State, for example, "You have completed that chore a number of times. Would you like to do another?" Finally, the youngsters may volunteer and decide to do the tasks in groups. With this variation, and at the youngsters' suggestions, follow through by honoring, accepting, and respecting their ideas.

ACTIVITY TITLE ## Responsibilities and Consequences

MATERIALS There are no materials for this activity on nurturing the social self through responsibility and consequences.

PROCEDURES With responsibilities and their related actions come consequences. When a youngster decides, for example, whether she would like pancakes or eggs, she is learning to shoulder her responsibilities and the consequences of her decisions. In deciding, the child assumes the responsibility and learns the consequence because she is given the freedom to do and try things. For instance, if the youngster chooses the eggs, she also accepts the consequences, and she may not eat the eggs. In this instance, you calmly take away the eggs and comment, "You can eat the eggs later if you choose to, and you can find them on the cabinet." (Make sure it is low enough for the child to get the eggs.) In this activity, learning responsibilities and consequences is a natural outcome of actions.

In nurturing the social self this way, avoid turning consequences into punishment. Punishment, for example, means saying, "I knew you wouldn't eat those eggs, and now I have to throw them away. Do you know how much eggs cost these days?" The consequences are thus turned into punishment.

VARIATION This approach can be modified to fit many varied situations. Such situations range from eating, to buying foods, to watching TV, and to shopping. For example, in a shopping situation, the youngster takes responsibility for helping you put away either the celery sticks or milk containers. In taking responsibility for putting away the milk, the child drops the plastic container and it breaks as it hits the kitchen floor. Again, your purpose to teach the child responsibilities and the consequences of her actions, rather than responsibilities and punishment. Responsibility and consequence of actions is learned when you hand the child some paper towels and say, "You might use these!" But the youngster learns that punishment is a consequence of responsibility if

31

you say: "I knew you would spill the milk. Can't you hold on to anything! Now, I have got to clean that big mess up! And, you can march to your room!"

Through such variations, youngsters learn responsibilities and consequences. If they learn to connect responsibility rather than punishment to consequence, they will come to you and out of trust share the results of their actions—a broken glass, lost toys, or hidden dirty clothes.

ACTIVITY TITLE ## Becoming Independent

MATERIALS For this activity on nurturing the social self through independence, no materials are needed.

PROCEDURES To start becoming independent, the youngsters must first feel safe enough to ask for your opinions in helping them decide between alternatives. In turn, you should show that you trust them to do what is sound and appropriate.

To begin this activity, wait until the youngster volunteers for a responsibility or needs to make a decision and comes to you for advice. For example, a young child may have the the responsibility of deciding which clothes to wear, which chore or task to volunteer for, which activity to do that day, or which toy to play with. When they ask you for you opinions and advice, you should talk over the alternatives, helping them decide (rather than telling). Then trust them to do the proper thing. In talking over the choices and consequences, for example, you might say, "Which one (or ones) do you prefer doing?" To younger ones say, "If you choose this, then you might _____ (insert a realistic consequence)! And, if you choose that, then you might (insert a realistic consequence)! Which one (or ones) do you prefer doing?" Make sure that you show them that you agree with their decision (or suggest a compromise when possible), and that you trust them to do what is appropriate.

VARIATION As a variation of this activity, you should think about and list the ways the children already showing independence. With this list in mind, and as the youngsters show these and similar ways of acting on their own, genuinely reward and praise them for these actions. In so doing, you are letting them know that you trust in them and in their decisions. With this variation, you are teaching the youngster that you trust their decisions and that they can feel secure in asking your opinions.

ACTIVITY TITLE ## Providing Opportunities in Being Independent

MATERIALS No materials are required for this activity in helping the youngster develop his social self through independence.

PROCEDURES This activity is aimed at providing opportunities for youngsters to develop independence. You will need first to guide the children into an opportunity for showing independence. After that, talk with them about the decision, and then trust them to do what they think is appropriate. For example, in going on a visit to relatives, ask the youngster if he would like to bring along a favorite toy. Talk with him about deciding which toy to take in the car if he needs help in deciding. Develop comparisons between the toys. For example, "Which one do you like the best? . . . Which one is easier to carry and hold as you are riding in the car? . . . Which toy would like to see Grandma and Grandpa!" After the child decides, trust him to care for the toy in the car and at the relative's place. Observe the youngster's actions and monitor his showing independence. Reward and praise these actions by commenting, for example, "You are really growing up because you can care for your toy at Grandma's and Grandpa's house!" In getting ready to return home, have them assume independence by taking the toy with them or deciding whether they want to take it home (after first checking out this option with your relatives). Again, trust their decisions, while praising and rewarding their actions.

VARIATION

Many opportunities can be developed for children to become independent by using these procedures. For variation, first determine the ways in which you want the youngsters to become independent. Then you need to develop the opportunities so that they can be on their own. To determine these ways, you might list ideas such as:

1. taking a trip by himself to a friend's or relative's house,
2. spending his money from his allowance and other monies that he has earned, and
3. keeping track of his own toys.

After listing such ideas, then decide on preparing the environment and arranging the opportunities so that youngsters can show that they are becoming independent. To help to decide on additional variations, listen and watch the youngster carefully to get a sense of when he is ready for more advanced opportunities for becoming independent.

ACTIVITY TITLE

Accepting Self by Reducing Difficulty

MATERIALS

No actual materials are required in nurturing the child's social self by learning to accept herself.

PROCEDURES

Children model what adults do, and often they try to complete tasks that are too large for them. These attempts may result in frustration, and after trying and trying again without success they may quit. These situations serve only to reduce the child's level of accepting herself and her actions, and the repeated frustrations may actually lower or reduce her self-acceptance.

When these repeated attempts arise and when the youngster continually fails in completing a task, try breaking the task into smaller units. For example, youngsters will try and try to move a heavy box filled with objects. As they repeatedly attempt these actions and as frustration increases, you might say, for instance, "I wonder what would happen if you carry two toys from the box at a time instead of carrying the box!" As another example, young children often pull rather than push objects. As frustration mounts, a simple comment might help, such as "I wonder what would happen if you push instead of pull it!" These suggestions, aimed at breaking the task down into smaller units, help to nurture the child's acceptance of self.

VARIATION

Nurturing the child's social self by helping her accept herself also means letting her explore, investigate, and attempt tasks that she chooses. For this variation, think back over today or this past week and identify the things you let the youngster do. When, for example, she attempts to put on her smock for the first time, let her paint in it even though it is not buttoned properly. Your praise, as she wears the smock she has put on herself, increases her acceptance of herself. As another variation you can also develop opportunities for the child to try tasks appropriate to her developmental level. These tasks should permit the youngster to succeed, and they assist her growth of self-acceptance.

ACTIVITY TITLE

Accepting Through Clear Messages

MATERIALS

For this activity of nurturing the child's social self by accepting himself, no materials are needed.

PROCEDURES

As teachers and parents, we often give the child equivocal mixed messages in response to his actions. In such messages you may give permission or accept his actions, but at the same time you introduce guilt and feelings of inadequacy. For example, you may tell a child that he can visit his friend but you really would appreciate his helping you. He receives a verbal "yes" with a subtle "no," which creates guilt. Mixed messages that produce guilt and feelings of inadequacy restrict and actually decrease accepting self.

Instead of sending mixed messages, try giving the child a clear "yes" or "no" with a reason, or simply say that it is up to him to decide. For instance, the youngster asks if he can do a particular task. You might comment, "Yes, because it needs to be done!" Or you could respond, "No, you can do it later because you might need help and I must complete this task now!" You can also leave the decision up to the child by saying, "You can decide!" With clear and straightforward messages, the youngster sees himself as someone of worth who is valued for his thoughts and actions.

VARIATION

You can practice giving the youngster clear messages that help to build self-acceptance in a number of ways. One good time is whenever the youngster asks for your opinion or says something. As another variation, you should try to avoid making statements that tear down and damage the self. Examples include: "Big boys don't cry! . . . You should love your brother (or sister)! . . . Look at the way you are treating your mother (or father)! . . . You don't respect me!" The use of these and similar comments is harmful to the self of the child. As another variation with older children, you can directly ask them to tell you, or in some way let you know, when your comments hurt or make them feel bad. In these instances, you use other comments and responses.

[2] Another key factor is nurturing the physical self. Opportunities that nurture the physical self and that help youngsters to cope with themselves and their world include such activities as:

1. selecting reference points,
2. finding a center of balance in space,
3. discovering shapes,
4. using small and large muscles, and
5. moving to determine height.

ACTIVITY TITLE **Referencing Our Physical Selves**

MATERIALS For this activity in nurturing the youngster's physical self by referencing body similarities, you need one large piece of white construction paper and a magic marker or felt tip pen.

PROCEDURES In nurturing the physical self, children must first learn body appreciation by referencing the similarities between themselves and others. Guide the youngsters to name the ways in which their bodies are similar. Similarities include, for example: two eyes, one nose, two ears, two arms, and legs, head, shoulders, and others. After identifying these items, write them on the construction paper. Each of these items can then be discussed.

VARIATION Some of the physical similarities listed can be used as comparisons that make children special, interesting, and unique. In turn, this variation emphasizes referencing of the individual's physical self from others, as well as the appreciation of the body self and others. For example, all children have hair, but their hair colors differ. Rogelio may have black hair, and that is good. Janet may have brown hair, and that is also good. This variation can be repeated for other body parts, such as eyes and their color, shoulders and their height, or faces and their colors.

As a second variation, comments are made on the ways the youngsters' bodies work. With this variation, you need to emphasize one or two things children do well with no comparisons among them. For example, you might say, "Carol runs fast! . . . or Sam jumps high!" Such comments should identify special physical attributes of each child.

ACTIVITY TITLE **Referencing Through Songs**

MATERIALS In nurturing the physical self by referencing body parts, no materials are needed.

PROCEDURES With this activity, youngsters learn to appreciate their physical selves and their uniquenesses. Children's songs and finger plays that emphasize the uniqueness of their physical selves include: "I Am Special" and "I'm Glad I'm Me!"

35

I Am Special
(Sung to the Tune of "London Bridges")

I am special, yes, I am!
Yes, I am!
I am special, yes, I am!
Very special!

I can talk, and think and love,
Think and love,
Think and love,
I am special, yes, I am.
I am special.

(Author Unknown)

I'm Glad I'm Me
This is the circle that is my head.
This is my mouth with which words are said.
These are my eyes with which I see.
This is my nose that is part of me.
This is the hair that grows on my head.
Now, what is there I have not said?
This is my face that you can see.
Yes, I am glad that I am me.

(Author Unknown)

VARIATION   Although many other songs, games, and finger plays can be used to nurture the physical self through referencing of the body, they should not emphasize winning and losing. These variations, like the core activity, emphasize songs, games, and finger plays that all children in individual and group settings can play. Some of the common variations are: "Did You Ever See a Lassee," "London Bridge," "Farmer in a Dell," "Ring Around a Rosy," "Mulberry Bush," "Hokey Pokey," and "Drop the Handkerchief!"

ACTIVITY TITLE   Referencing Bodies in Space

MATERIALS   For this activity, an H-shaped bar in indoor settings or an outdoors tree gym and a walking ladder are required.

PROCEDURES   Referencing bodies in space nurtures the physical self by encouraging the youngsters to stabilize relations between self and others in spite of their body movements and differing spatial orientations. With the equipment used in this activity, children should have the time and freedom to climb the bars and to hang their bodies down by their knees. As they hang from their knees, guide them to observe and comment on the fact that both feet are "up" and "higher" than their bodies. In this position, they can see their hands, head, and shoulders relative to their feet. Children learn that body movement can change their referencing points. Guide them to see and to tell about various objects around them as they hang upside down. Help them use their body parts as points of reference in observing and describing these objects.

VARIATION   As another variation, the youngsters can hang down from their hands. Guide them to observe and to tell about their body parts and the objects around them using this new reference point. For another variation, they can climb to the top of the equipment to observe and to tell about objects and their shapes from above. This referencing of the body in space permits the youngsters to see the tops of objects and to view things from the top down (rather than from the bottom up as they hang by their knees).

ACTIVITY TITLE   ## Finding the Body's Center of Balance

MATERIALS   This activity in nurturing the physical self by having the child find his center of balance requires no materials. One of the variations requires a child's see-saw or sawhorse with a board or plank four feet long whose width is wide enough for sitting with the two legs placed on either side.

PROCEDURES   To help the youngster appreciate her body and find her center of balance, locate a cement curb that is about four inches wide. Make sure that the curb is either away from traffic or on a cul-de-sac or infrequently traveled street. In guiding the youngster to walk along this curb, make sure she learns to use her arms to balance her forward movements. She acquires this sense of balance with each forward step, each of which changes her body's relationships among its physical parts.

VARIATION   Walking backward or sideways on the curb requires the youngster to find different centers of her body due to the changing tasks and to reestablish the relationships among her body parts. As another variation, two youngsters sit on opposite ends of a child's see-saw, board, and sawhorse. They move up and down the plank, thus learning to sense body balance in relation to its movements. In their efforts to establish balance, they learn to develop a center of balance and to understand that their movements to and from the fulcrum change the relationships among their body parts.

ACTIVITY TITLE   ## Finding the Body's Center in Jumping

MATERIALS   In nurturing the physical self by establishing balance by jumping, this activity requires three or four objects about eight inches high (such as unit blocks or bowling pins).

PROCEDURES   Place three to four objects, one behind the other. Each of the objects should be separated by twelve inches. Guide the child to jump over each object on both feet (or on one foot) without stopping. Through successive jumping without stopping, the youngster learns to find his body's center of balance.

In learning to find the body's center through jumping, the youngster can play hopscotch or a similar game that requires skilled jumping. With this variation, the youngster also learns to sense weight distribution during movement and body balance. In hopscotch or any similar game that requires skilled hopping, the youngster should be able to hop on one foot to an indicated spot, hop-turn around, and repeat the jumps without falling. Requiring greater degrees of weight distribution than hopping over the blocks, this variation can be practiced over and over again to improve the spontaneous sensing or conscious conceptualization of finding the body's center in space.

ACTIVITY TITLE   ## Moving and Discovering Shapes

MATERIALS   In nurturing the youngster's physical self by moving and discovering shapes, for each youngster you need six sticks or building slats twelve inches long and a piece of chalk or washable felt tip marker.

PROCEDURES   With chalk or magic marker, draw a four-foot square on the floor. Using body parts and body movement, guide the youngster to:

1. identify the number of sides to the square,
2. locate a reference point that marks the beginning of her movements around the object, and
3. balance her body and body movements.

For example, the youngster sits along the sides of the square. Then, she gets up and walks along the lines that form the sides of the square. The child can hop and then crawl along its sides. Try to use additional movements so she can discover and understand this square shape. These additional movements include "giant-stepping," jumping, running, walking, skipping, and tracing by moving one finger along its sides. You can use the same procedures for nurturing the physical self by using other shapes such as circles, rectangles, and triangles.

VARIATION   As a variation, the youngster moves the sticks or slats to form the shapes of a square, a rectangle, and a triangle. After the shapes are formed, such movements as walking, hopping, or giant-stepping can be used. As another variation, using either the chalk or wood outlines, similarities among the shapes can be observed. These similarities include the number of sides and their respective lengths.

ACTIVITY TITLE   ## Using Body Directions

MATERIALS   No materials are needed in this activity of nurturing the physical self by learning directions through body movements.

PROCEDURES   In learning about the physical self, the youngster discovers that direction is a course or a line on which the body moves or faces. Making sure that there is plenty of space for body movements, the youngster sits on the floor. Guide the youngster in learning to use body direction by moving his body to get as "little" or "tiny" as possible. Instruct him to curl up and make himself so "little" he can't be seen. You will need to urge him to squeeze his body up. The child can also see how tall he can get with his feet and knees on the floor. While holding his balance in a standing and then in a kneeing position, the youngster lifts up one of his feet from the floor. In the same two positions, he then raises one knee above the floor. Now ask him to turn to the left and then to the right. Ask him to walk around the room with his arms held as high as he can. And then, while you guide him, have him hold his arms as low as he can, again walking around the room. As the child follows the suggestions, he integrates parts of his body with the directional movements of turning or facing in one or more directions.

VARIATION

As variations, try some make-believe rather than real situations. For example, ask the child to pretend that his feet are stuck to the floor, and guide him to move his body in all possible ways (without moving either foot). To encourage other forms of body movement and direction, have the youngster pretend to be various animals such as elephants, birds, or horses. Pretending to be these animals, he shows how they walk, run, jump, or hop. In addition, guide the youngster to do the same movements like the make-believe animals but with one limitation. For example, have him pretend to be an elephant who hops only sideways or on one foot. In this variation, the child senses and feels movement from a particular point of reference.

ACTIVITY TITLE

Using Small Muscles

MATERIALS

For nurturing the physical self by developing small muscles and body movements, the required materials are 24-inch shoe laces, along with round and/or square wooden beads with holes drilled through them.

PROCEDURES

Help the youngster to string the point or tip of the shoelace through the beads, thus developing small muscles and eye–hand coordination. The beads can be put on the shoelace in any fashion or order. Later, after the youngster masters and plays with the task, guide him to put the beads on the lace in a particular order. The orders can be based on color—such as repetitions of the green/red/blue sequence—or on shape—such as sequences of round/square. The youngsters can also make up their own orders.

VARIATIONS

There are many variations of nurturing the physical self by developing small muscles and body coordinations. For example, you can change the types of materials. In addition to shoelaces and beads, you can use:

1. blocks for stacking,
2. pegs and pegboards for putting pegs into pegboards,
3. puzzles for taking apart and putting together,
4. plastic containers for pouring,

5. clay and similar substances for squeezing, pounding, and rolling,
6. adult clothing for buttoning and unbuttoning, and
7. locks and keys for locking and unlocking.

All these variations focus on developing the physical self and small muscle growth and body movement.

ACTIVITY TITLE   **Practicing Large Muscles**

MATERIALS   To nurture the physical self by practicing large muscles and body coordinations, you can use tricycles, wagons, pedal and go-carts, scooters,and other riding vehicles.

PROCEDURES   Simply provide one or two types of riding vehicles for the children. They can use the wheeled vehicles in their own ways. Legs, feet, arms, trunks, and other body parts move in singular and coordinated fashion as the youngsters move from location to location.

VARIATION   Many variations are possible, such as changing the materials. For instance, with an old mattress, children can tumble, jump, and roll backwards and forwards. Objects of differing weights provide practice in lifting and carrying. Other types of objects give practice in pushing, pulling, catching, throwing, and climbing. Children can also develop the physical self by crawling, twisting, and using other body movements that require large muscles and body coordinations.

ACTIVITY TITLE   **Moving to Determine Heights**

MATERIALS   For this activity in nurturing the physical self by moving to determine height, you need several hollow wooden blocks and a sturdy wall made from concrete, brick, or tile that is two or three feet above the child's head. For the variations, an outdoor play platform, ladder, a tape measure, and a 5'x1' strip of paper are used.

PROCEDURES   In moving to determine height, provide the youngster with several hollow wooden blocks, placing them at the foot or base of the wall. The youngster stacks the hollow wooden blocks against the wall. She may repeat the stacking processes by climbing up and down several times and by adding one or two blocks with each repeated set of movements. As the youngster gets closer to the top with each repeated step and peeks over the wall, she acquires a feeling for the height of both the blocks and the wall. She also experiences the physical movement as she lifts her leg, reaches with her arm, places her foot on the steps leading to the pile and to the stacked blocks themselves, and climbs up and down.

VARIATION   A variation of moving to determine height is the use of an outdoor play platform several feet above the ground with a connecting ladder. This set, which can be either purchased commercially or home-made, resembles a "mini-treehouse." In this variation, the youngster needs the time and freedom to climb up and down the ladder to get into or out of the play platform. The child senses kinesthetically the height of the play platform.

For another variation, measuring tape is glued or stapled to the paper in length-wise fashion; the height of each child is marked on the paper and her name placed alongside the mark. So that no child in the group can be labeled the "tallest" or "shortest," you need to include the height of another youngster whom you know who is taller than the tallest and one who is shorter than the shortest ones in the group.

[3] Nurturing the effecting self depends on opportunities that encourage:

1. problem solving,
2. resourcefulness,
3. happiness,
4. confidence,
5. competence,
6. sharing negative feelings,
7. understanding feelings, and
8. accepting others.

ACTIVITY TITLE **Solving Problems**

MATERIALS This activity, focusing on nurturing the effecting self by practicing problem-solving, can be completed without specific materials.

PROCEDURES Throughout their daily living and learning routines, children encounter many opportunities to practice and learn problem-solving. Almost everything the young child does requires problem-solving to navigate through the physical and social worlds. In attempting to tie his shoelaces, to put on and button or zipper up his coat or sweater, to carry heavy or bulky objects from place to place, to push or pull things in his wagon, or to paint on an easel, the youngster may encounter problems. With these and other opportunities, he needs the freedom to try to master these and other problems on his own. You need to accept and praise his efforts and solutions. A corollary to this procedure is waiting and letting him attempt problem-solving without rushing to solve the problem for him (unless of course he is about to hurt himself). Then, accept and praise his efforts—even though the product is a tangled or knotted shoelace, a sweater that is not buttoned properly, or a picture with large blotches or running paint. All the child's efforts and endeavors in problem-solving in his world say to him, "I did it!" And your praise of his solutions reinforces a positive effecting self.

VARIATION A variation of the child's attempts at solving problems is to guide him indirectly by breaking down the steps for mastery. You can use this variation with children especially when they begin to show frustration

after successive and repeated failure in problem-solving. In these instances, you can guide them by saying, for example, "You might put this puzzle piece in here! ... Try putting this button through this buttonhole and see if that might help! ... I wonder what would happen if you dipped half rather than the whole brush in the paint." Such variation permits success in solving problems.

ACTIVITY TITLE Becoming Resourceful

MATERIALS In nurturing the physical self by facilitating the youngster to become resourceful, no materials are needed.

PROCEDURES Becoming "resourceful" means developing the ability to think about a number of alternatives and to understand that there are no "right" or "wrong" answers for these situations. To develop, practice, and extend this capacity, youngsters can be guided to think about alternatives as immediate situations arise. For example, you are helping the youngster wrap a birthday present for her friend, and there is not enough wrapping paper for the gift. In this situation, you can develop alternatives by asking, "How can we wrap the gift and make it look really pretty, even though we don't have the time to buy some more birthday wrapping?" In actually identifying several options, you are modeling, showing, and practicing resourcefulness by brainstorming alternatives. You demonstrate that there are more ways of tackling this situation and that there are more answers to it than one "right" or "wrong" one.

Other situations arise, for example, when one child tells another, "You can't play with me!" or when one youngster grabs a toy away from another. In either of these two situations, you can model and provide the opportunities for becoming resourceful by commenting, "What are some of the things you can do when Johnny took your toy or said you can't play!" By brainstorming alternatives and options to these immediate situations and concerns, you give youngsters the tools to practice and to learn resourcefulness.

VARIATION As a variation, you can also contribute situations and provide opportunities for children to brainstorm alternatives. You simply need to find time in which to identify alternatives to these contrived situations. For example, Knox (1981, 72–73) suggests to begin brainstorming by asking the following questions:

1. How can we decide where to eat in a short period of time when one wants to go to the Dairy Queen, one wants to picnic in the park, and one wants to go home?
2. What are some of the things you can do when we go to a shopping center and you get lost?
3. What are some things you can say when you leave someone's house after you've had a good time?
4. What are some things you can say if you accidentally bother somebody?

ACTIVITY TITLE ## Knowing When and Why You are Happy

MATERIALS No materials are required in this activity of nurturing the effecting self through happiness.

PROCEDURES By recognizing happiness, children, parents, and teachers can assist its growth. Happiness can be recognized in a number of situations, and children can learn to recognize such situations by adult modeling. For example, you have just finished a task that is personally pleasing. Make sure that you recognize and share this happiness with the child through statements such as, "I have finished painting the room, which really makes me happy. And it looks so beautiful." By showing that you are happy, voicing that feeling, and giving a reason for your happiness, you help youngsters to understand and to recognize what happiness is. You provide them with a model they can use.

VARIATION As you use these procedures in helping children recognize and share reasons for happiness, a variation is to observe them for situations in which they show happiness. In watching children in particular routines, you can see them showing cheerfulness. In such situations, you can reinforce—and at the same time have them recognize—their happiness by commenting, "You really seem to be happy as you _____ (insert whatever the child is doing)!" Recognizing and providing a possible rationale for happiness help children become aware of their feelings.

ACTIVITY TITLE   ## Happiness in Retrospect

MATERIALS   In nurturing the effecting self by having youngsters recognize happiness in their previous day's routines, no materials are needed.

PROCEDURES   Identify times during the day that you can talk genuinely with the children. These times often include mealtimes—breakfast, snack, lunch, or dinner. After the youngster is able to recognize and explain why she is happy in these situations, ask her at mealtimes to tell about one or two situations that have happened that day to make her happy. Prompt and reinforce her comments. You could also genuinely give examples of situations that made you happy during the day. In addition, make sure you accept the child's responses that show she is or was "unhappy."

VARIATION   As a variation, this same procedure can be used during other times of the day. For example, you could ask the youngster, "What made you happy this morning (or afternoon)?" You can use the same procedures at more specific times during or at the end of the day, such as at bedtime, while riding in a car, while watching TV, and at play.

ACTIVITY TITLE   ## Creating a Happy Atmosphere

MATERIALS   This activity helps to develop nurturing of the effecting self by creating a happy atmosphere. No specific materials are required.

PROCEDURES   Knox (1980, 68–69) explains that it is basically impossible to make children happy,

> . . . but by looking at [their] strengths, by encouraging them, by expressing appreciation for what they have done, by demonstrating affection for them and by being real with them, we create an atmosphere in which it is more likely that they will be happy.

Creating an atmosphere that fosters happiness means remembering to praise them for their particular and specific skills after they accomplish something. Second, you can also show appreciation by hugging and using other forms of physical or verbal affection. And, by being real, genuine, and honest with them in daily living and learning routines, you develop favorable atmospheres in which happiness can develop and evolve. Look back over the week to see where these three principles are used to help develop a happy atmosphere for the youngster and for yourself.

<table>
<tr><td>VARIATION</td><td>As a variation you can plan genuinely to use these in your everyday actions and activities with youngsters in school and in home settings. Ask yourself, "How can I use them in planning and preparing for playground or backyard activities (or other activities, such as going on a field trip and doing tasks or chores)?"</td></tr>
</table>

ACTIVITY TITLE	Feeling and Being Competent
MATERIALS	In nurturing the effecting self by showing the child that he is competent, materials are not needed for this activity.
PROCEDURES	The young child does many things by himself, including going outside in the yard to play, going off to school, visiting with relatives, helping at school or home, and making choices. These and many other things are done by the youngster outside of your guidance. In these instances, trust is at the roots of feeling and of being competent. Telling him to have a nice time and that you will see him after he finishes playing (or visiting, helping, etc.) tells him he is competent. In addition, you are showing that you trust him to do the appropriate things while playing, visiting, or performing other endeavors. Saying to the child, "Be a good boy! . . . Be nice to Grandma! . . . Behave yourself!" or asking "Were you a good boy? . . . Did you behave yourself?"—along with other such actions and comments—does not build his competence.
VARIATION	A variation is to give the child the freedom to do things that he chooses at school or home and to trust him. By setting a positive and trusting tone for the youngster as he begins endeavors, you allow competence to evolve.

ACTIVITY TITLE	Reexamining Expectations for Confidence Building
MATERIALS	To nurture the effecting self by reexamining adult expectations for confidence building in children, no materials are needed.
PROCEDURES	A teacher might examine for several moments some of his or her expectations for the youngsters. For example, are they required to print their names? Are they asked to entertain themselves? Do they have to sit still for ten minutes? As a parent you need to ask yourself whether each expectation is appropriate for your child. If you criticize and point out her shortcomings and tell her that you are disappointed in her, you need to adjust your expectations. After reexamining your expectations, you may need to reset them to what the child can do presently and then adjust them based on what she can do later. Thus you contribute to her growth in competence. In addition, a closer match is achieved between what the child can presently do and what you expect. The reexamination and closer match develop confidence in the effecting self.
VARIATION	As a variation of reexamining expectations, determine which of them are not appropriate to the youngster. Inappropriate expectations need to be modified and changed. After listing the ones that need to be

45

changed, determine how you can modify and make them more appropriate to the child. You might adjust your expectation of tying her shoe to something that is more appropriate, such as being able to put and pull a shoelace through one or two of the shoe holes. In turn, provide the opportunity to practice and praise her actions and activities as she shows competence in these and other endeavors.

ACTIVITY TITLE **Sharing Negative Feelings**

MATERIALS To complete this activity on nurturing the effecting self by learning to share negative feelings, no materials are needed.

PROCEDURES In learning to share feelings, the youngster should be able to express negative ideas. Teaching the youngster that he can share negative feelings without being penalized or punished helps to develop the effecting self. He learns to understand that expressing a negative thought does not make him a negative or "bad" person. In addition, repressing negative thoughts creates fear, anger, and guilt in the youngster, which hinder the growth of the effecting self.

The procedure in showing the child how to express negative feelings requires you to model and practice this tool with him. In this procedure you need to listen to the child's negative feelings without judging them, even though they may be directed at you or at others. For example, the youngster might stomp into the house and say, "Sally is dumb, I don't want to play with her!" To react without judgment, you might respond with "You feel hurt because Sally won't let you play with her!" Or the youngster might even say, "I hate you!" Again without judgment, you might reply, "I know that you are mad at me right now and that's okay! But we have to leave the beach to meet Dad who's taking us out for dinner!" This procedure of acceptance requires reflection on what the child says, along with your acceptance of the negative feelings without judgment.

VARIATION A variation is to use "I" rather than "you" statements. "You" statements attack and humiliate the child. They build a hostile atmosphere that arouses guilt feelings and fear, thus reducing the effecting self. You can practice the tool of expressing negative feelings—that is, use "I" rather than "you" messages—by saying, for example, "I don't like the messy floor because others may fall over the toys!" rather than, "You children are messy and belong in pig pens!"

ACTIVITY TITLE **Understanding Feelings**

MATERIALS To understand and nurture the effecting self by understanding feelings, no materials are needed.

PROCEDURES The youngster learns to develop her effecting self by understanding her feelings. First develop a list of feelings, which should include happy, sad, afraid, anxious, disappointed, proud, excited, surprised, and others. In addition, ask the youngster to contribute some of them; you may be surprised at her contributions. Her list provides insight into her effecting self. Then ask, "I feel happy (or sad or anxious) when _____!" and have the child complete the statement by explaining her feelings and identifying the conditions under which she feels that way. You should complete one or two of them yourself so she understands the activity and learns that you also have feelings of happiness, sadness, or others. You may need to guide and prompt!

VARIATION

After listing the various feelings, guide the youngster to understand what is making her feel happy, sad, or anxious. Ask her to identify the conditions in which she feels in a happy, sad, or other kind of mood, and help her to understand why she feels the way she does. Then guide her to identify possible ways in which she can change these feelings. For instance, the child might say, "I feel sad when I can't put the puzzle together!" In an attempt to identify possible ways in which she can change her sad feelings, she might say "by asking for help . . . by working with another puzzle . . . by watching how the puzzle pieces fit in before taking the puzzle apart." Then the youngster can decide which one is most appropriate. This variation shows the youngster that she can control and change her feelings, as well as make her own decision.

ACTIVITY TITLE

Viewing and Accepting Feelings in Others

MATERIALS

For this activity in nurturing the physical self by viewing and accepting feelings in others, several children's literature books are needed. Some of the texts for children, among others that focus on feelings include:

1. Joan Griesman, *Things I Hate* (New York: Behavioral Publications, 1973).
2. Terry Berger, *I Have Feelings* (New York: Behavioral Publications, 1971).
3. Lillian Moore, *I Feel the Same Way* (New York: Atheneum Publications, 1967).
4. Judith Viorst, *Alexander and the Terrible, Horrible, No Good, Very Bad Day* (New York: Atheneum Publications, 1972).

PROCEDURES

These and other children's books can be read to the youngster. If he can read, he can read them to you and his peers. After the reading, review the text and focus on the character's feelings and his understandings of them. For example, for the book, *Alexander and the Terrible, Horrible, No Good, Very Bad Day*, ask, "What feelings did Alexander have?" Or, "How did Alexander learn to understand his feelings?" By reading and understanding that other youngsters have similar feelings and that feelings can be changed, the child uses the character as a model.

VARIATION

Additional books whose theme mirror some of the youngster's personal feelings can be selected. Again, use questions that focus on the character's feelings and how he or she comes to understand and change them. As another variation, the youngster can make up pretend or real stories about feelings, telling about them and drawing them. Drawing and otherwise expressing themselves about being in a lonely, happy, sad, or any kind of mood help the child understand his thoughts about people, situations, and events.

[4] TIPS

1. Nurturing actions fundamental to the social and physical selves, especially the effecting self, are largely internal. They develop through opportunities provided the child by parents and teachers rather than through direct and didactic teaching.

2. To help nurture various actions fundamental to the children's social, physical, and effecting selves, the parent and teacher must first of all model and practice these actions with the children in natural settings.

3. In the development of nurturing, the consequences of children's decisions should be regarded as the outcomes of their decision-making and not as punishment.

4. The youngsters should be allowed freedom to make choices that are genuine and possible for them to carry out.

5. Break down a large task into smaller ones if the youngster shows increasing frustration in doing the bigger one.

6. Children's stories about youngsters' feelings and understandings of self can be read over again a number of times, and the entire story or short passages can be acted out in pretend play.

7. Let youngsters become responsible for tasks that they want and choose to do; learning responsibility should not become confused with performing a duty.

8. Your answers and responses to children's questions should be straightforward and clear. They should be either "yes" or "no" with the appropriate reasons or a statement showing them that "you can decide." When you decrease your mixed messages, you help to produce an increasing acceptance of self in children.

9. In helping youngsters to nurture their physical selves through body referencing, the best group games to use are those that focus neither on competition nor on winning and losing.

10. Times throughout the day when you are not hurried or rushed are ideal in providing opportunities for nurturing the social, physical, and effecting self.

Role-Taking

ROLES OF THE CHILD IN CARING

Role-taking is the ability of youngsters to become persons, objects, situations, or events other than themselves, as shown through their motor and/or verbal role enactments. Taking the perspective of the other requires youngsters to "step into" different shoes and to transform themselves into that other. For children between the ages of three through eight, role-taking is natural and spontaneous, and it provides them with a personal feeling of mastery of their worlds (Caplan & Caplan, 1973).

Caring experiences through role play assist children to develop and practice receptive and expressive language. A careful examination of role-taking and caring abilities shows the contributions that role-making makes to caring, which are:

1. growth in imaging,
2. increased recall,
3. developing novel forms, and
4. learning socially appropriate communication.

Growth in Imaging

As a reciprocal relationship between individuals, caring lends itself easily to role-taking. Just as youngsters are cared for and protected by their parents and teachers, they must in turn show and demonstrate caring for these significant adults in their lives. To do so, youngsters must "step into the shoes" of, and essentially the role of caring from, the adults. Hence neither caring nor role-taking goes on in a one-way direction. Children model their caring on the roles they take from the adults around them. Through role-taking, youngsters identify with caring routines, try them on for size, and develop and expand ways of using them in life-like settings. Caring gives children the opportunities to try out caring acts and activities, or to modify and expand them as others react to these routines through role-taking. Role-taking permits children to practice and expand their mental concepts of viewing, understanding, and expressing caring actions and activities. The building blocks of caring rest with the growth of children's receptive and expressive thought and language. For example, children show caring acts, such as helping and sharing with others, to the extent that they have practiced and developed sound mental and language concepts for caring.

Increased Recall

In this contribution, role-taking provides the rehearsal and practice needed for the memorization and recall of caring acts and activities. For example, children who role play "Washing the Family Dog" are actually rehearsing and practicing that episode. They are thus better able to recall and to use caring routines in the same or similar situations. The quantity of caring actions shown by children is directly proportional to the amount of their recall and rehearsal through role-taking.

Developing Novel Forms

Developing novel forms of caring acts and activities relates in part to the improvising element in role play. Through the capacity to improvise, the youngsters bridge gaps between what they have already experienced and the demands of the current role. For example, young children in a role-taking episode of "Going to the Circus" begin to brush the hair of a "pretend" lion before it performs in the circus act. Brushing the hair of the pretend lion is an improvisation that evolves from within the role play setting. Although they have had no direct experience with "caring for lions," the youngsters improvise by developing new forms of caring to fit this role-taking episode.

Learning Socially Appropriate Communication

In caring, socially appropriate language and actions are modeled after family members, peers, and significant others. In a role-taking episode, one child says to another, "Don't be afraid 'cause I'll be there with you!" This and other language provide youngsters with opportunities to "play" at life and to enrich their social caring skills. The socially appropriate language through role-taking serves caring and easily integrates them into real life social situations.

This chapter provides you with several ways of using role-taking in the caring routines of young children, which can be used to actively nurture caring acts and activities with young children in home and in school settings.

[1]   Learning to be a friend and showing characteristics of friendship to others constitute a reciprocal process and a key to caring. Try some of the following role activities in caring through friends and friendship.

ACTIVITY TITLE   ## Helping: A Visit Through the Neighborhood

MATERIALS   Get a sheet of paper and a pencil or crayola. Before your visit, you also need to locate places in the neighborhood that help people and animals. These places, for example, can be supermarkets (which help people provide for their food needs), hospitals (which help people and animals when they are sick), clothing and cleaning stores (which keep people provided with clothing), and numerous other establishments.

PROCEDURE   Take the youngsters on a field trip to the selected locations in the neighborhood and community. Before the field trip(s), make sure you provide the children with an objective or purpose for the visit. For example, "We are going to visit the supermarket, post office, and fire company. As we visit these places, see if you can name the ways people help other people (and/or animals). When we return to the school (or home), we can name these ways of helping others and role play how they help them." Take careful mental or written notes of helping situations, and you and the children can point out these events during the visit. Upon returning, generate a list of helping situations and write them down on paper: for example, people buying food for themselves and their pets, clerks helping to stock and bag the food items, people helping others fight fires in their homes, and so on. After making up the list, have the children role play each of these situations (that is, what was done and how was it done). Then exchange roles, and practice the helping situations over again.

VARIATIONS   For role-taking, introduce that idea the children help others. Ask them to think about and identify ways in which they help others. Examples could include helping the adult keep the room clean and helping other children put their arms into their jackets. Each of these situations is then role played by the individual child or group, and they in turn exchange parts for additional practice at helping.

ACTIVITY TITLE   ## "A Friend in School and Home"

MATERIALS   Gather eight pieces of cardboard twelve inches long and four inches wide. With a felt pen, write the following eight phrases on each of the pieces of cardboard:

1. washing dishes,
2. emptying the wastepaper basket,

3. setting the table for a snack (at home or school),

4. putting things back into their places,

5. making the bed,

6. reading or telling about a favorite story,

7. caring for yourself (such as feeding, brushing, walking the family or classroom pet), and

8. cleaning up the table (or work area) of trash.

If the very young child cannot read, present these (or other) experiences orally to the child. You also need various objects that are real or miniature replicas that are suggested by the situation.

PROCEDURES All of these eight situations portray common everyday experiences that focus on making friends by showing children's caring toward themselves and toward significant others. Present each situation separately to a child or to a group of youngsters. Invite them to role play the experience. If children in a group role play the episode, guide them to expand the episode, as well as to define and assign roles. After the children have been shown and have practiced the situation a number of times, discuss the meaning of the episode for making friends. For example, ask, "How are you making friends by washing dishes?" Make sure you guide them toward—but do not tell them—the exact answers to questions used in the discussion. Work with them at their own (not on an adult) level of thinking.

VARIATION You can use numerous other situations that require children to show friendship roles in helping themselves and others. But these situations must first be experienced by youngsters before they can be asked to show any role-taking episode. Familiar caring experiences can encourage children to be and to become friends. Unfamiliar ones do not facilitate making friends because the children have no experiential foundation.

Excuse Me!

MATERIALS   There are no materials for this activity on being polite and showing politeness as characteristics of friendships. Yet you need to recognize and to be aware of situations that occur in the home and at school in which being polite encourages friendship between children and between the child and adults. Essentially, the activity requires the adult to carefully observe the youngsters' actions and activities for the "right" moment in which they can or have shown politeness through friendship.

PROCEDURE   Watch the youngster carefully as she interacts with members of her peer group, with sisters and brothers in the family, and with adults at school and home. Try to "catch" her showing politeness in a friendly encounter. Examples include:

1. As the youngster is drawing a picture, she asks, "May I use your yellow crayon?"
2. She helps another child put his arm into his jacket sleeve and says, "Excuse me, can I help you with your jacket?"
3. As the youngster is helped by another in some way or fashion, she says, "Thank you!"

These and numerous other situations form the keystone for building politeness and for helping and establishing friends. After the child has shown any of the numerous forms of politeness to peers, siblings, and/or adults, guide her to "play back" her actions. Say, "That was a very good way of showing politeness!" Guide her into rehearsing the situation by saying, "Let's now pretend-play what you did and said because it shows that you were polite and were a friend!" At the conclusion of the role-taking situation, ask the individuals to exchange roles and role play the situation another time. At the end of this second playback, discuss politeness—"how" it was shown, "why" it is important, and "how" it helps being a friend. The discussion on the "how's" and "why's" is tailored to the children's and not to the adult's level of thinking.

VARIATIONS   The same idea—that of the child's being polite to another individual— can also be extended to an adult's showing politeness to another adult. Before trips (or field trips to the supermarket and to various other business establishments), ask the youngsters to watch for instances in which clerks and other adults show politeness to other adults. Guide them to recognize these instances at the most appropriate times and as they occur. Upon your return to the school or home, guide the youngsters to role play what the adults did and said to show politeness to others. At the conclusion of the role play, discuss the characteristic of politeness using the same questions as previously outlined.

ACTIVITY TITLE Sharing Friendship

MATERIALS Paper and pencils or crayons are needed. In addition, materials appropriate to the role play situation are used.

PROCEDURE Ask the children to name their favorite friends at home and school. Then write down the responses of the youngsters as they are dictated. With the youngsters, talk about why they listed them as friends, as well as the conditions and situations in which they showed some of the qualities of friendship. As the children identify the people, the why's, and the conditions under which friendship is shown, keep writing down the information. For example, a youngster could say that, "Tim is my friend!" For the "why" part of the discussion, he might add, "Tim helped me!" For the friendship conditions, he might state that Tim helped him zipper up his coat when he was having difficulty. (You may need to guide the children in pinpointing conditions.) Other examples include:

1. "Sally . . . sharing . . . shared her toys with me,"
2. "Shanda . . . shared interests . . . we play blocks together,"
3. "Reynoldo . . . play games . . . Reynoldo lets me play games with him and his friends!"

After you have completed the listing of names, why's, and conditions, the children in turn role play these special friendship situations. Make sure that the youngsters exchange parts so they become the "initiators" as well as the "receivers" of friendly acts.

VARIATIONS In addition to having the youngsters identify friendship conditions, the parent and teacher can offer situations to extend the role play. In using this variation, make sure that the conditions and situations show a variety of qualities basic to friendships. These include showing: (1) dependability, (2) cooperation, (3) sharing, and (4) common interests.

ACTIVITY TITLE Reading and Role-Playing About Friends

MATERIALS A children's book that focuses on being a friend or on showing friendship is the major requirement for this activity. These books should have as their underlying themes such friendship qualities as (1) caring, (2) depending on someone, and (3) helping one another. Examples of two classical children's texts that focus on such qualities are: 1. Sarah Asheron, *How to Find a Friend* (New York: Gosset & Dunlap, 1964). 2. Syd Hoff, *Who Will Be My Friends* (Evanston, Ill.: Harper & Row, 1960).

PROCEDURES Read the story book to the youngsters, making sure that you emphasize the friendship situation with the pitch of your voice. After reading the text, discuss the friendship situations with the children by asking open-ended questions. The open-ended questions permit the youngsters to put themselves into the role of the major characters and events in the story. Begin the procedure with such questions as "How was _____ (insert the name of the main character in the book) a friend?" Or, "How did he/she show friendship?"

After the youngsters respond to the questions, guide them to role play the situations in which the main characters (and/or events) show particular qualities of friendship. In addition, role play other episodes from the children's literature books that show the growth and development of friendships. Practice these role-taking episodes again, and make sure that every child has the opportunity of playing the main characters in the story.

VARIATIONS   After the role-taking episodes, the youngsters can be encouraged to draw one or two things from the stories that show "what a friend is," "how to become a friend," and "why friendship is important to everybody."

ACTIVITY TITLE   ## A Story of Friends

MATERIALS   For this activity, you need a number of felt materials, cut-outs, and a flannel board (or a regular plywood board covered with felt.) Trace or draw figures of two girls, two boys, one adult, and one dog or cat on felt. Also include house and car "figures." Then cut them all out.

PROCEDURES   Give the felt figures to the child or group of youngsters. As you hand each of the figures to each child, ask her to identify and name it. Second, guide the youngsters in developing and telling a story with the cut-outs. Make sure that the story deals with friends, friendships, or some form of helping, sharing, or cooperating. For example, say to the youngsters, "Tell a pretend story about these friends and the games they play together!"

With either younger or older children, accept the stories they tell about their friends. The stories themselves are more important at this time than the way they are told. Ignore broken rules of grammar or the fact that an episode has no discernible beginning, middle, and end. You may also want to prompt or cue them if they show difficulty in making up and developing their stories. After they tell their stories about friends, ask "How did these individuals show their friendships to each other?" Emphasize the actions and deeds mentioned by the children and the fact that showing friendship requires being a friend. In discussion, also bring out other qualities of caring, such as co-operating and sharing.

VARIATIONS   Ask the child or group of youngsters to tell a different story about friends and about the important qualities of individuals caring for individuals. Make sure that all the felt cut-outs are used in this second story. Repeat the previous questions with their focus on friends, friendships, and caring.

ACTIVITY TITLE   ## Three Wishes About Friends

MATERIALS   Paper and pencil are the only materials needed.

PROCEDURES   Discuss and talk about "wishes" and what they mean. Ask the youngsters to name and explain three wishes they have about friends. These wishes could include, for example:

1. "I wish I could do things with my friends!"
2. "I wish I could be like my friend!"
3. "I wish that I had friends!"

Accept all the children's "wishes" concerning friends. After they have given their wishes, make sure that they explain them, to give you a better understanding of what these wishes are and what they mean to them. After naming and explaining, guide the children to role play and to act out each of these wishes. In the role play, guide them to focus on the qualities of friends and on the characteristics of caring they would like to show. Make sure that the children exchange and play roles of themselves as well as of the pretend friends they might like to become.

VARIATIONS   The child can also draw his wishes about friends. After the youngster has drawn his wishes, make sure that you ask for explanations of them. The child can also role play these wishes about friends and friendships. Similarly, guide the children to identify the qualities and characteristics of friends they admire.

ACTIVITY TITLE   ## Puppet Play and Caring

MATERIALS   You need a hand puppet and a children's story or book. The hand puppet resembles and represents the main character in the story. It can be either purchased or made from home-made materials. However, the puppet should be easily manipulated by the youngster. The children's book or story should be carefully chosen. The character in the text should show the qualities of caring, cooperating, and dependibility through his or her friendly acts and activities. These books can be borrowed from the local school or public library.

PROCEDURES   Read the story of the caring friend to the youngster. Discuss the ways in which the child in the story shows and displays caring actions of a friend. You may need to guide the youngster to recognize these qualities. After the reading and the discussion, introduce the puppet and let the youngster manipulate and play with it. After the child has the opportunity to use the puppet, say to him, "This puppet is _____ (insert the name of the main character in the story). We just read about him (or her) and what he (or she) did in the story." Continue the guidance by saying, "Show what _____ does and says in the story." Continue the guidance by saying, "Show what _____ does and says in the story to show that he/she is a friend." Have the youngster role play the story using the puppet, and prompt him to show additional qualities of being or showing a friend.

VARIATIONS   You can use the puppet over again in other stories read to the child. Following the same procedure, have the child enact and show the role

of a friend. In addition, the youngster can also make up stories based on the qualities of friendship and use the puppet to enact them.

ACTIVITY TITLE **Being a Friend to the Classroom or Family Pet**

MATERIALS   Pets found in the classroom and home are ideal resources for this activity. If no real pets are available, the youngster can have a "pretend" pet that can be used in this activity.

PROCEDURE   Discuss how and why we care for our pets. The how's could include caring for pets through feeding requirements, grooming, healthful exercise, buying licenses, and taking them to the veterinarian when they are ill. The why's include such items as loving them, their dependence on us, and our reliance on them. Following the discussion, youngsters role play—a number of times—the ways of caring for the pet and showing friendship toward it. After acquiring these helping and caring routines, the children show these actions directly with the pet. These responsibilities can be changed around so that every youngster has the opportunity of actually showing the how's and why's of caring and of being a friend to the pet. Make sure that you monitor the children's actions in these actual follow-through routines of caring and being a friend to a pet.

VARIATIONS   In addition to working with an actual or pretend pet, youngsters can draw "caring for their pets." The drawings of the pets can change depending on which animals the youngsters decide to call their pets. After they complete their drawings, discuss the how's and why's of caring, of being a friend to a pet, and of receiving its friendship.

57

ACTIVITY TITLE Pictures About Caring for Pets

MATERIALS Look through a number of family magazines and journals to find pictures of pets as friends and caring for pets. Make sure that the pictures show a number of different kinds of pets and the numerous ways of showing caring.

PROCEDURES Ask the child to describe and to talk about what is happening in the pictures. Guide her in the discussion and focus on how the pet is cared for, why it is being cared for, and how the individual and the animal show that they are friends. Guide them to discover what a pet is and the characteristics that both the individual and the pet show as friends. Repeat this procedure with several of the other pictures. Finally, ask the youngsters to go back over the pictures that were discussed and choose one of the pets they would like to have. In turn ask, "Why would you like to care for this pet?" Then ask each youngster to show how she would care for it and be its friend. In this role play, she can show a number of acts and activities that show caring for and being a friend to the pet.

VARIATIONS Ask each youngster to choose another picture of a favorite pet. Repeat the same procedures with this and other pictures of pets chosen. In addition, the child can also draw the various routines of caring for and being a friend to pets, and discuss them with the parent or teacher.

[2] As members of school and family groups, children have relationships to significant adult "others." These relationships constitute another key factor that helps shape their roles in caring by practice through role-taking. The following activities use different types of role-taking to facilitate the caring of children as members of families and school groups.

ACTIVITY TITLE Caring in Family Groups

MATERIALS Look through old catalogs from Montgomery Wards, Penneys, and Sears, as well as family magazines and journals. Find pictures of family group members doing things together and showing various types of caring. These pictures should show several types of family activities such as recreation work, and bedtime routines, sharing thoughts, making decisions together, and cooperating to complete a task.

PROCEDURES For each picture, ask the youngsters to describe the actions of the family members and the way they are caring for one another. For example, ask, "What are the people in this family doing together? . . . Tell about what they are doing?" In inquiring about caring, you might say, "How do the family members in the picture show that they are caring for one another?" Guide and prompt the children in their descriptions and discussions. As each picture is described and the caring situations discussed, decide which of the pictures the child relates to best. After these "best" pictures are selected, ask the children to role play the situations portrayed in them. In these role play sessions, give emphasis primarily to practicing the caring routines in the pictures. As the role play unfolds, encourage and reinforce them for elaborating on the caring routines. At the end of the role play, change the roles of the actors and have them rehearse the episode again.

VARIATIONS   The child is asked to draw members of his family working together at a particular task or recreational endeavor. After discussion of the picture the youngster is asked to enact the role play episode.

ACTIVITY TITLE   Adults' Jobs at School, Home, and Work

MATERIALS   This activity of identifying jobs and of understanding the importance in caring for individuals does not need any materials.

PROCEDURES   Ask the children to describe the jobs that are performed by parents at home and work. Also ask them to talk about the jobs done by teachers and by other significant adults, such as police and fire officials. Next, discuss the importance of these jobs to others. In the discussion on the importance of jobs, pick up and guide the children's ideas about jobs and how they show caring. For example, the parent washes dishes, prepares meals, irons clothes, repairs the home, goes to work and visits friends and places of interest. The teacher, for instance, works with children, cleans and dusts the classroom, helps each individual youngster, and empathizes with them as specific occasions arise. The importance of other jobs includes helping to fight fires, keeping buildings from burning, and helping people who are lost.

All these jobs and others are important because they show caring by and for others. The way each job shows caring is mentioned through adult guidance and prompts. The children are asked to show what each job is and how they are performed by role-taking. The caring element of each job mentioned by the youngsters is also shown through role play. To insure that all jobs are practiced and that their caring elements are shown in the enactments, make sure that the youngsters have the chance of role playing a number of them.

VARIATIONS   After role playing the jobs, the youngsters can be asked to represent the workers' actions by drawing pictures of them. Ask the children to explain their pictures and the caring elements shown. Again prompt and guide them in their explanations of the caring actions shown in the pictures.

ACTIVITY TITLE   Child's Jobs at School and Home

MATERIALS   No materials are needed for this activity focusing on children's jobs at school and home.

PROCEDURES   Ask the children to identify the jobs and chores they do at home and school. After identifying them, guide the youngster to explain what they do on their jobs. For example, in emptying the trash at home and the wastepaper basket at school, the children show the actions of "picking up and walking with the object" and "emptying it into a larger container." As each job is explained, guide them to describe how they are showing caring for others. Emptying the trash and paper baskets, for example, shows the caring of individuals because these receptacles can then be used by group members at school and home. Prompt and guide the youngsters in identifying the caring actions in each of the jobs. After completing the discussions, ask each youngster to role play the job he does either alone or with others. In the reenactments, make sure that the caring actions in the job are shown and explained.

VARIATIONS

Pictures of children performing varied jobs can be obtained from journals found in the home and school. The pictures are discussed with the youngsters, and the various types of caring shown in these illustrations are explained. Again, prompt and guide the children in their recognition and explanation of the types of caring shown through the roles. The new jobs and chores identified in the pictures are practiced through role play. Make sure that each youngster has the chance to enact and practice a variety of jobs and caring-related elements.

ACTIVITY TITLE   Nonverbal Ways of Showing Caring

MATERIALS   No materials are required for this activity of showing caring actions using nonverbal communication.

PROCEDURES   Begin this activity by asking the youngster to tell you how she lets others know what she needs and how she feels. The obvious and most

commonly mentioned way is "talking" or "speaking." Guide the child to mention another way of showing desires and feelings through the use of motor actions. Prompt her to mention that feelings of caring are conveyed through motor actions and body movements (that is, without verbal communication). You need to model caring through role playing to show young children that caring can be shown by "smiling," "putting your arm around your friend's shoulder," "hugging one another," "shaking hands," and many other means! Although children and adults always use nonverbal ways of showing that they care for one another, they rarely think of this method as communciating because it is so natural and spontaneous.

After the youngsters model the caring actions using body movements, ask them to think of how they can show others that they care through motor actions. Accept and prompt all motor responses, and ask others to identify what is communicated. Since there is no "right" or "wrong" answer, accept all the children's verbal identification of the caring roles that are expressed. In addition, you need to explain that many types of caring can be shown by a single motor or nonverbal action. This explanation prevents children's feelings from being hurt because their nonverbal mode was "incorrectly" guessed by their peers. Repeat the procedures until all children have taken their turns. Next, have the children practice each other's motoric actions that show caring in nonverbal ways. Again, have them guess the caring action that each one is showing.

VARIATIONS   Throughout the day, ask the youngsters to observe others (including adults) as they show caring actions through motor and body movements. At the end of an hour, half-day, or day (depending on the age of the child), ask the youngsters to recall the instances observed. In turn, have them practice through role play the particular form of caring they observe.

ACTIVITY TITLE   Caring Through Significant Others

MATERIALS   Look through your favorite comic strips and books to find comic characters showing and displaying caring routines with others. Comic strips such as "Peanuts," "Nancy," and contemporary comic books show caring acts and activities. Clip these examples and mount them on cardboard backing from soap boxes obtained from local supermarkets.

PROCEDURES   Hold up the comic strip examples and ask, "What are _____ (insert names of the comic strip characters) doing in the comic strip?" As the children interpret and explain the characters' actions, guide them to identify and describe the caring actions they are showing toward others. After these preliminary procedures, have the children decide which of these characters they wish to role play and ask them to enact the caring actions shown by them. When hesitations occur, prompt the children, and permit them time to elaborate and expand on these caring actions through their role play. Make sure that the major roles are changed, and continue to practice these actions as long as the children show interest.

VARIATIONS | Ask the children to find examples of their favorite comic characters. Also ask them about their favorite television shows as sources of caring actions. Repeat these procedures and have the children role play the caring acts and activities of their favorite characters.

ACTIVITY TITLE | ## Some Famous Families

MATERIALS | You need pictures of currently famous families and of storybook families. For example, newspaper clippings showing the activities of families of our national leaders can be used. In addition, gather commercial or make hand-drawn pictures of notable families in the literature. The famous storybook families should include characters like Mary Poppins, the Old Woman Who Lived in the Shoe, Mother Goose, Pinocchio, and others. Further pictures of notable television families can be used.

PROCEDURES | Hold up one of the pictures and ask the child to explain what it is about! After the youngster has given you her explanation, guide her to identify whether it shows several important traits of caring. For example, ask, "Do you think the picture shows that the family members are friendly toward one another? . . . Why do (or don't) you think so?" The same questioning procedure is used over again with other caring traits, such as kindness, happiness, helping, cooperating, working toward a goal, listening and communicating, having fun with one another, and others. After the youngsters have identified these caring traits and explained them in the pictures, practice these characteristics by role playing the characters in the picture. As before, guide and prompt them to rehearse these caring traits. At the end of the role playing episodes, have the youngsters exchange role and rehearse these traits again.

VARIATIONS | As a variation, the child can be encouraged to identify an additional trait (or traits) that she feels is important in showing caring. In addition, she is asked to choose one of her favorite pictures and to tell about these traits through the character's actions and activities.

ACTIVITY TITLE | ## Guessing Caring Actions

MATERIALS | Gather four or five pictures of individuals showing caring acts and activities. Make sure that each picture shows no more than one caring action. Examples of one-category pictures of caring actions include, as examples:

1. a girl walking her dog,
2. a police official helping a man cross a traffic intersection,
3. one boy with his arm around another boy's shoulder,
4. one girl sharing her toy trucks with another in a play session.

In addition, you need an 8½ x 11" piece of cardboard as a cover for the pictures.

Hold up the cardboard with its longer side on the surface of the table, and place one of your pictures behind it. Make sure that the child can see only one-half of the picture, and that the other half is covered by the cardboard. When you ask the youngster to describe how the individual might be showing caring actions, you force her to mentally represent possible caring actions to complete the picture. Accept all the youngster's responses and descriptions of caring. Now show the other half of the picture and ask the youngster to describe the caring actions. Make sure she knows that there are no "right" or "wrong" answers and that her guesses are "correct." Repeat this same procedure with the other pictures.

VARIATIONS The adult can reverse the procedure and ask the child to hold up the cardboard with one-half of the picture showing. In reversing the roles, the youngster directs the same question to the adult. With this variation, you should suggest other caring actions and activities not previously mentioned by the child or in your discussions.

ACTIVITY TITLE **Caring Through Materials**

MATERIALS Gather together objects and materials that are used in the home and school to show caring for the environment and for self and one another. For example, objects and materials from the home might be a broom or a toothbrush! In addition, toy objects from home, such as children's trucks, cars, and dolls, can be used as if they were real cars and children. Objects and materials from the school might include puzzles and other toys that need to be put away so that others can easily find and use them, as well as pots, water, and detergent. Toy objects from the school, such as Lincoln logs and cars, can also be used to represent real situations and settings.

PROCEDURES All the objects from the house and school can be used by the child to show caring situations. For example, ask the youngster to show through role play what you do with the broom, the toothbrush, the pots, the water, the detergent, and other real materials. For toy objects, ask the youngster to "pretend that you are driving the truck (or car) and show how you care for a passenger while driving!" With the doll, the youngster can pretend he is the doll and show how he dresses himself! For the Lincoln logs and cars, a town or city intersection can be constructed, and the child can demonstrate what he does to show caring as he drives down the intersection in a car where individuals are attempting to cross the street! In all these situations the child is asked to imitate the use of real or pretend objects in varying types of group settings.

   After the child has shown caring in these role play sessions, discuss the caring routines and how they were shown or represented. Guide him where appropriate.

VARIATIONS For variation, ask the child to represent the caring actions or activities suggested by the objects before he can use it. In turn, the caring actions are discussed.

63

ACTIVITY TITLE	Recognizing Feelings

MATERIALS   Three 5x8″ pieces of cardboard and a felt pen are needed. On one of the cards draw a happy face. On another card, draw a sad face. On the third one, draw a neutral face that shows no feelings.

PROCEDURES   Hold up each one of the cards successively. With each card, ask the youngster, "What feeling does this face show to others?" Further, ask, "Why do you think the child feels this way?" Guide and prompt the child's responses to determine and extend her recognition of individuals' feelings and the situations that may have caused these responses.

After the youngster understands and recognizes "happy" and "sad," try other feeling and feeling dimensions. For example, the recognition of surprise, fear, and empathy leads to other relevant dimensions of feelings. After recognition of these various feelings, the youngster is asked to "show these feelings" through role play. After she practices these feelings, discuss the relationship between recognizing individuals' feelings and showing caring to those who show these feelings. Guide the youngster, through discussion and role play, to describe and show how she might respond to those who are, for example, sad, angry, or afraid.

VARIATIONS   Collect from old magazines and journals pictures of children in family and school groups showing various feelings. Ask the child to identify and describe the feelings of the youngsters in the pictures. Through

prompting, ask her to show reciprocal caring actions that could be made to ameliorate the feelings represented by the youngsters in the pictures.

ACTIVITY TITLE

Recognizing and Practicing Caring Words

MATERIALS

You need 5x8″ index cards and a felt tip pen for this activity on recognizing and practicing care words. On each card, print one caring word for family and school groups, such as helping, sharing, loving, cooperating, trusting, or listening. Additional cards can be made for other caring words. These cards make a caring word bank.

PROCEDURES

The first step in this procedure is to develop an initial recognition of the printed words. This goal can be easily achieved by using the following two-step teaching routine:

1. While holding up the word card, ask the child, "What does this word say?"
2. Then, "Point to the word that says 'helping'!"

Repeat this teaching procedure as often as necessary to teach the child the elementary recognition skills for each word.

After the youngster learns to recognize several of these caring words, you are ready to have him practice the words through role play. Place three of the word cards before the youngster—let's say helping, sharing, and, trusting. Direct the child by saying, "Point to the word that says 'helping'." After he correctly points to the word card, ask him to show through his actions what that word means. In enacting that word, the youngster can use his own body and any object or set of objects he chooses. Older children tend to use more objects to assist their enactment and understanding of the caring words than younger ones. Prompt and guide the child in this enactment. In addition, you may become involved in the role play yourself. Particularly when the child hesitates for a period, you may want to model and act out several of these caring words individually or with him. Complete the enactments and practice of the remaining caring words.

VARIATIONS

After the youngster recognizes and practices these caring words, you can act out a caring word. Then ask him to point to the word that identifies or names the set of actions that he has observed. After the youngster gets the idea of pantomiming and then identifying the caring words shown through these actions, ask him to act out words of his choice, and you identify them. The list of caring words can be expanded, and these procedures and variations can be used over and over again.

[3]   In caring, youngsters encounter situations in which they serve as counselors for themselves as well as for others. Making decisions, sharing information, listening to others, and helping them with various

personal, individual, and group endeavors are among the important skills of caring as counselor through role-taking. The activities that follow focus on caring routines in which children practice the roles of counselor for themselves and for peer group members.

ACTIVITY TITLE ## Let's Decide

MATERIALS No specific materials are needed for this activity on decision-making and choices as a skill basic to caring and considering.

PROCEDURES Introduce this activity at the child's level by having her identify and explain a decision she has made outside the area of caring. For example, "Did you ever have difficulty in deciding and choosing between two toys (or between two types of activities, foods, or whatever)?" Have the child describe and explain the situation or situations, while making sure that the dilemma (either this *or* that) is brought out. After this description ask, "How did you finally decide which one to choose?" Prompt her where necessary. Try to guide her in identifying the criterion (or criteria) used to decide, regardless of whether the reason is individual ("I liked to do this better than that!") or group-based ("Mommy, the teacher, or my friend helped me choose!"). Next give the youngster the following situation, which can be role played immediately after reading or practiced after discussing and resolving it.

> Pretend you and two other friends are walking home from school. Both of your friends live close to your home. One friend says, "Let's walk home this way!" The other says, "Let's walk home another way!" (You can use the names of streets and children to make the situation more realistic and specific.) The two children begin arguing about which one of the two ways they should use to go home. Since they are your best friends, how would you help them decide which one of the ways to walk home?

Placed in the role of friend and counselor to both youngsters, the child must help them resolve the problem. As before, prompt her for a criterion that assists decision-making, such as one way is shorter than the other and/or one way goes past the hobby shop, and they can see the toys in the store! This situation is ideal for practicing through role playing. Since children are continually faced with these situations of choosing and deciding, try other examples based on their daily living experiences. Follow the same procedures, and practice them through role play strategies.

VARIATIONS The children should also know that adults have to make decisions and choices as part of caring and considering for themselves and others. Describe several of your experiences to which the youngsters can relate. Ask them what they would do, and then practice the decisions using role play procedures.

ACTIVITY TITLE People Working and Caring Through Their Jobs

MATERIALS This activity shows people working with people—talking and discussing a common problem or interest in a caring setting. The materials include pictures and photographs of such people and such situations as two plumbers who are planning to repair a leaky sink valve, fire officials helping one another "suit up" for a fire, or people deciding on procedures at a business meeting. In addition, gather some tools and other concrete objects that represent the jobs and tasks people are performing in the caring settings.

PROCEDURES With these pictures, photographs, and tools, build a "learning center" by displaying all these materials neatly on a table for the children to see, work with, and use. After they become familiar with their objects in their own way, ask the youngsters to find a picture or photograph of people working and using these tools. Further, ask them to tell what the people in the illustration are working on and doing together. Accept all the responses that are appropriate to the pictures or photographs. Then say, "Pretend that the people are talking to one another and helping each other finish their job!" Continue by inquiring, "What might these people be saying to one another as they work together!" As the children explain, guide them to recognize that they could be discussing ways (or alternatives) to complete and/or perform jobs together. Also focus on ways they might be helping one another decide on procedures and on how helping each other to make decisions is "caring for others and for the jobs they are doing!" Next ask them to practice caring through role play by showing what these people do and say to one another as they work together to cooperatively complete the job. In similar fashion, use the same procedures with several of the other tools, objects, and illustrations.

VARIATIONS The youngsters practice the same episode again, but this time ask the children (and/or adults) to guess what job is being done and how it is being completed. Next have the children (and/or adults) guess how the actors are showing, caring, helping, and decision-making as they carry out the role episode.

ACTIVITY TITLE Recalling Caring at Home and School

MATERIALS No materials are needed to perform this activity in helping youngsters recognize and recall situations in which family, school, or sibling groups show caring as counseling.

PROCEDURES To set the stage for recall, say:

Today and yesterday, all of us have either watched or seen your parent(s); brothers, and sisters at home, or friends at school, help and share with each other. Working together means cooperating with and caring about others and about the things that you and

67

others do. [Here give an example that you recall that shows the youngsters the concept or focus.] Now try to remember an experience [situation or event] that you saw or shared in which people were caring by helping others.

Have the youngster explain in detail the situation he saw or participated in! Ask the children to recall and share their experiences or activities. Review the experience you choose as an example in the story, and highlight the aspect of caring as counseling. As others have the opportunity to recall and share their experiences, choose one situation that clearly shows actions and activities of family or school groups caring by helping others and making decisions. After you clarify this example, have them role play and practice it. Exchange the actors' roles, have them rehearse the episode again, and pick another situation that was recalled and go through the same procedures with the children.

VARIATIONS   Give the children, or have them identify, other examples of caring in which family or school group members help each other discuss, plan, cooperate, or carry out an action or activity. They can also be explained, and acted out through role play.

ACTIVITY TITLE   ## Listening to Others

MATERIALS   You need two hand puppets. These puppets can be either purchased at local department, toy, and learning stores or made with old worn-out socks (by stuffing them with paper or yarn for the head, sewing on buttons and cloth for the eyes and mouth, and putting on clothing or body parts).

PROCEDURES   The adult puts one puppet on one hand and the second one on the other hand. Holding the puppets so that they are "talking" to one another, read the following script:

> *First puppet* [to the second puppet]: "I have had a real 'bad' day today. Everything went wrong! I fell off my bike and hurt my knee. My favorite toy that I always play with is lost. My mother scolded me for scuffing up my new shoes."
>
> *Friend puppet:* "We all have 'bad' days. Don't feel badly." [The friend puppet pats the first puppet on the shoulder.] "You will feel much better tomorrow!"

Put the puppets away and out of the child's sight. Ask, "What did the first puppet say to his friend? . . . Why did the first puppet feel so 'badly'? . . . How did the second puppet make his friend feel better?" Accept such answers as "Don't feel sad!" and the like. Give the child one puppet, and you put on the other. Ask the child which part she wants to play, and rehearse the episode again. Add additional content by improvising as the occasion arises in the enactment. Exchange parts and practice again. When the episode is completed, ask, "How did the puppets make each other feel better?" Prompt and guide her for

responses, using the "caring as counseling" theme. These responses could include, "Because they shared feelings! . . . They helped each other feel better! . . . Because they are friends!"

VARIATIONS   Enact similar play settings with the puppets; have one share feelings with the other, who listens and provides empathic responses. The same procedures and similar questions can be used again to have the youngster understand the importance of listening in caring as counseling.

ACTIVITY TITLE   Drawing What I Do

MATERIALS   You need three pieces of white construction paper, 8½x11". In addition, this activity requires crayons or a set of felt tip pens of different colors.

PROCEDURES   The youngsters draw three different pictures for this activity. Each drawing is completed successively. In the first, ask the child to, "Draw a picture of yourself and your pet (either that you have or that you would like to have) and how you care (or would care) for it!" The second picture contains a drawing of the child and his parent (or teacher) doing a favorite activity together. In the third one, ask the youngster to draw a picture of himself and a pretend companion (or real friend) doing something together, such as playing a game, building a castle, eating lunch, and so on.

Upon completion of all three drawings, ask for an explanation and description of each drawing. Make sure that you probe and guide the child's descriptions of what caring actions he is showing toward his pet, his companions, and adults. Ask, "How does your pet (companion, parent, or teacher) show that it (he, she, Mommy/Daddy, or the name of the teacher) cares for you?"

Next extend the child's representational thinking from a description of caring. For each drawing, give him a pretend situation that focuses on and requires him to respond to caring as counseling. For example, using the drawing of the youngster and his real or pretend pet, comment, "Both you and your pet care for one another!" Ask, 'Show what you would do and say to help when it became sick!" Prompted by these and other questions, the youngster shows and says what he would do with his pet (companion or adult) in each situation. Prompt and guide the responses so that the child is required to identify particular action steps that he would perform in each of the caring as counseling situations.

VARIATIONS The youngster completes additional drawings of caring situations that he experiences. These caring themes for the drawings can be based on other sources, such as favorite television programs or children's literature books. The same procedures are used with these additional drawings to focus on caring as counseling.

ACTIVITY TITLE ## Creating a Story on Caring

MATERIALS One sheet of lined paper and a pencil are needed for this activity. On the piece of paper, write, "The Special Things I Like to Do with Other Children!"

PROCEDURES As an initial introduction to this activity, say, "All of us like to do special things!" Continue the introduction and give examples of some of the special things that you like doing. Some of these, as examples, might include "I like going to the circus, to the movies, and to dances!" Ask the youngster, "What special things do you like to do?" Prompt the child and have him identify as many as possible. Next tell the youngster, "Now, having named some of the special things you like to do, we are going to try something different. What are some of the special things you like to do with other children?" As the child identifies them, you can list them on the piece of paper. As before, prompt where necessary. After the child lists as many as possible, quickly go over the items and identify some that suggest caring as counseling. For example, some of these items could include: "helping my friend . . . cooperating with . . . or sharing my toys with . . . " Next, each of these situations of caring as counseling can be practiced using role playing. After the child has acted out these special situations, discuss the element of caring as counseling with him. Prompt him where necessary, and again rehearse the episodes.

With the additional items on the list, describe the situation and highlight, emphasize, or develop the caring as counseling element. The child's responsibility is to guess the special event being described.

ACTIVITY TITLE **Using a New Caring Action with Another**

MATERIALS One lined sheet of paper and a pencil (or a chalk board and chalk) are required for this activity of practicing a new caring action ·with another.

PROCEDURES Develop a list of possible ways in which children might show caring as counseling with a friend, peer, parent, or teacher. The list should include:

1. help another reach a decision,
2. listen to another,
3. solving a problem with a friend,
4. sharing my toys with another,
5. volunteering to help my teacher or parent with a job,
6. making my parent's or teacher's job easier,
7. helping my pet learn a new trick,
8. showing feelings for another."

In addition, ask the youngsters to think up other ways of showing "caring as counseling"! As the situations are identified, add them to the list.

When the list is complete, explain and give an example of each one to the children so they understand these caring as counseling situations. After the description say, "Choose one of these ways of showing caring with another that you have not done before and that you would like to try out!" Wait several minutes until the youngster has decided on one of them. If the youngster hesitates or needs assistance, help her decide. Then continue, "Try out and show this new way of caring with a friend, sister, brother, mother, father, or teacher! After you try it out at home or school, we will talk about it!" As the children try out their new ways of showing caring as counseling, ask them to explain what they said and did and the reactions of the others. As they are explained, highlight and focus on the caring as counseling element.

VARIATIONS The youngster can choose other new ways of showing caring as counseling from the list and try them out at home or school. Follow the same procedures for discussion. After trying them out, the children can also practice them by role play.

ACTIVITY TITLE **Charting the Ways of Showing Caring**

MATERIALS For this activity, a number of materials are needed. First, you need two or three pieces of oak tag or heavy-weight drawing paper measuring

18x24". Second, cut out a number of pictures of caring as counseling from family magazines or journals. Make sure that the pictures show a number of caring as counseling situations and a variety of people (such as adults to adults, children to adults, children to children) showing these actions. With masking tape, tape each of the pictures in list fashion along the eighteen-inch side of the paper. Along the top of the paper, write each of the children's names. When the pictures fill one side of the paper, use the other pieces of paper until all the pictures are used and taped into place. After these charts, which represent different caring as counseling situations, are completed, you are ready to begin the activity.

PROCEDURES

Ask the youngsters to explain each of the caring situations. Prompt and guide them to focus on the caring as counseling element, that is, especially on what the individuals are saying and doing—how one person is caring for another and the other reciprocating in some fashion. Depending on the quality of the picture and on the ages of the children, you may have to ask them to "pretend" in order to describe what the individuals are doing and saying in the situations. Next ask the children to role play the situations to determine their level of understanding. Finally, ask them to try several of these caring routines at school or home. After they have done so, ask them which ones they used and place a tally mark or X under their names and alongside those situations represented in the pictures. Repeat this process of charting over a period of time, such as a week or a month (in the case of older children). Then discuss the caring as counseling situations used the most by the youngsters.

VARIATIONS

Pick up on and discuss those caring as counseling situations that have the fewest tally marks beside them. Ask the children to focus on these situations during the following week, and record the children's accomplishments.

As another variation, ask the youngsters to find additional pictures of caring as counseling, tape them to the chart, and follow the same procedures.

ACTIVITY TITLE

TV Characters and Caring

MATERIALS

Some drawing paper and crayons are required for this activity.

PROCEDURES

Introduce the activity by asking the children to name their favorite television shows and television characters or actors. Ask them to describe why they like the shows. Further question them on why they like the television characters they have identified. Prompt and guide them to describe the actions and activities of the characters and actors. Then ask, "Which of your favorite television characters show that they care about people and their feelings in how they act toward othes?" Again prompt where necessary if the children hesitate or if they are unable to identify their favorite "caring" television characters. Ask, "How do you know that _____ cares for people and their feelings?" Continue, "What does _____ do and say that lets you know he (she or it) cares for people and their feelings?" The children should describe some of the caring actions that they have observed their characters perform.

Next have them draw pictures of their favorite television characters performing acts and actions with others (such as people or animals), and ask them to talk about their pictures. Prompt and guide the children in explaining their pictures of television characters as "caring" others, based on the actions and activities they perform. Finally, have the youngsters role play and practice caring as counseling through the roles of their favorite television characters.

VARIATIONS

Keep a list of the favorite television characters the children have identified. Have them role play the actions and activities of these various television "actors" in the context of caring as counseling situations. Exchange roles among the children. In addition, as a few of the children play these individuals, you can have the others name them and explain the caring as counseling actions they are performing.

ACTIVITY TITLE

Writing a Story About Caring

MATERIALS

You need several large pieces of writing paper measuring at least 20x24". Make sure the surface of the paper can be written on with a felt tip pen. In pencil, draw straight, horizontal lines on the paper. These lines should be spaced enough to write sentences between them in manuscript form. Two or three inches between the lines should be enough for clear and legible manuscript print.

PROCEDURES

The purpose of the activity is to have the individual child or group of youngsters develop and dictate a story about children who show caring as counseling! As the story is dictated, your task is to copy down and write their words with felt tip pen on the lines drawn on the paper. The story dictated by the youngsters can show helping, cooperating, listening, empathizing, and other group forms of caring as counseling. The best results in "Writing a Story About Caring" are obtained when the youngsters have experienced caring as counseling situations. And, for younger children it is even more important to use actual caring as counseling experiences as a basis for their written stories. To initiate this activity, for example, watch and wait—or plan—for the children to have a caring as counseling experience.

Another important idea in conducting this activity is to copy the children's contributions down as they dictate them. Changing, modifying, or altering the choice of words decreases the children's responses. Putting their thoughts down on paper to make sentence sense is acceptable. As the children are dictating, it is also acceptable to prompt and guide them in completing or extending their thoughts. After the children complete the dictation, make sure that you read the story in its entirety before practicing it through role-taking. Having completed this procedure, give the passage a title, ask the children to divide up and assign parts, and role play it. The story and role play episode can be practiced again with different actors playing the roles.

Additional stories can be dictated and practiced through role play following the same procedures. As another variation, you can write your own caring as counseling story and ask the children to enact the episode.

[4] TIPS

1. In working with children you will come across numerous incidental experiences in home and school that can be used to encourage caring actions. These incidental experiences that "catch children" caring are reinforced through adult praise and by providing opportunities for their additional rehearsal.

2. Learning caring roles through role-taking perspectives requires you to prompt and guide children's activities and actions. Only through adult prompting and guiding do youngsters learn to develop and practice role-taking activities that encourage growth of caring. The prompting and guiding are done at an appropriate time and sensitively offered by the teacher and parent.

3. In developing caring actions of children through role-taking perspectives, you need to model caring actions throughout the day for them. You can model through your comments, such as "You are feeling happy today! . . . You have colored your picture really well!" You can also model through your nonverbal actions—putting your arms around the shoulders of children, hugging them, patting them on the shoulder.

4. Encourage the youngsters to show caring actions of friendship, as well as caring relations to significant others in school and in family groups. Encourage them also to counsel and guide themselves and others in varying situations. In this context, "encouragement" means providing a supportive environment and a constructive atmosphere where the children can not only attempt but also succeed in showing these actions.

5. In developing caring roles through role-taking perspectives, the environment in home and school must have a quantity and variety of materials within them. Providing ample "dress-up" clothing, concrete materials, and objects that can be used for improvisation is crucial in developing caring. The quantity and quality of materials support and enrich the learning and development of caring through role-taking.

6. Use television programs to develop the caring actions of youngsters through role-taking. A number of very sound children's television shows beautifully illustrate friendship, family, and school group caring and caring as counseling. Remind them to watch these programs, so you can use their content for dramatic, sociodramatic, and puppet plays.

7. In learning and practicing caring actions using role play techniques, children must receive experiential and self-reward through these enactments. Experiential and self-reward obtained through

these enactments helps children learn, develop, and use these caring routines.

8. In learning and practicing these caring actions and activities through role perspectives, children must control their own play behaviors rather than being controlled by the adult. Effective control means that you guide and suggest where appropriate, rather than direct them.

9. In these role enactments, permit youngsters the freedom and flexibility to improvise, extend, and expand on your suggestions in showing caring roles through perspective taking. The more they expand and extend caring roles through their own creative thinking, the more they learn and use them in their daily living.

10. After completing role-taking episodes, you may need to prompt and guide the children so that they do *not* criticize or evaluate how well each "played" his or her role. Evaluating the children decreases their personal interest in doing these actions, decreases the probability that they will learn effective and constructive caring routines, and decreases their motivation to use role play.

Consideration

FOR OUR OWN AND OTHERS' NEEDS

Much like caring, consideration is a *mental* process that must be developed in children. In this respect, consideration can be defined as

1. the act or process of considering, deliberation, meditation,
2. a circumstance to be considered, a factor in forming a judgment or decision,
3. thoughtfulness or solicitude,
4. a thought produced by considering or a thoughtful opinion.

Yet very much unlike caring, which is primarily a *feeling* process, consideration is a process of learning about the effects of our actions, about causes and effects, and about the consequences of our actions and the actions of others. Hence this chapter takes the perspective that it is necessary to think about all aspects of our being, both mental and emotional.

In terms of consideration, young children need to be made aware of planning as an important part of their development. Planning implies a view of the future, as well as the consideration of necessary conditions, neither of which do young children naturally consider. So one of the goals of this chapter is to provide experiences conducive to developing this awareness and these abilities.

Further, many experts agree that much of the way people relate to their world and to the people in it is determined by their experiences in the early years. Several activities for parents, teachers, and children are included that deal with personal biases and prejudice. Understanding and accepting differences in people is vital for young children if they are to be positive functioning adults in a pluralistic society. With the world growing smaller each day, we must prepare children to live in the community of the world.

The third section of this chapter deals with the consideration of the needs of others. During the egocentric period of their lives, children find it difficult to gain a perspective of the needs of others. Yet again it is important that we offer experiences, at an early age, to promote such consideration,

While participating with your children in the following activities, keep your mind open to learning as well as to teaching.

[1] Considering the necessary conditions and the effects of their behavior on others is an important aspect of the affective/cognitive development of children. Try the following activities to facilitate this development.

ACTIVITY TITLE **Fighting Behavior**

MATERIALS To do this activity concerned with the self-control of aggressive feelings, you need paper, pencils, and the opportunity to view a contact sporting event! Boxing, wrestling, football, or lacrosse are good examples.

PROCEDURES Watch the contact sporting event and talk to the child about physically aggressive behaviors that children and adults use. Make a listing of the aggressive actions that the child can remember using and how he felt.

You will need to explain what aggressive behaviors are. You may describe them as "angry actions" or the things they do to other people that they don't like. Children will usually list things like pushing, hitting, biting, throwing things, yelling and screaming, taking things away, messing up the others' things, spitting, making faces, and the like. To get the child warmed up, you might remind him of a situation when he was in the role of aggressor and what he did.

After you have let the child talk about those actions and feelings, you need to turn the conversation to how it feels when someone acts like that toward him. Here again a good starter is to bring to mind a time when the child was in role of victim rather than aggressor. If necessary, you might ask how it felt when someone hit or punched him. List the responses, about how it felt to be the victim, next to the corresponding aggressive act and feeling, as follows:

Aggressive Behavior	Feelings	Feelings as Victim
1. Hitting	Powerful	Mad, sad,
2.	Angry, upset	Angry, hurt, etc.
3.		

Ask the child if he realizes that others feel this way too. Even though this is a yes, it will undoubtedly lead to a discussion of considering the effects of your actions on others.

VARIATION

After viewing the sporting event and listing the child's aggressive behavior, talk with him some more and list the aggressive feelings and actions that he thinks adults have. Place a star by the adult aggressive action that the child has actually observed. The list of children's aggressive acts will probably be more extensive than the list of adult aggressive behavior.

This exercise provides an opportunity to discuss self-control and the appropriate ways to release aggressive feelings—language, sports, hobbies, and so on. (See Chapter 6.) Make a list of the appropriate ways children can vent aggressive feelings.

ACTIVITY TITLE

How Does Your Garden Grow?
(What We Need to Grow)

MATERIALS

This activity on considering people's needs for growth and development calls for chart paper, a red-and-green marker, radish seeds, a container that is five or six inches deep, soil to fill the container, water, and a sunny place. Or pictures of plants and people in good and poor condition will also do.

PROCEDURES

Begin this activity by planting the radish seeds in the container. If planting is not possible, display the pictures. Depending on the child's knowledge, either elicit from her or explain the necessary conditions for the plants to live and grow. Categorize these conditions as food and protection (such as nutrients from the soil, water, and sunlight). Explain how too much sunlight, wind, erosion, or animals can harm the plant. Your explanation need not be in-depth. Use the green marker to list the plants' needs.

After planting and cleaning up, make a comment like, "I'm sure glad I don't have to water you every day! . . . or, It's a good thing I didn't have to plant you, so you would grow." Next ask the child what she thinks has been necessary for her to grow and develop. List these with the red marker. Children's responses are usually all physical like food, clothing, and shelter. Accept the child's responses and lead her to think about the needs we all have of security, love, creative expression, acceptance, mastery, self-concept, and so on.

Help the child brainstorm how we fill these affective needs and how we can fill these needs for others.

VARIATIONS

To demonstrate the effects of deprivation, plant several containers of seeds and subject them to different conditions. Put one in a closet (no sun), don't water another, do everything right for the next one, and so on.

After the plants have come up and shown signs of deprivation, discuss the needs of plants and people. Display the pictures of people in good and poor condition, and allow children to brainstorm the reasons for the differences in condition. (Relate them to the plants.)

ACTIVITY TITLE	## Considering Your Growth

MATERIALS   This activity on self-growth requires a tape recorder or paper and pencil.

PROCEDURES   The purpose of this activity is to help children become aware of how everyday experiences contribute to their personal development and to aid in their self-understanding.

Each day for a week, you and the child either write down or tape record your responses to the following questions:

1. Did you meet anyone new yesterday? Who? Where?
2. What new things did you try?
3. What was the nicest thing you did for someone yesterday?
4. What was the best thing that happened to you?
5. Think of yesterday: What did you learn about yourself?

Set aside a time during the weekend to share your responses. This sharing of insights can lead to greater understanding of self and each other.

If you find that the child has little to report, then some planning of his experiences is indicated.

VARIATION   Record these impressions on sheets of construction paper and construct a mobile at the weekend session. Another alternative is to collect or to draw pictures to represent the experience and develop a collage at the end of the week.

ACTIVITY TITLE   ## It Takes Time to Grow

MATERIALS   Long strips of paper or strings, clothespins, and small squares of paper, pens, magnifiers, and a measuring tape are needed for this activity.

PROCEDURES   The intent of this activity is to provide some perspective for children on the process of growth and development.

Young children find that they cannot do many things. Lots of times they hear, "Wait until you're older" or similar things. This activity will give them a chance to see the time-line of development.

While talking about how and when we learn things, as well as about how our body grows, cut two pieces of paper strips. Depending on your age and on the child's age, decide on a length to represent each year of life. Two inches is usually good. So if you are thirty and the child is five, one piece will be sixty inches and the other will be ten inches long. Together the two of you fill in the strips by activities you were able to do at various ages: dressing yourself, feeding yourself, tying your shoes, reading, playing organized sports, cooking, sewing, driving, earning money, staying up until nine o'clock, and so on.

Discuss the necessary growth and development that must take place for these abilities to develop.

Using the same format, list the important events in your life and when they happened: birth–school–graduation–first car–death of a parent–marriage–child was born–and so on . . . Discuss these and share your feelings of each with the child. Call on the child to describe his important events to you.

ACTIVITY TITLE   ## My Dad Can Beat Yours

MATERIALS   No materials are needed for this activity for dealing with children's jealousy.

PROCEDURES   Children often exhibit feelings like:

> "Mine is better than yours."
>
> "My house is bigger than yours."
>
> "My Mom is prettier than yours."
>
> "I can do it better than anyone!"
>
> "My Dad can beat up your Dad!"

These statements reflect fear or jealousy. This fear stems from a feeling that they are going to lose something that is important to them, usually attention or affection.

To deal with such feelings, you must first accept the feelings that the child is having. Then you can let her know you understand and finally to reassure her of your intent.

The next time you are confronted with a statement reflecting this type of feeling try:

1. Reflecting the feeling—"Your house is bigger than theirs."
2. Then reflecting the intent—"You want me to know that you have a big house."
3. Lastly, reassuring—"I'd like (love) you no matter what!"

VARIATION   Think of the times that you have felt jealousy. What did you say or do to express the feelings? Was it effective? What caused you to "get over" the jealous feelings? How can this introspection help you to facilitate children's ability to deal with negative feelings?

ACTIVITY TITLE   ## If (*Condition*), Then (*Action*)

MATERIALS   This activity demonstrates that necessary conditions must be met before certain things will happen. It makes use of no materials.

PROCEDURES   The intent of this activity is to demonstrate the influence of situational conditions in considering your actions. Teaching children about the necessary conditions for events to happen will help them plan.

Begin this activity by having the child respond to a series of statements of the following form:

If *you're* happy, then _____.

If *you're angry*, then you _____.

If *you want (don't want) to do something*, then you _____.

If I try *hard*, then _____.

Let the child respond to a few of these. Then you respond as well.

The next step is to describe some of these situations to the child. For example, if it's a nice day, we'll have a picnic. If Dad gets here in time, we will go to the show. If we feed the fish a lot, it will grow fast. And so on.

After describing each situation to the child, change each statement to reflect the situation where the condition is not met. Then ask him what will probably happen. For instance, if it rains today, then what will happen? If Dad is late, what will happen? What will it mean if we feed the fish only a little or not at all?

VARIATION   Use physical objects to show that necessary conditions must be met. Good examples are electric toys with and without batteries, building with blocks using round shapes and square shapes for foundations, creating activities, science experiments.

ACTIVITY TITLE   I'm Listening!

MATERIALS   This simple activity for developing listening skills requires paper, crayons, and a way of keeping time for two minutes.

PROCEDURES   Tell the child you have a game to play. Explain that she will get two or three turns talking about whatever she would like to talk about for two minutes. The only rule is that the listener may not interrupt the speaker until the two minutes are up.

Although usually it's best for you to go first, if the child has a topic, let her go first. What you talk about doesn't matter. Observe the child while you're talking. What did she do that let you know she was or was not listening attentively?

Now it is the child's turn. While she is speaking, over-emphasize any of your behavior that shows you are listening:

1. Shake or nod your head.
2. Smile and use other facial expressions to reflect what she says.
3. Sustain eye contact.
4. Lean toward the speaker.
5. Make appropriate accepting sounds like hmm, ah, ah-ha.

When the child's time is up, the two of you talk together about how you could tell the other was listening. Point out the five aspects mentioned, and demonstrate them to the child.

Ask the child to use as many of these techniques as possible during your turn. Provide some feedback as to how well she let you know she was listening this time.

During the child's next turn at speaking, try to exhibit behavior that communicates that you are not listening: look away, frown, fidget, yawn, and so on. When her turn is over, discuss the difference in behavior and feelings in the two sessions.

Continue as long as both of you would like practicing good listening skills.

VARIATION   For groups of children or the whole family, try this. On strips of paper write: (1) "Good Listener" or (2) "Poor Listener." Divide the group into threes and assign roles of speaker, listener, and observer. Have the listener choose one of the slips and play the role of good or bad listener. Rotate the roles around the group until everyone has tried each role. Let each observer guess which role the listener played and why he or she thinks so.

Now do a demonstration of the five listening behaviors: (1) head movements, (2) facial expression, (3) eye contact, (4) body posture, and (5) accepting sounds.

Let the groups take turns practicing receiving feedback from the observer.

ACTIVITY TITLE   ## Saving to Buy

MATERIALS   To convey the value of money and of saving money, you need an empty, cleaned, bleach bottle, along with masking tape, shoe polish, a sharp knife, and a sheet of white paper.

PROCEDURES   Place all the materials on the floor or table where the youngsters can work easily. Begin by suggesting that you make a bank together. While the child is wrapping the bottle with tape, you can discuss where and how children get money. This discussion will vary depending on the age of the child. While he is working, you can make a list of possible resources for future reference. When the bottle is wrapped, the child can rub it with shoe polish to give it a finished appearance.

Have the child choose some object of desire that he will be saving for. Write down the cost and draw this item at the top of a page; add the date and tape it to the "nose" of the bank. Instruct the child that each time money is put into the bank, the amount is to be written on the paper. Periodically, you and the child add up the total. When enough is saved, make a big deal of cutting open the bank and buying the item.

Point out to the child how long he has been saving and elicit the feelings he has about:

1. achieving the goal,
2. the length of time, and
3. the worth of saving on a regular basis.

VARIATION   Take a trip to the bank and open a joint savings account with the child. Be sure that the bank employee explains the operation of the savings account. You can reexplain things later at home. Help the child make a savings book for his own bank at home. (While at the bank be sure to take the child into the vault. It's neat.)

ACTIVITY TITLE **Who Decides?**

MATERIALS This activity on considering who makes decisions requires a piece of poster board, construction paper, glue, markers, and scissors.

PROCEDURES Introduce this activity in a discussion on decision-making. Display the materials and, with the child, make a "Who-Decides" board. Down the left side of the poster, list all the family members' names. Using the construction paper, make three pockets for each person and label them "Always," "Sometimes," and "Never." Make one large pocket at the bottom. The board will look like this.

For the decisions pocket, make strips of paper to fit into the pockets. On each strip, write decisions that affect the child. Samples are bedtime, eating time, the amount of allowance, TV shows, toys, spending money, buying new clothes, the time for going outside, chores, and the like. Let the child sort the decisions, each into the pockets that show who makes these decisions.

Lead the discussion to touch on areas of your concern. This might be an increase in the child's decisions or yours. Make sure that it is clear that all decisions are made for the good of the individual and the family.

VARIATION Make a deck of cards by writing or illustrating decisions and events that have an effect on the child. Samples are no movies this week, staying in your room, extra money in your allowance this week, a trip to the arcade games gallery, thirty minutes extra homework, one week's restriction, and so on.

Have the child draw a card and tell what could have happened to cause this decision to be made. Who probably made this decision?

ACTIVITY TITLE ## How I See Myself

MATERIALS To complete this activity on self-expectation, you will need white paper, a marker, strips of colored paper, and glue.

PROCEDURES This activity works best with small groups of elementary-aged children. It can also be effective in a one-to-one setting with younger children.

Give each child a piece of paper and instruct them to fold it into three sections, label the top section "Yes," the middle "Sometimes," and the bottom "No."

Using a list of descriptive phrases that describe different types of people, have the students write the statements in the appropriate boxes on their own paper. You may need to write the list for copying. For younger children it is necessary to cut the strips of colored paper, and let them glue them in.

Here are some ideas to include, but be sure to use some of your own and to elicit others from the students.

1. Enjoys being with people
2. Enjoys being alone
3. Once starts something finishes it when he or she has to
4. Likes being the boss
5. Prefers being outside
6. Usually does things only _____
7. Is good at a lot of things
8. Makes friends easily
9. Prefers to be alone
10. Makes others feel good

The point to be made in the discussion of the list is that how we see ourselves influences the way we behave and how we see others. The listing we create can serve as a list of our expectations of self.

In closing ask the students to circle the description that we would like to be examples of and to put a line through those negative aspects that we would like to change. Point out that the ones circled also indicate the positive aspects that we see in others.

VARIATION To see how others view us, pair the children off and have each child do the listing as though he or she were the other child. After they complete their listings, have them share their perceptions with each other.

Have them label their papers something like:

Susie as though she were Jane

[2] The first step in teaching about personal biases is the recognition of our own biases and prejudice. The two tools to combat biases and prejudice are experience and knowledge. Try the following activities to provide the experiential and knowledge base that will help your children understand prejudice and accept differences in people.

ACTIVITY TITLE **A Different Definition**

MATERIALS Music from various cultures and times—classical, rock, jazz, pop, easy listening, or whatever. Recordings can be borrowed from your local public library.

PROCEDURES Play a variety of music for the children while they are occupied with other activities. As the other activities are completed, ask questions about the music. You might begin by asking which ones they liked. They probably won't be able to describe the music well enough to identify it, so you will need to play back parts to let them select.

This should be a positive experience (they will like some types of music). It will provide opportunities for discussion of the music's origin, rhythm, content, lyrics, and authors. By discussing all aspects of the music, children see that different people, sexes, and cultures are appreciated worldwide.

VARIATION Set up an art gallery displaying painting, prints, sculpture, and other works of art from various eras, cultures, and media. For each, provide a description of the piece and of the creator. Have a discussion period about the gallery, stressing the contribution of people of all types.

ACTIVITY TITLE **Culture Collage**

MATERIALS To complete this activity on awareness of cultural differences, you need a variety of pictures of people, products, architecture, and other subjects from various cultures. You also need glue, scissors, and a large piece of paper or cardboard.

PROCEDURES Cut out the various pictures and place them, by culture, in separate envelopes. With no introduction, hand these to the child and ask what she sees that is alive and different in the envelopes. As the child describes the contents, listen intently and accept any comments.

Next explain that different cultures are represented. You may have American, Oriental, African, European, or any area represented. Stress that, although people live in different parts of the world, they have the same feelings and needs. Suggest the collage idea, and let the child mix or categorize the pictures any way she wishes.

VARIATION Mount the pictures on pieces of cardboard, and label the envelopes with the name of the culture and the shape of the country. On the back of the pictures, indicate the correct envelope. Let the children use this 85 as a sorting game.

ACTIVITY TITLE	Awareness Trip
MATERIALS	Although no materials are necessary for this activity, the adult must have an itinerary for the trip.
PROCEDURES	After the children have gained some idea of the variety of cultures in our world, suggest that you all take an imaginary trip. Use several chairs, chalk on the sidewalk, a large box, the bed, or anything that will add to the confined feeling of being on a plane. Make a big thing of having everything ready and of taking off on the trip.
	After you are "in the air," take the role of tour guide. Announce the country you are about to land in and remind them to be polite. Disembark from the plane and talk about all the things you are seeing. While describing all of these things, encourage the child to add things they think they would see. Interpose questions to reinforce concepts, for example, "I wonder what they mostly eat? . . . How they get around? . . . What they make a living from?"
	When you return from the trip, let them share their adventures.
VARIATION	Rather than a plane, board a train and see America. Be sure to have stops in ethnic areas of cities, in farm lands, in migrant labor camps, on an Indian reservation, and at historical spots.

ACTIVITY TITLE	Learning Together
MATERIALS	This activity for collecting information on different cultures requires writing paper, pens, envelopes, and stamps. You will also need to contact a teacher to get addresses.
PROCEDURES	Children often comment on the different cultures they see represented on TV or on visitors in our country who wear clothing from their countries. The next time this situation arises (or you can create it), get excited and tell the child you want to know too.
	Use the writing materials to send short notes to various embassies in Washington. These embassies will send you many brochures describing their countries, cultures, and tourist attractions. These materials will also provide much information for you and your child. They will also be useful for other activities in this book.
VARIATION	Use an encyclopedia to find out as much as you can, with the child, about various countries. If possible make photocopies of maps and pictures, and develop a "Worldwide" coloring book.

ACTIVITY TITLE	The Eye of the Beholder
MATERIALS	You need pictures of three males or females. Choose pictures of adults about the same age that look very different—fat and skinny, different complexions, with or without glasses, tall and short, and so on. You also have to have scrap paper and pencils.

PROCEDURES Number the pictures 1, 2, and 3. Ask the group of children to look at the pictures and write the number of the most attractive on a piece of paper. Have the children, one at a time, tell which is most attractive to them and why. After a discussion, point to each picture and ask the children what is not attractive and whether they can think of what type of person would choose this one as most attractive. The idea is that beauty is in the eye of the beholder.

VARIATION Do the same activity with pictures of flower arrangements. Discuss the ways the flowers are alike and different. Lead the discussion into the similarities and differences of people and of people's preferences.

ACTIVITY TITLE ## Are You Prejudiced?

MATERIALS This activity on determining the extent of sexual prejudice requires paper and pencils.

PROCEDURES Make a checklist of the following items with check spaces for boys, girls, and both: quiet, strong, emotional, noisy, weak, want to look nice, good, afraid, brave, bad, in charge, give in. The list should look something like this:

	Boys	Girls	Both
Quiet	_____	_____	_____
Strong	_____	_____	_____
Emotional	_____	_____	_____
Noisy	_____	_____	_____
.	.	.	.
.	.	.	.
.	.	.	.

Ask the children to complete the checklist. Now have them complete the following statements by using the checked items:

Boys are _____.
Girls are _____.

Lead a discussion to determine which listing seems more positive or negative. Do you think your sex is portrayed well?

VARIATION Make listings of the things boys do, of the things girls do, and of the things both do. Circle the one that you consider positive and draw a line under the negative. Who has the most positive? The most negative? What kinds of things are on both lists?

ACTIVITY TITLE ## I'm Gifted Too! (IQ)

MATERIALS No materials are needed to learn about how IQ's are determined and what they mean.

This activity is basically for parents to acquire knowledge. As children approach the middle elementary grades, it is appropriate to explain IQ to them and to clarify the ways we are all gifted.

IQ stands for Intelligence Quotient. An IQ is a score derived from the formula $IQ = MA/CA \times 100$. MA stands for mental age, and CA stands for chronological age. To determine a child's mental age, we usually give a general abilities test. Chronological age is the number of years and months since birth. So if a six-year-old has a test score that gives a mental age of six, then his or her IQ would be figured so:

$$IQ = 6/6 \times 100$$
$$= 100$$

As you can see, 100 is an "average" IQ. Actually an IQ of 90 to 110 is considered in the average range.

Many people treat this IQ score almost as a magical yardstick by which to categorize children. Although it is a useful tool in planning experiences, the IQ score really tells us very little about the person. Probably the most valid assumption that can be made from an IQ score is the child's ability to take the test. Obviously, children who have never seen a circus could not answer circus questions, or farm children know little about inner-city experiences. So the particular test that is administered is the key—a fact demonstrated by researchers who administered different IQ tests to children. Perhaps the overall IQ should be determined by a series of tests covering the cognitive, affective, and psychomotor domains.

Whether your children are categorized as "gifted" or as "slow learners" according to IQ scores, it is important that you focus on the gifts they have and build a positive concept of self and others.

VARIATION When your child mentions knowing someone who is gifted or a slow learner, draw him out. Make listings of how the two are different and alike. Point out the positive aspects of each, and explain how the IQ and giftedness are determined.

Point out gifted artists, scientists, humanitarians, and others who were gifted in other than academic ways.

ACTIVITY TITLE ## Mom and Dad (Male/Female Stereotypes)

MATERIALS This activity points out the stereotypical roles fostered at home. To do this activity, you need two large pieces of paper and colored markers.

PROCEDURES On one paper write "Mom" and on the other write "Dad." If photographs are available, add them too.

Ask the child to list all the things that Mom and Dad do on the appropriate pieces of paper. Make sure that the child uses only one color. After discussing his listing, choose another color and expand the listings. The child will probably be surprised at all the things you do that they don't know about.

Discuss the listings and explain the reasons for dividing up the
tasks and activities the way they are. Use another color of marker to list

all the Mom-things that Dad could do and all the Dad-things that Mom could do.

Make it a point to actually change some of these roles for the child to see.

VARIATION   Choose a day on a weekend or holiday for Mom and Dad to change roles. Make sure that the role reversal is complete.

ACTIVITY TITLE   Prejudice in the Media

MATERIALS   This activity on prejudice in the media requires paper, pencils, and access to media.

PROCEDURES   Use the paper and pencil to design a checklist of areas you wish to investigate. Our example will be on sex role stereotypes in TV cartoons, but you can just as easily pick race, age, or cultural stereotypes in print, on TV, in advertisements, or on the radio. Change the areas to fit your needs.

Cartoon Titles

	Boys	Girls
Number of Characters		
"Good guys"		
"Bad guys"		
Problem solvers		
Smart ones		
Silly ones		
Asks for help		
Is afraid		
Fights		
Strong		
Saves the day		
Works with tools		

Who are:

Sit with the child while viewing a cartoon, and the two of you use the checklist. Discuss the roles portrayed for the different sexes. How are they different? Which role, boy or girl, would the child want to play? Are these roles "true to life"? Is this the way the child sees boys and girls?

Try to make the point that these experiences influence the way children grow up to view sex roles.

VARIATION With the child, write a story that has only girls in it. Then write a story with all boy characters. How do the stories differ? This can give you a clear view of your child's sex role stereotyping.

ACTIVITY TITLE ## All Alike But Different

MATERIALS This activity on distinguishing an individual from a group requires a collection of stones, potatoes, or walnuts, and a bag.

PROCEDURES With a group of children or the family, have each person select one of the group of objects. Instruct them to really look at their choices. Notice the shape, texture, color, smell, unique properties, and any other distinguishing characters. Tell them to "make friends" with it.

After allowing enough time (three to five minutes) for familiarity, hold up your object and tell a very personal story about it. This should include all the unique points. For example, this rock was once a part of a huge boulder; I can tell by these sharp edges. Once it was in a stream, see the green color? It was scooped up and put into the bag to be sold at the garden store.

Let each person present her new friend to the group.

Place all the items in the bag. Ask everyone if she thinks all of the objects are the same. Then ask if they could pick out their "friends" out of all those in the bag.

Pour the items out of the bag, and let everyone try to find their "friend." (Some may not, but that isn't important.)

Lead a discussion stressing that people are all unique but that we

are each a part of groups. Would we want to be judged as an individual or a group?

VARIATION   Using strips of paper of different lengths, create a picture of how we fit into groups:

All the People in the World
_____

Our Sex
_____

Americans
_____

Our Race
_____

Our State
_____

Community
_____

Family
_____

ME

Use this chart to discuss other groups we are a part of and how we are alike and different.

[3]   The major goal of teaching principles of consideration to children is for them to develop a consideration and a positive regard for others. Try the following activities to develop consideration of others.

ACTIVITY TITLE   Tasks "Two" Do

MATERIALS   To do this activity on cooperation with others, you need a handful of paper slips and a pen.

PROCEDURES   Prepare slips of paper with tasks that two people could perform together or that two could do easier than one. Sample ideas are moving heavy objects, washing dishes, collecting dirty clothes or garbage cans from all over the house, or washing the car.

Explain that everybody must get someone else to work with on the task. The time limit should be flexible to allow everyone time to complete the tasks with a partner. Have the slips returned or provide a checklist to tell when everyone is done.

Initiate a discussion about how the two children were able to work together and help each other. Were there any problems? How many helped the same person that helped them? How did it feel to ask someone for help? How did asking for help and being asked to help differ?

Have everyone list regular tasks that two people could do easier than one. Will it be easier to ask for or to offer help in the future?

VARIATION   In the classroom or home you can provide a listing that includes both task-oriented and "free time" activities. Ask everyone to choose a person that he would choose to do the activity with. After allowing plenty of time, ask him to write or discuss why that person was chosen. Then discuss how each of us act and why we act in ways that would make people want to do things with us.

ACTIVITY TITLE **Others' Limitations**

MATERIALS To complete this activity, you need paper, pencils, crayons, and a variety of pictures.

PROCEDURES Before introducing this activity to the child, prepare two sheets of paper, one with the following code written on it and the other with the code and translation.

$< O\Sigma 1$	$\Sigma 1$	X	$)\theta I$	$X (<\Sigma V\Sigma< *$
T H I S	I S	A	F U N	A C T I V I T Y

Present this page to the child and ask her to read it to you. Of course she will not be able to do so. Press them to read it—"Read it to me. . . . What do you mean you can't read it? . . . Come on, read it!" Don't push too hard but cause a little frustration.

Convey the idea that the feelings she experiences must be similar to the feelings that nonreading children feel in schools. Ask what other feelings nonreaders must have. Can she think of limitations that other children or she herself has? Some children lack coordination, so they aren't very good on the playground. Some have speech problems, perceptual difficulties, or other problems.

Now give the translation to the child. Ask about her feelings now. As a follow-up, she can invent her own code using shapes or colors.

VARIATION A similar activity, especially for younger children, is to discuss various physical handicaps. After discussing the limitations and feelings of handicaps, suggest that you try to see what it feels like to "experience" a handicap. Try a variety of the following:

1. Stuff her ears with cotton to simulate hearing loss.
2. Tie up an arm or leg to immobilize it.
3. Wear a blindfold for a period of time.
4. Keep large pebbles or a gag in her mouth.

Try several at once to simulate multiple handicaps.

ACTIVITY TITLE **Environment and Mood**

MATERIALS This activity on understanding the effect of our immediate surroundings on us requires transportation, drawing paper, assorted crayons, and a tape recorder.

Talk with the child about how it feels to be playing in a very quiet place alone and in a loud place with lots of noise. Point out times when it is appropriate to be loud or soft-spoken. Perfect examples are on the playground, at a party, with someone working nearby, or nap time.

Discuss the difference in feelings and how it affects actions. You might use waltz and rock music to demonstrate. Point out that surroundings should be considered when we plan our activities, much as nursery school teachers plan out active and quiet areas.

As a demonstration, take the child to the public library. Take the tape recorder along and record for a few minutes. At the library have the child choose two books to look at and allow enough time for him to finish one. Next take the child, book, and recorder near a busy intersection with automobile and pedestrian traffic. Turn on the recorder and tell the child he can look at the other book now. Obviously these two conditions differ for reading purposes.

After returning home, discuss the two situations and listen to the tape. Which place was better for reading, for singing songs, for jumping rope, for calling out to friends?

Use the paper and crayons to recreate the two scenes while listening to the tape.

Try the same type of activity in light and dark places. Leave on the lights and lively music at nap time. Hammer and saw while the child is involved with a quiet activity.

VARIATION Cut out various scenes and activities from newspapers and activities—such as parks, playgrounds, libraries, city streets, country farm scenes, homes, pastoral scenes, baseball players, children talking on the playground, cooking or building with blocks.

Place the scenes in an envelope with paper clips and the activities in another envelope. Have the child match the scenes with the appropriate activities.

ACTIVITY TITLE ## Ecological Concerns

MATERIALS This activity increases our awareness of the environment. It requires grocery bags, poster board, markers, glue, scissors, and construction paper scraps.

PROCEDURES This activity works best with groups of children, but it can be done with one child or the family.

Plan a litter-collecting trip around the school or neighborhood. Instruct the participants to pick up all the litter they see and try to fill the bag.

After the collecting trip, spread the collected litter on a table top or floor. Have each participant choose a piece and describe the who, when, and why of the litter. When everyone has had a turn, have an open discussion about litter and about the people who litter. Include why litter is bad, other forms of pollution, times when you have also littered, what the world will be like in twenty years if this continues, and what we can do to prevent litter and pollution.

As a culminating activity have each participant make an "I'm Against Litter" poster to display in the home, school, or neighborhood.

Have the children participate in a "Recycle Me" contest. Collect a variety of throw-away items that have potential for reuse, such as newspapers, medicine bottles, plastic bottles, sheets, boxes, egg cartons, string, paper, milk cartons, styrofoam containers, or old clothes. Display these and have a contest to see who can brainstorm the most reuses for the collection. Award the winner a choice of the items.

ACTIVITY TITLE ## Saved for Sunday

MATERIALS To do this activity designed to emphasize consideration for material objects and the household, you need a cardboard box with a piece of paper attached to the outside. Materials for decorating the box are also appropriate.

PROCEDURES Talk with the household members (Chapter 6) about the need for everyone to keep his or her things put away. Point out the times that kids have left toys out, parents have left tools or newspapers out, and so on. Be sure to point out instances that involve everyone without focusing on any individuals.

Explain that the "Saved for Sunday" box is to help everyone care for his or her things and for the house. Any items left out of place will be put into the box, and no one will be allowed to use them until Sunday when the box is emptied and all items are put back into place. The rule as to how long the items can be left out, before going into the box, should be decided by the group. It could be an hour, a half-day, or anything that is out at bedtime.

VARIATION The idea, entitled the "Miscellaneous Box," is the same as for the previous procedure, but the items can be removed from the box and put into their proper places at the end of each day.

ACTIVITY TITLE ## The Work Ethic

MATERIALS To complete this activity on understanding the place of work in our society, you need paper and pencils and a daily newspaper.

PROCEDURES Begin by having everyone describe what work means to him or her. As new points about the meaning of work are mentioned, make a complete listing of *all* the feelings described. Then add the answers to the question, "Why do people work?"

Now that you have a listing, all of you, together, classify each entry as a positive or negative reaction.

As you discuss each of these aspects of work, new ideas can be added to the list. By the time all of the ideas are classified as positive or negative, you will probably have the ideas that people work in paying and nonpaying activities, that they work for personal satisfaction, that they work to help others, and that nearly everyone works in one way or another.

Now use the want ads in the paper to classify the available jobs as possible occupations for yourself, according to the education required, the salary range, the amount of personal satisfaction you would feel in that job, or any other aspects of work interesting to you.

VARIATION The same listing generated in the first part of the activity can be used. Make an additional listing of the ways that the children feel they work now! Include the why's of work for them. Compare these two lists, pointing out the similarities between the work they do and the work adults do.

ACTIVITY TITLE ## Getting Ready to Go

MATERIALS Stick-on labels and markers are needed to do this activity, which is designed to expedite that troublesome time of leaving the house.

PROCEDURES Begin this activity by discussing how it feels to have to wait for people. Children may have difficulty understanding why it's difficult for adults to wait. So you need to explain the reasons well enough for them to at least get a feel for it. Next explain that you have an idea that will make getting ready to go easier for you and for them.

Do this as a game. Pretend that there is a call inviting you to go somewhere. (You will actually go somewhere.) Tell the child that you and she must get ready to go.

Give each person a stack of the labels and instruct them to put a label at each place they must go to get ready to leave. If child is older, she can write on each label what she had to do at that place. With younger children, you can retrace their steps after you are ready to go and write in what they did at that place. Common stops on the road to "getting ready to go" are, the bathroom, dresser, closet, toy or book shelves, the refrigerator, and perhaps a few other places.

Now that everyone has completed preparations, each participant takes everyone else around the house explaining what he or she did and why. All participants should be encouraged to suggest ideas to help each person find solutions to problems about getting ready to go.

Obviously, this activity must be done when you aren't in a hurry to leave. Now you are all ready to actually go somewhere—to a park, to get a taste treat, to visit someone, to a movie. As you are leaving the house and on the way, be sure to talk about the difference in getting ready to go when there is plenty of time and when you are in a hurry. Suggest that tomorrow or sometime soon you would like to try an emergency "getting ready to go" drill. This way everyone has his or her labels to follow, along with the ideas from the group to get ready with no hassles.

VARIATION This activity can be done at school or with groups of children by having each child make a list of the things she must do to get ready to go somewhere. This list can include getting ready to go downtown for a short while or on a more extended trip. A second listing can be made for an emergency box or bag that would allow the child to be ready to go in a moment.

This exercise can also be extended to encompass the general and emergency procedures of the school. It is an excellent way to provide a clear understanding of what is expected in case of an emergency at school.

ACTIVITY TITLE   ## How Can I Help?

MATERIALS   This activity will help the child discover ways to develop consideration for and ways to help various family members. All that is needed is paper and pencil.

PROCEDURES   Begin this activity by making a listing, with the child, of all family members in the household. Ask the child what each person would really *like* to do and what tasks each person *has to do* on a regular basis. Explain that time is an important determiner of how many things we get to do.

Next ask the child what things he could do to help each family member get the "must-do" tasks completed, so they would have more time to do the things they would like to do. List these beside each person's name.

Help the child plan and implement some of the ideas. The family members will provide the necessary positive reinforcement.

VARIATION   Help the child list home-made presents he thinks each family member would like. Then provide materials so he can make one gift for each family member. Have a special party where the child can give each person the gift and share their feelings.

ACTIVITY TITLE   ## Ring-a-Ding (Telephone)

MATERIALS   For this activity on the considerate use of the telephone, you will need two toy phones or the materials to make them (toilet paper rolls and an egg carton, string and a box), a telephone book, paper, and pencils.

PROCEDURES   If toy phones are not available, make two phones by cutting egg cups from the carton and attaching one to each end of the toilet paper rolls to resemble a receiver. Attach the strings to the receiver and the box to finish your telephones.

To emphasize the importance of the phone, role play the situation of a child having to contact the police or fire department in an emergency. The role play stresses the need for reporting your address and telephone number.

Make a card with each child's name, address, and phone number, and help the child to work on memorizing them. Allow plenty of time for the practice use of the phone in emergency situations.

Use the phone book to make a listing of important emergency numbers.

VARIATION   Rather than stressing the emergency aspect, have the children practice good telephone manners. Structure these manners in chart form:

1. Greeting: "Hello!"

2. Identifying yourself: "This is _____."
3. Asking: "Could I speak to _____."
4. Ending the conversation: "Thank you, good-bye."

ACTIVITY TITLE **Teachers Are People Too**

MATERIALS No materials are necessary to do this activity on recognizing the teacher as a person.

PROCEDURES Many times I have seen my classroom students in the grocery store. Their usual response is "What are you doing here? You're supposed to be in school!" They actually think that you live in the school.

Discuss the fact that the teacher is a person with the same feelings and needs as anyone else. They have families, friends, hobbies, and other interests—the same as anyone. Many teachers also have other jobs. Talk about why teachers choose to teach.

Give the teacher a call, and arrange for having the teacher's family over for dinner or for a visit to the teacher's home. Arrange for you, the child, and the teacher to meet downtown while shopping or for lunch.

Draw the child out about who the teacher is and what other roles the teacher might fill.

VARIATION In the old days the teacher's desk was often lined with apples. Today we often get books, stickers, pen and pencil sets, and other school-related gifts.

Do some research on the teachers' likes and hobbies. Help the child pick the next gift for the teacher to be associated with a nonteaching activity.

[4] TIPS

1. Lasting effects come from early experiences.
2. Familiarity leads to acceptance. Provide early experiences with many people.
3. Stereotypes and prejudices are passed on from parents and teachers to children. Consider the model you provide.
4. Sex role behaviors are among children's first learnings. These learnings have a social rather than a biological base.
5. Children are always listening, and generally they take things literally. Be careful what you say that might lead to prejudice and stereotypes.
6. An awareness and acceptance of the multicultural aspects of our world is necessary for our children to grow to be fully functioning adults.

7. To teach consideration and acceptance, you must behave in considerate and accepting ways.

8. Our society is founded on accepting ideals. Democracy, religion, science, and law are the tools with which to fight prejudice and to promote acceptance.

9. To break the "cycle of prejudice" teachers, parents, and children must take an active role.

10. One of the main ingredients for producing happy children is developing a consideration of self and others.

Expectations

A SENSE OF SELF AND SELF-CONFIDENCE

The expectations we have of and for children are very influential in establishing their sense of self and self-confidence. Expectations also have a direct impact on children's behavior.

Two conditions must be met if we hope children will strive to live up to our expectations. The first is that the expectation must be reasonable in terms of the situation and the child's developmental level. The second is the quality of the interpersonal relationship between the adult and child. The adult must be viewed as a person that is trustworthy, friendly, warm, and somewhat self-confident. If the adult is not trusted or not clear about his or her own self-expectations, then it is difficult to communicate clear expectations to children. Once this relationship is established, the child can integrate the others' expectations and perform accordingly. Specifically, "If he [or she, the adult] thinks I'm a leader, then I must be. If he thinks I can't do it, then I guess I can't."

A goal that all parents and teachers have for children is the development of their ability to set realistic personal goals. Our expectations of children have a strong influence on this area of development. To influence others and to function successfully, in the adult world, children must learn to set and strive for realistic personal goals.

By establishing these realistic expectations and helping children establish realistic personal goals, we will be modeling caring. At the same time we are providing an atmosphere conducive to children's development of a sense of success and ability to effect their world. As children develop a sense of self and self-confidence they are more able to trust others and to share of themselves.

This chapter therefore approaches expectations by focusing on the effect that they have on actions. It concentrates on helping children to learn to set personal goals and on how to establish realistic expectations of self and others. These activities will hlep children to develop a positive sense of self and self-confidence.

As you try these activities, bear in mind that all individuals are unique in the values they hold, in the desires they have, and in their personal characteristics. So be open and show caring while participating in these activities.

[1] Parents' and teachers' expectations and self-expectations have a definite effect on children's behavior and on the development of their self-confidence. Try the following activities keeping focused on you and the children's action.

ACTIVITY TITLE **Realistic Expectations**

MATERIALS This activity on understanding child development requires a pen and paper.

PROCEDURES Many factors influence how much a child can do. The quantity and quality of his experience, his intelligence, his training at home, his education, and others. Although as individuals children develop at their own rates, there are ranges of behavior that can be expected at given ages. It is also important to understand that children do not develop in all areas at the same rate. At different times their affective, cognitive, and psychomotor domains may exhibit surges or lags in development.

The following is a very brief description of the expected development as related to age. For more in-depth readings on the range of behavior you can expect at various ages, ask your physician, your child's teacher, or the local librarian. Read through the entire listing of behaviors. Focus on the listing for the age earlier than your child's. If your child has not exhibited a number of abilities, then plan activities to promote their development:

One to two years of age: Talks in short sentences, transfers objects from hand to hand, forms attachments to and carries familiar objects, drinks from cup unassisted, walks about unattended, does without stroller, plays with other kids, masticates food, eats with spoon, identifies food substances, names objects, makes marks with crayons, pulls off socks and gloves but can't put them on, climbs stairs alone but creeps down backwards.

Two to three years of age: Relates experience in sequence, communicates toileting needs, initiates play activities, puts on and takes off large articles of clothing, can get drink unassisted, eats with fork, avoids hazards, cuts with scissors.

Three to four years of age: Plays cooperatively with peers, walks down steps, seeks attention, buttons and zips, takes some responsibility for tasks, can tell complete stories, takes care of toileting with help.

Four to five years of age: Expanding vocabulary includes descriptive words, shows interest in competitive games, can follow rules, draws with intent, dresses self (no tying), the "world" is expanding to include the neighborhood.

Five to six years of age: Coordination is much improved, can use skates, bikes, wagons, remembers and writes simple words, sophisticated vocabulary, seeks social contacts, makes up intricate stories.

Six to seven years of age: Well developed language skills, conceives and completes projects, gets snacks alone, has a sense of time, can use knife for spreading, bathes self with help.

Seven to eight years of age: Uses knife to cut, seeks cooperative play situations, takes care of personal hygiene, tells time to the quarter hour, clear differentiation of reality and fantasy.

Eight to nine years of age: Uses tools adequately, has basic reading skills, bathes self without help, does household chores.

Nine to ten years of age: Very independent, gets about town alone, makes friends on own, cares for self.

VARIATION   Make a list of skills and abilities that you expect your child to have at two, three, and four years of age. Use the preceding list and other readings to check the accuracy of your expectations.

ACTIVITY TITLE   ## Task Analysis

MATERIALS   To complete this activity on setting expectations, you need paper and pen.

PROCEDURES   When we, as parents and teachers, have an expectation of children, it is important to make it a "reasonable expectation" (see "Realistic Expectations" in this chapter). Task analysis is a way to adapt our expectations to the child's developmental level and to provide successful exprience for the child.

Every task consists of necessary conditions that must be met if the task is to be completed. It is convenient to think of this as a step-by-step sequence. Very complex and very simple activities can be broken down into their component parts. Reading is a complex interaction of visual discrimination, memory, auditory discrimination, comprehension, and other subcomponents. Dressing yourself is also a series of activities that requires a variety of skills—large motor coordination, fine motor control, body parts, and concepts.

Develop a chart similar to the one following, to determine the components and necessary skills for completing a selected task. Adjust your expectations to match the areas that you feel the child can successfully complete:

Task	Components	Skills	Approximate Age You Think It Should Be Done
Toileting	Development of control muscles	Ability to communicate need	_____
	Recognition of need	Getting to bathroom	_____
	Knowledge of appropriate actions	Use of facilities	_____
		Development of coordination	_____
	Getting to and on toilet		_____
	Use of toilet paper		_____
Dressing	Choosing clothes	Knowledge of body parts and appropriate clothing	
	Putting on articles		
	Lacing, tying, buttoning, zippering	Large motor coordination	_____
		Fine motor development	_____

In the case of toileting you would expect a five-year-old to complete the activity. You would expect three- to four-year-olds to communicate the need, get to the bathroom, and possibly use the facilities, but you would expect them to need help in the areas requiring fine motor coordination. A two-year-old might ask to use the toilet but would need help.

In the case of dressing, the two- or three-year-old could put on large articles, the three- to four-year-old could even button or zip, but even up to six the child might need help lacing or tying.

Try this exercise with activities for older children too—mowing grass, running errands, cleaning bathroom, and so on.

Before you ask a child to do the activity, you, the adult, should do it, while noting the step-by-step procedure necessary to complete the task.

VARIATION Use this idea as a tool in evaluating your children's development. Analyze some tasks and take your children through the activities. What steps can they complete alone? What is their attitude? Are they confident or fearful?

ACTIVITY TITLE Expectations of Self

MATERIALS This activity on expectation requires paper and pencil.

PROCEDURES Depending on your expectations of the participants, develop a list of simple expectations either on your own or with them. A sample list might be: get up in the morning with one call, make the bed, personal hygiene, come when called, help around the house, do addition home-work problems, spell six words, sing two songs, do ten push-ups. These lists can be very general or very specific.

After presenting the list or developing it with them, ask, "What are some things you can do that are not on the list?" Accept any responses and allow them to add to the list if they like. Now ask if they can't do some things well or easily. Do they expect to be able to do these in the future? How long? How will they get better at it?

While stressing the expectations we have of ourselves, this activity also provides an opportunity to discuss the expectations that others have of us.

VARIATION Use this as a time to talk about "what you want to be when you grow up."

The usual firefighter/nurse/lawyer/Indian chief response can lead to an interesting discussion of what you must do to develop the skills necessary. You can also introduce the other possibilities of careers to the children.

ACTIVITY TITLE ## The Other's Perspective

MATERIALS This perceptual awareness activity will require paper, paint, paper mache or clay, a table, two chairs, and a doll.

PROCEDURES Children do not think with the same logic as adults. It is sometimes very difficult for them to understand our explanations of limits and expectations. This activity should help them realize that they will not understand some things at their developmental level and that adults see some things differently from children.

You must take care not to approach this activity with an I-told-you-so or condescending manner. Promote the feelings of being open and of exploring while doing these perceptual awareness tasks.

Using paper mache or clay, make a set of "mountains" on a table top. Be sure that one side is relatively smooth and the other is rough and has valleys. Near the end of the day, place a chair on either side of the table so that only one side of the mountain can be seen.

Place the child's doll in one chair and seat the child in the other. Talk about the earlier activity of making the mountain, and ask the child to describe what she sees. After allowing a full description of her side of the mountain, ask what the doll is seeing on the other side of the mountain.

Young children will describe the same scene or say that they are seeing the same thing.

Show the child the other side of the mountain. Then explain that one of the things that happens as you grow is that you learn to see things not only your own way, but in the way other people see them also. You can practice this through other activities in this book.

VARIATION With older children, use self-made inkblots as a stimulation. Have each child make a set of three inkblots by pressing paint between the folds of a sheet of paper.

Have the children write their impression of the inkblots, and have each child present the inkblots to two other children. Let the children compare the three responses.

Lead a discussion stressing that people see things differently and that experiences play an important part in how we perceive things.

ACTIVITY TITLE **I Turned Out OK**

MATERIALS To do this activity on establishing expectations, you need no materials, but you may wish to have a pad and pencil or a tape recorder handy.

PROCEDURES Find a time when you can do some uninterrupted thinking. Let your thoughts wander through your childhood. What incidents and memories, both positive and negative, stand out the most? Think about them and try to remember the role that your parents played in them. As you remember them, try to identify the times that they make you feel good. What did they do or say that made you feel good?

Many people raise their children very much the way they themselves were raised. After all, "If it was good enough for me . . . !" This attitude is easy to understand because being reared is about the only training in childrearing available. Even though parents are great, however, they do not always do the things necessary for their children to reach parental goals. So, as you do this introspective activity, you will recognize attitudes and actions of your parents that you have had to "overcome" in your own growth process. Use these insights to influence your own parental values and to make decisions related to your own childrearing practices.

VARIATION Make listings of your own childrearing goals. Next to these, list the goals that you think your parents had when rearing you. Connect the goals that you and your parents have in common. Concentrate on the other goals that you have and make a listing of what you will do differently or extra as compared to what they did. You might try a listing of the same sort for the ones you had in common.

ACTIVITY TITLE **Home and School Together**

MATERIALS Depending on the idea you wish to reinforce, a different set of materials will be needed. In general you will need paper, pencils, crayons, scissors, a ruler, glue, tape, and a box.

PROCEDURES We all have school-associated academic expectations of children. To make these expectations clear and meaningful to children, we must not only discuss these expectations but actively participate.

Using a shoe box or a similar box, help the child decorate it with school-related pictures and words. For a surprise introduce the materials listed above as supplies for doing school things at home. This can also serve as a central place to store things brought from school.

By staying in touch with the teacher, you can provide materials for the development of the same concepts the children are working on in school. For working on math concepts you might provide a group of two-piece objects like people/hats, shoes/feet, bottles/tops, and other match-ups, to work on one-to-one correspondence, a color wheel to develop color recognition, number lines, flash cards, or work sheets. (Ask the teacher for specific ideas.) Work with the child to show your concern and consideration.

VARIATION

In a group or classroom provide "My House Box." In this box the children may keep some items that they brought from home. This works well for sharing time and as a preventive of some classroom disturbances. The My House Box can be a place for everything from home to remain except during specified times.

You may need to use smaller-sized boxes to fit in cubbies or lockers.

ACTIVITY TITLE
How Many Rules?

MATERIALS

To complete these activities on teaching of rules, you need paper and pencil.

PROCEDURES

We all have to live within a set of guidelines. For the adult world they are called "laws." For the child's world they are called "rules" or "limits." It is difficult to know what limits we should place on children to facilitate their development.

When the rule is made to protect children or property, we can feel very sure of the need for the rule. When the rule is to provide some not-so-concrete understanding or experience for the children, it is not so easy to evaluate the rules' appropriateness. Also, many rules are established for the convenience of the adult with little consideration of the child's needs. This activity provides some structure for evaluating the necessity of the rules.

First sit down and list all the rules you have for the children. Then read through them all and count them. Record the number of rules you have listed in the top right corner of the page.

In terms of the child's development, there are three main reasons for rules. Read these three reasons and, next to each of the rules you have written, place the number of the reason that applies to that rule. This rule:

1. protects the safety of the child, of others, or of property.
2. defines boundaries and allows the child to make choices and decisions within those boundaries.
3. provides experience that will help the child learn self-control and to demonstrate responsibility.

After coding the rules you have listed, try to plan the environment or your interactions with the child in ways to solve problems without establishing the rules.

VARIATION

Using the same listing, code it by the following three descriptions. This rule is:

1. for the benefit of the child.
2. for the benefit of the adult.
*3. important enough to the child and to the adult to be enforced *all the time.*

If the coding does not show an asterisk (*), then the rule is not worthwhile. These rules without the * will cause resentment, teach the child to ignore and sneak around them, and become a source of frustration to you.

ACTIVITY TITLE **Establishing Limits**

MATERIALS No materials are necessary to complete this activity on establishing limits.

PROCEDURES To truly establish limits for children, the rules must be reasonable, necessary, and enforceable ("How Many Rules" in this chapter). Unreasonable, unnecessary, and unenforceable rules do not prevent unwanted behaviors, and they serve only to develop negative attitudes toward authority.

When you feel you have established a necessary, reasonable rule, the following sequence of activities can aid in developing compliance with the rule, as well as a positive attitude toward following it:

1. Repeat and restate the rule often. It is necessary especially with young children, that you help them remain aware of the rules. It is hard to tell if children are testing rules or if they have just

forgotten. They will test the rules. So if the rule is necessary, then it must be enforced. (See "Consequences, Three Types" in this chapter.)

2. Plan the environment to make it as easy as possible to follow the rule. Temptation is hard to resist, even for adults.

3. Make expectations very clear and explicit. The rule might be, "Keep your room clean." This is not explicit. Provide a checklist to clarify it: bed made, dirty clothes in basket, clean clothes folded in drawers, toys put away, and so on. Let the child know when and how the rules must be followed.

4. Remind the child of the rule and provide a chance to comply with the rule *before* imposing the consequence of breaking the rule. This approach promotes responsibility for his own behavior and stress the rule's importance rather than his compliance.

*5. Focus on the child's ability to follow the rules. Reinforce the child when he does follow them. When children are reinforced for appropriate behaviors, those behaviors are more likely to be repeated.

By following this sequence you will foster the child's understanding of the importance of rules, along with a positive attitude toward authority.

VARIATION   For one day try to ignore an infraction of rules (except safety) and constantly reinforce his positive behaviors. You will be surprised at the results.

ACTIVITY TITLE   ## Consequences, Three Types

MATERIALS   This activity explores the types and uses of consequences. To complete this activity, you will need paper and pencils.

PROCEDURES   Enforcing rules implies that, if the rule is not obeyed, consequences will follow. Often the breaking of a rule brings its own consequences. For instance, if the rule to bring all toys inside is broken, the consequence might be that it rains on the toys or that someone takes them. Either would be a "natural consequence" of the action. Parents should let natural consequences serve as rule reinforcers whenever possible. For example:

1. Run on the grass rather than the sidewalk—skinned knees.
2. We all eat dinner at six—cold dinner if child is late.
3. Save some allowance for later—no money later.
4. We will all be ready to go—child doesn't go.

It is often necessary, however, to avoid natural consequences. Playing in the street, with electrical outlets, near hot stoves, close to valuable property, or when other people are involved. Also, rules that are established for the training and the future development of the child must not be ignored—homework, work ethic, eating habits, or personal hygiene. Situations in which you cannot allow natural consequences require you to impose a consequence, which can be of two types: (1) logical consequences or (2) authoritarian consequences.

Although both types of consequences must be imposed by the adult, logical consequences have a direct relationship to the inappropriate behavior. The use of logical consequences makes it much easier for the child to connect their behavior to the consequences of the act. If the child borrows things and does not return them, it is logical that you will not lend them again. Leaving toys outside could be followed by not playing with the toy the next day. Not trying all foods at dinner means no desert. Making a mess means you clean it up. Not finishing homework before playing means less play and more work time tomorrow. By imposing logical consequences you are tying together the act and the outcome. This can help children see the effect of their actions and to take responsibility for their outcomes.

The third type of consequence, authoritarian consequences, should be used only where natural and logical consequences are not possible or when they have failed to elicit compliance. Authoritarian consequences are usually considered to be punishment. There are consequences, unrelated to the behavior, that we, as adults, have judged to be necessary. Here again the use of consequences must be related to the necessity and importance of the rule.

The goal of imposing such consequences is to help children to develop self-control and an understanding of the importance and need for rules. Keep this in mind when using authoritarian consequences. Children often see these as arbitrary, and they do not connect their actions to the consequences. A good rule for parents to follow is twofold: Let the punishment fit the "crime," when possible. And extreme punishment doesn't pay.

Use the following example to design consequences for the rules you listed in the preceding activities:

Rule: Fold and put away all clean clothes.

Natural Consequence: Wear wrinkled clothes.

Logical Consequence: Child must iron and put away clothes.

Authoritarian Consequence: One week in house restriction.

VARIATION Using the list of rules developed in the preceding activities, sit with the child or in a family council and write out clearly agreed-upon consequences for breaking each rule. This session also provides the child a decision-making opportunity—"I can ignore this rule if I am willing to suffer the consequences."

ACTIVITY TITLE Changing the Rule

MATERIALS This activity on using flexibility in rule-making requires paper and pen.

PROCEDURES The rules we made should constantly be reevaluated. The major reason for changing the rule is usually that it is no longer necessary. For instance, you may have a rule for the six- or seven-year-old that says she cannot cross the streets to play. When the child is nine or ten, she is quite capable of following safety rules, and so the rule needs to be changed.

Another reason parents change rules is because the old rules are not working. If we continually challenge children with rules that are not working, you exasperate yourself and the children. This is counter-productive.

To change the way you treat the child, you must plan a very gradual process. A sudden "crackdown" will not work. This confuses children and causes personal resentment. Rather than changing all at once, focus on one rule or aspect of the relationship to work with. Plan an approach to this single problem, discuss it with the child and the family, and implement the plan. When you feel satisfied with the resolution of this problem, select another problem area to work on.

VARIATION   In approaching problem areas, it is vital that you consider the child's point of view. Choose a problem area and use the following format to approach planning or solution.

1. Write a brief statement describing the problem.
2. What are the child's *feelings* about it?
3. What are your *feelings?*
4. List the important aspects of the situation.
5. List outcomes you would like.

In entry 4, number the aspects starting with the most important. Do the same for entry 5, outcomes.

Make sure that your responses, in terms of most important aspects and outcomes, are congruent.

[2]   Many things influence the way children set personal goals. The following activities help parents and children focus on these influences stressing the positive and compensating for the negative.

ACTIVITY TITLE   **The Wish Book**

MATERIALS   To complete this activity on wishes and expectations for the future, you will need two book-size pieces of cardboard, paper, scissors, tape or glue, brass fasteners or a stapler, mail order catalogs, a hole punch, and markers. Crayons and various paper scraps are also useful.

PROCEDURES   Help the child make a binder with the cardboard and brass fasteners. Punch holes in the paper and put them into the binder. Decorate the cover carefully, including the title, "My Wish Book," and the child's name.

Divide the book into three sections. Section one is called "Things I Wish I Could Have." The second section is called "Things I Wish I Could Do," and the third section is "What I Want to Be."

Have the child cut pictures to glue into the appropriate sections.

They may also want to write or have you write a narrative description or picture captions.

As they work on different sections, you can help them realize which of their wishes have a reasonable chance of coming true and even make plans for making them come true.

VARIATION   Use the catalogs, have the children go through and put a circle around items they would like to have. Then ask them to go through and put a star on the ones they would *really* like to have.

Lead a discussion to determine which represents reasonable expectations. Also discuss what would have to be done if they are actually to get those items.

ACTIVITY TITLE   ## Labeling

MATERIALS   Paper and pen are all that are needed to do this activity on the effect of labels.

PROCEDURES   We use many labels in our society: handicapped, under-achiever, over-achiver, hippie, deprived, gifted, sissy. When you hear the word "minority," for example, what is the image that comes to mind?

A good way to point out the use of labels is to start a collection of them. Look in advertisements, newspapers, and books, and be alert to them everywhere.

We sometimes think of our children as fitting into categories. Lots of children have heard themselves referred to as slow learners, gifted, average students, under-achiever, and so on. Yet we forget how much influence a word can have. Think of times you have used words that convey expectations. Even cute little nicknames are strong influences on children. Do you remember the kids named Shorty, Tubby, Speed, Flash, Stinky, or Fred Sandford's son, Dummy? Much as when children use terms they have heard but don't understand, we as adults don't know for sure what effects these nicknames will have.

Using a piece of paper, list all the labels or not-so-nice nicknames you can think of. Use this as a list of words to avoid.

VARIATION   Make up a list of words consisting of nonsense syllables. Just by the sounds of the words, decide which are "good" and which are derogatory. Teach these to your family or group, and use only the positive ones for a day.

ACTIVITY TITLE   ## Everybody Does It

MATERIALS   This activity on peer pressure requires only paper and pencil.

PROCEDURES   I once read a story by Jack Griffin in *Guidepost* magazine. The moral of the story was that adults can't stand a kid who cheats. The bulk of the story related the experiences of a boy that made him feel it was OK to cheat. There were descriptions of an Uncle who shaved his income tax, of lying to an insurance company, of a high school coach teaching illegal blocking methods, and so on. These were all actions on the part of adults. In the end the boy was caught cheating on an exam, and his response was the same as he had been hearing all his life: "Everybody does it!"

Another similar problem often occurs when children want to participate in a fad or an activity. They support themselves with, "Everybody does it!"

The next time this rationale comes up, relate this story and ask what the child thinks of it. (You can also make up similar stories.) Using the paper and pencil, ask the child to help you delineate exactly what it is everybody is doing. By writing down the response, you have a place to start discussing the request and, if you approve of the activity, a kind of "contract" of what will be permitted.

VARIATION

Another way to approach the everybody-does-it situation is to ask for a written description of *who* is doing *what* and *why*. The who part of the question will help you and the child focus on the influential peers and their influence. The what will give you actual descriptions of the behavior from which to make judgments. The why will get at the intent of the participants or what they will be getting out of the activity.

ACTIVITY TITLE

What Would You Do If _____?
(Cause and Effect)

MATERIALS

This activity will provide practice in brainstorming consequences and actions. You will need no materials for this activity.

PROCEDURES

Tell the children that you would like to see what they would do if certain things happened. Design a few role plays that will seem real to the children. For example, "What would you do if you are waiting for your turn on the slide, and Tom pushes his way in ahead of you. . . . What would you do if your parrents (or teacher) punished you for something you didn't do? . . . What would you do if you really wanted a bike but didn't have enough money?

Assign roles and have the children play out the situations and outcomes. Have everyone discuss their feelings during the role play. Can anyone come up with other ideas?

VARIATION

Make a collection of "What Would You Do If _____" ideas. Use pictures for younger children and stories for older ones. Add new situations as you know the child is about to deal with them.

ACTIVITY TITLE

Death and the Life Cycle

MATERIALS

To do this activity, you need pictures of plants and animals in different stages of life: seed–a young plant–seedling plant–dead plant, a chicken egg–a chicken–a rooster–fried chicken, a fawn–a buck–a hunters' trophy, a pregnant woman–a baby–a child–an adult–an elderly person–a coffin.

Birth begins the life cycle, and death completes it. Children have an intense curiosity about both. Many children have no concept of death, and others, at a very early age, develop a fear of death. It is important for all children to understand the life cycle and to know that, in the end, all forms of life die. Every living thing has a natural life cycle. The cycle begins at birth, and the interim stages are growth, maturity, reproduction, aging, and death.

To develop an understanding of this cycle, use the pictures showing the stages of development of plants and animals. Let the children place the pictures in the appropriate sequence. Have the pictures numbered on the back so the children can check their ordering.

Discuss the cycle and the needs at each stage. Ask for the children's impressions and feelings about death.

VARIATION Display pictures of elderly people in various conditions and situations—health, working, with children, in the hospital, in groups.

Discuss the process of aging, relating it to a machine. The parts just wear out. We can replace them sometimes, but sometimes we cannot.

Point out that we will all die but that, as you grow older, you are getting closer to death. You might point out some facts about aging: In the days of Caesar's Rome, the average life was twenty-two years. In the pioneer days, people lived until around thirty-five, and in 1900 the average was less than fifty. Today Americans can expect to live until around the age of seventy-three. However, in the end we all face death.

This is a good time to discuss funerals, different cultural and religious beliefs about life, death, and life after death.

Create an atmosphere that is open and accepting about death and life. Do not promote fears of either one.

ACTIVITY TITLE **I've Got the Power!**

MATERIALS This activity on clarifying goals requires paper, pencil, markers, a large piece of poster paper, and a stapler.

PROCEDURES To set personal goals, children must feel that they have the power to decide. This activity helps them to clarify what they would do if they were all-powerful.

On the poster paper, write, "If I were all powerful I would _____." Cut squares of paper, and on the top of each write one of the following words or phrases: get rid of, start, stop, accept, reject, keep, create, forget, remember to, fight, accept, protect.

Have the children write or draw the things that they would do if they were all-powerful. Ask them to order the things so that the first thing they would do is on the top, the second next, and so on. Staple these together and share them with the group or family.

VARIATION Ask the children to list in order the ten jobs they would like to do when they grow up. Have them get into groups to discuss the reason for each

and what they would have to do in that role.

ACTIVITY TITLE	When I'm Fifteen!
MATERIALS	This activity on self-perception and goal-setting requires paper, pencils, crayons, markers, tape, and paint, if possible.
PROCEDURES	Ask the child to list as many strengths, positive traits, and skills as she can for herself. Now tell her to close her eyes and imagine that she is fifteen years old. Her body has grown, and all her skills, traits, and strengths have developed very well. Tell her to open her eyes and make a picture of how she looks at fifteen. Then ask her to write a description of that fifteen-year-old, what her life is like, what she thinks about, what her wishes and goals are.

Lead a discussion to draw out why she thinks she will be like this at fifteen. |
| VARIATION | Display pictures of older children dressed differently, engaging in different activities, alone, in groups, happy, sad, and so forth. Ask the child to choose pictures of people that are the way she will be when she is that age. Discuss her reasons for the choices. |

ACTIVITY TITLE	Time Capsule
MATERIALS	This activity on community and personal values requires grocery bags, personal items, paper, and pen.
PROCEDURES	Explain what a time capsule is and how it is used. Tell the child that you are going on a fantasy trip to outer space because the earth is so polluted that we can't live here any more. Since we will be gone, we will each leave a time capsule here so that anyone visiting the earth will be able to tell what kind of individuals we were.

Have the child collect the items and place them into the bag. (Limit it to one grocery bag.) Have him role play the visitor to earth and find the box. Ask him to tell you what he thinks about the person who left all these objects.

This activity allows children to express the way they hope others see them. |
| VARIATION | Do the time capsule activity as a listing of things that will convey to a stranger the character of the whole human race. Discuss which things must be included and why. |

ACTIVITY TITLE	Letters to a Novice
MATERIALS	For this activity on expressing expectations, you will need stationery, construction paper, and variously colored pens.
PROCEDURES	Introduce this activity to the children by explaining that a novice is a person who is new at something, someone with no experience. Describe a situation where a boy or girl around the age of the participants was found on an island where she had spent all her life alone. Now she was being brought to the United States.

113

Ask them to write a letter telling her the most important things she will need to know and have if she is going to get along here. Let them share their letters, then mount them on construction paper and display them.

VARIATION   Lead a discussion covering all a person's needs including basic physical, emotional, spiritual, and cognitive needs. Have the children prepare a listing of what they feel are their most important needs.

ACTIVITY TITLE   Trusting

MATERIALS   For this activity on evaluating your trust of children, you need paper and pens.

PROCEDURES   The expectations of parents and teachers have a lot to do with the way children see themselves. We are often so concerned with our responsibility for children that we forget that many of our demands are actually their responsibility. Use the following as a checklist to determine how much trust you have in the child. Do you:

1. insist on constant adult supervision, or allow children to "be in charge"?
2. assign a child to monitor the group when you are away, or let them be responsible for themselves?
3. keep your personal feelings private, or trust children with your personal feelings?
4. make children always ask for permission to change activities, or allow them to choose activities?
5. always provide direct evaluative feedback, or help children learn self-evaluation?
6. Do you manipulate children and the environment so that they make decisions you will approve of, or do you trust children to make their own decisions?

If you find that the first option is your gut reaction, you are demonstrating a lack of trust for children. This approach will not foster a sense of self-worth in children. Add to the list other ways you show trust of children.

VARIATION   Prepare a similar checklist for children to respond to. Do you trust yourself to:

1. complete homework, or do you want someone to check on you?
2. take care of pets, or do you need help?
3. decide what to do on Saturday, or be told what to do?
4. what to buy with your own money, or ask what to buy?

[3] To establish realistic goals, children must have an understanding of themselves and of the world around them. They must also develop the ability to judge situations and to evaluate behavior. Try the following activities to help children develop the skills necessary for setting realistic goals.

ACTIVITY TITLE **Do As I Say, Not As I Do!**

MATERIALS For this activity on parental self-disclosure, you need a sheet of butcher paper or cardboard large enough for an adult to stretch out on. You also need colored markers and a pencil.

PROCEDURES Rarely are we, as parents, able to live up to our expectations of our children. We expect them to be totally open and honest with us all the time, to share experiences with us, and *never* to lie, cheat, or steal. Yet generally parents attempt to keep their faults and weaknesses a secret. But sometimes we fail (see Everybody Does It). Examples might be our smoking, drinking, or speeding in a car. We would never want our children to do these harmful or illegal things. Nonetheless, children look to parents as models and often think of them as infallible. This activity helps children to gain realistic expectations of adults.

Ask the child to help make a picture of you. Lie down, face up, on the paper. Let the child use the pencil to trace around you including your feet, fingers, and head. After he has traced you, use a marker to go over the pencil lines.

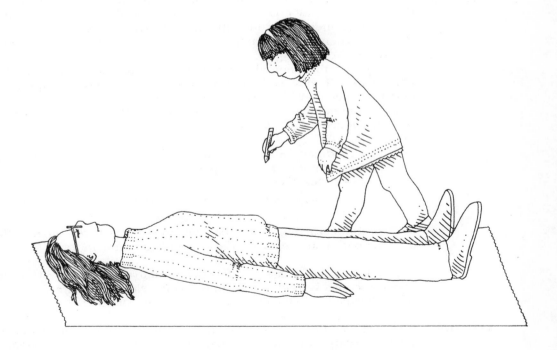

Then you and the child decorate the portrait (let the child do the face). As you do, talk at first about your positive traits, which might include talents like art and music, skills like carpentry and sewing, or personal characteristics like caring, loving, giving or softness. As you and the child mention these, write them around the tracing.

Continue this discussion until the portrait is complete. Then ask the child if any things about you are not so good or positive. Discuss these, and then introduce your own weaknesses that you feel comfortable discussing. Be sure to include that you try your best to do what you think is right for the child. If you feel comfortable enough to do so, let them know that you often have questions about the best thing to do for the child.

List these aspects of yourself on the portrait as well. Display the finished product and continue the discussion.

VARIATION
Collect pictures of yourself at various ages. While talking with your child, write a description of yourself at those ages. Also write what your dreams and hopes were. Help the child see that you were successful with some of your aspirations and failed at others.

ACTIVITY TITLE **Alternatives Are Sometimes the Answer**

MATERIALS
To do this activity on offering alternatives, all you need are paper and pencil.

PROCEDURES
Children must conform to many expectations and limits to function in the world of adults. Often children are not able to come up with appropriate alternatives for activities they wish to do. This activity is designed to encourage parents to offer alternatives to inappropriate behaviors.

Here is the general form of the verbal statement of offering alternatives: "Bobby [child's name], you may not (do the inappropriate behavior). You may (do the alternative)." This form of statement greatly reduces the number of no's a young child hears, and it is an effective tool for children of all ages. For example,

1. For a *toddler*: "Scott! You may not play with the *ashtray* (plugs, bottles, glasses). You may play with *these plastic cups* (nesting, blocks, tubes, hats)."
2. In the *nursery*: "Mary! You may not *take Susie's dishes*. You may *use these*."
3. In *kindergarten*: "Tom, no one may *throw rocks on the playground*. You may *throw these bean bags at the target*."

For one day, practice offering alternatives *every time* you must give directions or reprimands to the child. Notice the effect. Strive to offer alternatives to the child, whenever appropriate.

VARIATION
The best way to avoid reprimands and constant direction-giving is to plan alternatives to possible inappropriate behaviors. For example, have multiple copies of books and toys, provide places appropriate for

active and quiet events, remove tempting "off-limits" objects, and so on. Also make a list of all the inappropriate behaviors you have to deal with. Brainstorm ways to plan alternatives into the environment.

ACTIVITY TITLE **The Book or the Cover**

MATERIALS To do this activity concerning first impressions, you need scissors and a selection of current periodicals (such as *Time* or *People*).

PROCEDURES Often our first impressions are not accurate. When we as parents have expectations of children, we must take care to look deeply at behaviors, to get at the intent of the actions. Also important is to help children realize that first impressions must be reevaluated to insure an accurate perspective. Try this activity to emphasize how inaccurate first impressions can be.

Locate pictures of famous people involved in activities that are not characteristic of their image. Pictures of Ronald Reagan chopping wood, bankers with a shovel laying a foundation, or anyone engaged in a nonoccupational activity. Good places to find these are periodicals, like *Time* and *People*, or the newspapers. Present these pictures to the children and ask them to tell you what kind of people they are, what they probably do as a job, whether they have families, and so forth. After you all discuss their impressions, tell them the actual backgrounds of the people. Stress the idea that first impressions affect the way we relate to people. It is important that we remain open to changing impressions.

VARIATION We often hear children say, "Oh, I can't do that!" This is usually a reaction to their first impressions of what a task requires. Use the activity Task Analysis in this chapter to break the task down. Help children to see that their first impressions are usually inaccurate and that, by approaching the task step by step, they can do the activity.

ACTIVITY TITLE **Actions and Intent**

MATERIALS For this activity on intention, you need paper, pencil, and the scripts included.

PROCEDURES Judging people's behavior is difficult. Much has been written in the field of moral development concerning the effects of situations and of people's intent on the judgments passed by others.

How do children make judgments, given both the outcomes of actions and the intent of the person involved? For example, Johnny was getting a cookie, which was against the rules, and accidentally broke the cookie jar. Tommy was allowed to get a cookie and broke the jar. Sam, who wasn't supposed to have a cookie, got one but didn't break the jar. Who acted the worst? There is no "right" answer.

Such forced choice situations can be very helpful in seeing how children view moral decisions and in getting them to think about their actions. Two sample stories follow:

Story 1. Mary, Frank, and Sue saw a friend of theirs taking a bracelet from a store. Mary thought they should report the friend to the department store manager. Frank left the store immediately because he was afraid he would be accused of shoplifting also. Mary didn't report the friend because she didn't want the friend to get into trouble. Sue reported the friend.

Who did the right thing. Why? Who did the worst thing? Why? Can you think of something else someone could have done?

Story 2. Tom and Jane are boy and girl friends. Tom's Mother needed some medicine from the drugstore in the next town twenty-five miles away. Tom has no transportation and can't leave his Mom alone. He calls Jane for help.

Jane went to her friend Emily, who has a car, to ask for help. Emily said she couldn't help because she had a date.

Jane went to Chris and asked for help. Chris said he would but he had already told Randy that he could use his car.

As a last resort Jane asked Mike. Mike said sure, but only if when they got back he and Jane could stop and do $100 worth of repair to his car.

Jane agreed to do it, and Tom's mother was OK.

Who acted the worst? Were the friends' reasons acceptable? What else could have been done?

Try making up your own scripts that your children can relate to.

VARIATION   Use a list of negative behaviors like cheating, stealing, lying, spying, gossip, meanness, or hurting others. Ask the children to rank them from the worst to the least bad. Discuss the differences and what makes one different from the others.

ACTIVITY TITLE   ## The Family Code

MATERIALS   This activity on establishing general goals for parents and children calls for a loose-leaf notebook or folder, paper, markers, pens, a hole punch, and a piece of stiff paper.

PROCEDURES   A general statement of philosophy, including ultimate goals and a preference of methodology, is required of most applications for teaching positions. There is no similar requirement for parenting, and indeed training in parenting skills is a rarity.

In the olden days each family had its own coat of arms and a family code of honor, very much like King Arthur's Code of the Round Table. Design a Family Coat of Arms following the same format as the Me Badge activity (Chapter 1). In the individual section of the Coat of Arms, put major values that you want your family to have and to be passed on to the children: fairness, justice, honesty, freedom, activeness, awareness, sensitivity, strength, caring, consideration, feeling, a willingness to work hard and so on. Add personal touches for decoration like hobbies, work, family outings, special celebrations. Then display and discuss this Coat of Arms.

Using the notebook, write out The Family Code. This code may be the philosophy of life that the family holds, or the goals and the activities that the family intends to do.

Another approach is to write all the rules, regulations, and limits that you wish the household to consider. These should be worded in a positive way. For example:

Rather Than Saying:	*You Could Say*
No wasting of food.	We will consciously conserve food.
No running inside.	Walking is for inside; running is for outside.
No one is allowed to leave their things in the living room.	Everyone will keep their things in their room.

This code book is also a good place to keep the products of many activities in this book.

ACTIVITY TITLE **Turn Over a New Leaf**

MATERIALS To do this activity on classifying parental expectations, you need construction paper, markers, pens, scissors, and a tree branch.

PROCEDURES Fold each piece of construction paper in half. Find a large leaf to trace on the paper, or draw your own. Cut the leaves out of the paper. On each leaf draw a picture representing a personal characteristic or behavior. Label these with cute titles like, Mr. Messy, Lazy Larry, Tattle-Tale Tim, Sad Sadie, Nosey Nellie, Mr. Perfect, and the like.

On the other side of the leaf, on the top, write, "Are you a *(title)*?" Below this write, "How can you change this?"

Older children can write their own answers on the leaf and attach them to the tree branch. Younger children may need to dictate their responses or draw pictures. Plan times to discuss which new leaves have been turned over.

VARIATION Make a booklet out of the construction paper. On the front of each page, draw the pictures and label them. On the back draw a picture of the opposite characteristic of behavior.

Explain that the "Turn Over a New Leaf" booklet will show both the ways you hope children will not act and, by turning over a new leaf, the ways you hope children will act.

ACTIVITY TITLE **Hobbies**

MATERIALS This activity on developing skill areas through interests requires pen and paper.

PROCEDURES Most parents would like their children to be skilled in at least one area. This is obvious by the number of very young children involved in gymnastics, piano, violin, dance, and other pursuits.

Make two listings, including all the things you wish you could do well and the things you hope the child can do well. Look over the two lists and draw connecting lines between abilities that appear on both lists. From this create a single list of the things you hope that both you and the child can do well.

Sit with the child and discuss the listing. Together the two of you select two areas that you are interested in.

On separate pieces of paper use these areas as headings. On each brainstorm as many experiences, activities, and hobbies you can think of to facilitate skill development in that area. This will be a final product from which to choose a mutual hobby for you and the child.

VARIATION After discussing what a hobby is and what the child's interests are (see I Love to _____), set up some guidelines for a hobby tour. Depending on the age and ability level of the child and the hobbies chosen, these rules will vary. (The choice of hobbies is limitless: puzzles, models, sports, music, collecting various items, whatever.) In general try:

1. This time is to be devoted to a specific hobby.
2. The hobby can be changed only after a specific length of time.
3. The hobby must develop some skill area.

ACTIVITY TITLE I Love to _____!

MATERIALS This activity on clarifying desires requires paper and pencil.

PROCEDURES You and your child should both participate in this activity.

List the things you love to do. List at least five and no more than ten. After writing these down, go back over the list by placing a 1 by the one you most love to do, a 2 for the next, and continue until you have ranked them all by number.

Discuss the number of items you listed. Was it hard to think of things or were there so many things that ten didn't cover everything? Next use the following code to look at each listed activity. Place the codes next to the activity.

$ If it costs money
A If you do it alone
P With people
B For having done it recently (within two weeks)
C If it involves taking a chance
G If you think it produces personal growth
X If it is on both of your lists

Discuss your and your child's listing. Do the rankings match? Have you many X's? Are the items you ranked 1 to 5 also the ones with the most symbols? Do you see any patterns? Discuss these aspects with the child, and try to interpret self-expectations from the listings.

VARIATION Ask your child, "If you could do anything you wanted, what would you do?" After a response ask, "What else?" When the child can no longer think of things, go over the list and, for each response, ask why that one was chosen. The answers to the question "Why?" will give you insight into what the child's expectations of life really are.

ACTIVITY TITLE | **Contracting**

MATERIALS | To do this activity on contracting, you need paper and pencils.

PROCEDURES | Contracting is a very useful tool in helping children establish realistic goals. The basic requirements of a contract are that it is:

1. fair,
2. clearly stated,
3. generally positive,
4. individualized, and
5. structured so that performance is immediately rewarded.

Initiate this activity one morning. Ask the child what she expects to do that day. List these expectations and then include any activities that you expect her to do. Design a contract similar to the following one, and both of you sign it to indicate your agreement.

Child's Name   *Adult's Name*

Goal: To perform all tasks agreed to.

Agreement: Before 4:00 o'clock I will straighten my room, take out the trash, and trim the hedge.

Consequences:
1. I will be allowed thirty minutes extra TV time tonight, or
2. No extra TV time.

Date: _____   Signed: _____

_____

After trying these one-day contracts, extend the contracts to cover a week or a month. Finally suggest that the child move into self-contracting, checking with you for only approval of the rewards.

VARIATION | Explain to the child that we often expect to do too much. Let her know that you are conducting an experiment and that the consequence will not really be imposed. Then present the child with a contract that you feel cannot possibly be met. Make sure it's a short task.

After the child has attempted the task, discuss the feelings that this inability to meet the contract caused. Can she relate this feeling to other situations in real life? Invite her to swap roles and to assign you a impossible task.

ACTIVITY TITLE | **I'll Show You Mine
(Sexual Experimentation)**

MATERIALS | No materials other than paper and pencil are needed for this activity on responding to children's sexual experimentations.

PROCEDURES At a very young age children discover that sensations from the genital area can be very pleasant. When children understand the relationship between stimulation of the genital area and the pleasurable sensation, they will quite normally participate in self-stimulation (masturbation). Playing doctor is also a common experience.

A parent's response to early masturbation and sexual experimentation can be very influential to the later sexual development of the child. This activity will help you to become aware of your own feelings toward the subject and to develop ways of dealing with the situation.

Write a short description of your feelings about early sexual experimentation. Is it bad, normal, OK, damaging, a part of growing up, or what? Can you recall your own early sexual experiences? Were they guilt-producing? How did your parents react? Think of what you have written. Is this the experience you hope your child has?

In general I recommend that your reactions be casual and accepting. Masturbation and sexual experimentation is a normal activity. Let the child know that you are aware of this activity.

It is important, even at this early age, that you convey the private aspect of sexual activity. Many children will participate in sexual activities in public. A good response is, "I know you want to do what you're doing. Find a private place to do it." Or, "I know that feels good; you need to find a place to be alone." To condemn them for their action will generate guilt and not help in sexual development.

VARIATION Use a book, for children, on human development. Point out the genital areas of both the male and female.

Lead an open discussion allowing the children to share their experiences. Introduce your own feelings and stress the idea of all sexual activity being private. Make it clear that the act is not bad but also that over-indulgence is not good. (Excessive masturbation may lead to a preference of self-stimulation rather than heterogeneous sexual relationships.)

This is also a good opportunity to introduce the fact that some adults have had bad sexual experiences or have grown up misinformed about sex. These people are sick and need help to overcome their problems. Sometimes these people expose themselves to or touch children. The children need not worry about these people but should be aware of them.

[2] TIPS

1. Knowledge of the individual and of child development is necessary to establish reasonable expectations.

2. Realistic expectations promote successful experiences and a positive self-concept.

3. Unrealistic expectations either will not challenge a child to grow or will provide experience with failure.

4. Parents' and teachers' self-expectations are the basic models for children's expectations of self.

5. People try to "live up to" the expectations others have for them.

6. Children learn what they live.

7. Mutual trust and respect is one of the goals of teaching and parenting.

8. Your attitudes about and toward children are reflected in their attitude toward themselves and others.

9. To be a positive functioning adult, you must be able to set personal goals.

10. Fear of failure is a major cause of unsuccessful experiences. Help children treat failure as a growing experience.

Self-and Self-Esteem

HOW CHILDREN SEE THEMSELVES AND OTHERS

Children have a basic instinct to explore and to experiment, an instinct evidenced by their constant grasping, moving, jumping, and throwing—all to test themselves. Although the self is basically the total world for young children, they begin to relate to their environments and to the objects in it through their own physical selves. They gratify themselves through their experiences, and this gratification then leads children to seek more experiences. As they continue to do so, they become active, curious "learners."

So, before young children can become other-directed, they must first develop a sure and positive sense of self. Only then can their experiences become contributors to the way children view themselves and their abilities to grow. Such a view of self, called *self-esteem*, is a major influence on the way children behave as they grow and develop.

The other most important influence of the development of self-esteem is the way children are seen by significant others, such as parents, grandparents, sitters, siblings, peers, and teachers. The old axiom that "You see yourself through the eyes of others" has much to say in the way we relate with young children. If parents or teachers are constantly telling children, "You're *too* little" or "*no*, not yet—wait until you grow bigger or older," the children learn that they are not very competent. If, on the other hand, we encourage children to try things and let them experience the natural consequences of their action (not damaging ones, of course), they are then encouraged to try new things and are better equipped to handle possible failures.

If children see themselves through our eyes, they must certainly see, at least partly, how we view ourselves. Insofar as how we see ourselves is a strong influence in the development of the child's self-esteem, it is vital that we, the significant adults, be sensitive to the child's view of self and be aware of our own beliefs and level of self-esteem.

Children and adults alike approach tasks and experiences with expectations and preset beliefs. If our children are to be successful in this world, our responsibility is to help them believe that they are able to meet the challenges of life with competence and skills. To develop these skills, parents and teachers must not only provide opportunities for children to make decisions and to act upon them, understanding the consequences but not fearing them, but they must also support them in their growth and development. These decisions, in the beginning, affect the child directly.

The purpose of this chapter is to offer some ideas about attitudes and activities for the home and school that:

1. help children and parents learn about themselves, together,
2. develop a positive view of self and others, and
3. provide avenues for dealing with a realistic view of self and others.

While approaching these activities, keep in mind that what you think and especially the way you "are" with children will have the most impact on your children's development.

Each of the following activities contribute to the ways children see themselves, as well as to the way they see you as their parent or teacher. These activities assist the growing relationship you establish with the children.

[1] Self-esteem and the personal self are important aspects of a child's development. Try the following activities.

ACTIVITY TITLE **Routines**

MATERIALS You will need crayons or markers, and chart paper for this activity.

PROCEDURES List the activities you anticipate the child to be involved with for an hour (or a half-day or the total day), in the order most likely to be followed. Mark each activity with a simple picture depicting the actions required for the activity: a toilet for the bathroom, a sand box for outside, or books for quiet time. As each activity is completed, point it out on the chart and let the child mark it off. This chart also gives you a recordkeeping system for your child's daily activities. Of course, the child will do things not included on the chart, so you will want to add these activities.

VARIATION	Make a pocket calendar for the youngster. Have him mark the days he would like to do certain things. You will have to help him understand that he can't do everything in one day and that there will be other days to do things.

ACTIVITY TITLE Individual Schedules

MATERIALS	For this activity, you need note pads, primary pencils or crayons, paste, scissors, and catalogs.
PROCEDURES	Help the child find or draw pictures of activities that she likes to do or would like to do. Make a sizable collection for them to use. Use the collection of pictures to help the child list and identify (picture) the activities she did that day. You can help her remember and sequence the activities. Either immediately or on another day, use the picture collection to help the child list or plan the schedule for that day.
VARIATION	Older children may wish to plan several days or a week. Use the listings as starting points for discussing how the child spends time, what causes the choices, and the importance of a balance of activities.

ACTIVITY TITLE Parental/Teacher Awareness-Listings

MATERIALS	Select several sheets of paper and pencils.
PROCEDURE	Develop a list of your personal goals for the children. Place a star by the goals you feel competent of achieving with them. Circle the goals you feel are not being achieved. Compare and discuss these goals and your concerns with a peer, professional, or spouse who is familiar with the child. Ask yourself:

1. "Are the goals reasonable or unreasonable?"
2. "Are you pushing the child?"
3. "Are your concerns common among parents of this age child?"
4. "Do you both see the children in the same light?"

Reach a solution as to which goals are reasonable and which need to be adjusted to meet the needs of the child. Focus on one goal and make a plan to accomplish it. The plan consists of deciding on the goal to work with and of writing out specific ideas to achieve that goal.

VARIATION	Expand your goals by reading about and discussing children's development and by learning with a peer or friend. Make a list of goals that are appropriate to various age levels of children.

ACTIVITY TITLE Anecdotal Records

MATERIALS	A notebook and pen are needed for this activity.

PROCEDURE Observe the youngsters as often as possible and in a variety of situations—alone, with our children, with strangers, sitters, and watching television. Keep a written log of the kinds of things they do and how long the activities hold their attention. Also write your opinion of which experiences they enjoy. For example, "John seems to be really enjoying the new car. He rolled it back and forth about twenty times before he started picking it up!" These anecdotal records will provide you with a "picture" of the child's development over a period of time. You will also have a record to compare with your goals and personal assessment of the child's strengths and weaknesses.

VARIATION Many people actually keep a series of photographs along with the anecdotal records to provide a pictorial record of their children's learning as well as development.

ACTIVITY TITLE ## Bathroom Routines

MATERIALS A small poster board, colorful markers, clear contact paper, a crayon or wax marker, and visuals such as soap, toothbrush, wash cloth, and the like are needed for this activity.

PROCEDURES As the child matures, encourage him to perform daily hygiene tasks independently—bathing, brushing his teeth, or brushing his hair. Also, with the child, develop a chart of daily bathroom tasks. As you teach the child the tasks and make the poster, discuss the relationship of the tasks to good health. On the chart use pictures to identify the necessary activities and include a word to describe each activity: picture of a toothbrush—teeth, pictures of soap and washclothe—face, 2 pictures of the toilet—flush. Attach the crayon or china marker (available at an art supply store), so the child can mark the tasks performed. Each day discuss the chart and plan ways to help him complete more activities independently. (The contact paper protects the poster and allows you to wipe off the crayon each day.) Don't expect immediate success with the youngster; it takes time. Keep track of the youngster's progress by listing each completed task and the date successfully completed.

VARIATION For children who are having great difficulty following through with these routines, provide a "reward," such as a visit to the zoo.

ACTIVITY TITLE ## Fun in Food Groups

MATERIALS To complete this series of activities, you need a variety of foods from each of the four food groups: meat and fish, fruits and vegetables, breads and cereals, milk and dairy. You will also need to use the kitchen, some paste, scissors, and pictures of various common foods.

PROCEDURES Begin introducing the food groups by discussing the foods the youngster usually eats and to which groups the foods belong. Using labels from foods or pictures from advertisements, make a collage depicting a variety of foods from each food group. (Make sure the four groups can be seen within the collage.) Make a collage by pasting the cut-out food

127

pictures in random, overlapping patterns. Display this collage to stimulate discussion of foods, nutrition, and the food groups. Plan a menu for a day with the child using the food groups as the basic framework for planning a balanced diet. For example, say, "Each day we need three servings from the milk group, four servings from the fruit and vegetable, four from the bread and cereals, and two from the meat group. What three servings from the milk group would you like?" You and the child prepare and enjoy these foods while discussing the relationship between healthy bodies and the way we think, feel, and act.

VARIATION   Using empty cartons or the actual foods, make a four food groups mobile by hanging the items from a coat hanger. You can also use advertisements glued to empty cereal boxes.

ACTIVITY TITLE   More Fun with Food Groups

MATERIALS   These activities require a variety of foods from each food group. You also need cooking facilities, transportation to local supermarkets, paste, paper, food coloring, paint or ink, and a sponge.

PROCEDURE   Set aside four consecutive days to stress the food groups. With the children coin a cute name for describing one of the food groups for each day: for example, Bobbie's Banana Day (fruit and vegetable group), Marvin's Milk Day (milk and dairy group), Sid's Cereal Day (bread and cereal), and Frank's Fish Day (meat and fish).

On the day designated as Bobbie's Banana Day, do several activities throughout the day involving those foods. For example:

1. have a raw fruit and vegetable tasting party,
2. visit the local Farmers' Market with the youngster,
3. slice various fruits and vegetables and press them into an ink- or paint-soaked sponge, and
4. make an assortment of prints on paper.

On milk and dairy day, visit a dairy, of course. Crack and beat some eggs and talk about the difference between the yolk and white of the egg. (Be sure to save the egg shells.) Make butter by shaking some heavy cream vigorously in a small jar. Have a smelling and tasting party, trying several strong and mild cheeses. Crumble and color egg shells with food colors. Use these to make a texture collage, by gluing them onto stiff cardboard (obtained from the dry clearners). Use your child's imagination and your own to design enjoyable experiences around each food group. Be sure to stress the need for a balanced diet and the interrelations of our bodies, minds, feelings, and energy with the foods we eat.

VARIATION   Sid's Cereal Day, for example, gives you a chance to eat several types of grain and grain products—wheat, rye, corn, and the like. Make some new dishes for meals. Look at several raw grains and notice the difference Talk about nutritious versus sweetened breakfast cereals. Bake some bread. For Frank's Day, visit the fish and meat market. Ask the manager to show you everything. Discuss and look at some other sources of protein. Find out why meat is important to us. What do people eat if they don't eat meat?

ACTIVITY TITLE | Avoiding Sexual "Stereotypes"
Or What Am I—A Boy or a Girl?

MATERIALS | You need photographs of a variety of playthings such as dolls, trucks, jacks, books, and so on, along with paper and pencil.

PROCEDURE | Sexual stereotyping is most definitely a learned thing. Children learn these stereotypes from many sources such as television, toys, books, school, peers, other adults, and especially parents. To keep your child free of stereotypes, you must first try to rid yourself of your own. Make a listing of the stereotypes you hold as an adult, such as particular jobs for men and women—doctors and lawyers are men's roles, while waitresses and secretaries are women's roles. Can you think of exceptions to your own stereotypes? Where do you think you got the stereotypes?

Ask your youngster some questions as you play with her. Can a boy play with dolls? Can a woman drive a dump truck? Can women play baseball? Can men be secretaries? Can women be garbage collectors? Can men and women be school teachers, maids, doctors, lawyers, police, or firefighters? What will you be when you get a job? Accept any answers you get without lecturing. Note the types of stereotypes your child is acquiring and try to expose her to situations that will help her grow beyond them. Show the photographs and ask, "Is it OK for boys and girls to play with this? Why?"

VARIATION | Begin the discussion with the fact that men and women are different but that the gender does not preclude either from jobs. Continue by showing photographs, reading stories, and visiting people that typically do not hold the position they are in.

ACTIVITY TITLE | Mirror, Mirror

MATERIALS | This activity requires full-length and hand-held mirrors, a people puzzle, or child's picture book.

PROCEDURE | Let the youngster handle and play with the puzzle and/or picture book of a person (clothed or unclothed). After the child has become familiar with them, sit down and do the puzzle or read the book with him. During this time stress the names of the body parts and their locations on the body. Have the child touch his own leg, arm, and head as you talk about that part of the puzzle or book. (This is a good time for tickle-tickle games too.)

After doing the puzzle or the book, talk about the different things that parts of your body do for you. For example, *arms* lift things, *hands* hold items and wave good-bye, and *feet* move. Let the child play in front of the mirror for a while. Let him experiment with the hand-held and full-length mirrors, too. It's very difficult to manipulate the hand mirror to see your back; you will probably have to help. (Lots of people never see their backs until they are adults!) Give a series of directions so the child can see different parts of the body in motion. For instance, "Swing your arms like a monkey!" "Jump as high as you can!" "Pretend to wash your face!" "Tie your shoe and watch yourself in the mirror." "Pick up the shoes." "Lean over and look through your legs at the mirror!" Keep up the discussion of the body. This is also a good time to discuss the relationship between nutrition, health, body, and mind. Make a list of the body parts and check the ones the child knows! Work on experiences to "teach" the others.

VARIATION   Put the mirrors, book, and puzzle out for the child to experiment with. As questions arise, take him through the same discussion but let him initiate the activities.

ACTIVITY TITLE   I'm Important Too!

MATERIALS   You will need large pieces of paper (people size), several felt tip pens, crayons, or paint.

PROCEDURE   Let your youngster dress in her favorite clothes with the restriction that they are colorful. Have the child stretch out on the paper! Carefully trace around the body with the felt tip pen. Let the child color the portrait, making sure to include the colors of the clothes and as many details as possible.

Now you have a full-size painting of the child. You can let him know just how special he is. While you are naming the ways and showing how special—identify the special talents the child has and why you love him. Write these talents and reasons in colorful language all over the page.

VARIATION   The child cuts and pastes pictures of things that are important to him. These importances may include household tasks, family groups, pets, artistic talents, and the like. Then you make a list with pictures of the ways the youngster is important to you. Compare lists.

[2]   Nurturing self-esteem is a basic aspect of developing the self and self-esteem. Try the following activities.

ACTIVITY TITLE   Expressive Faces

MATERIALS   Paper, crayons, and an empty coffee can are needed for this activity. In addition, find some visuals, for example, of children fighting, of a mother and child smiling, of youngsters crying, of people playing, and so on.

PROCEDURE   Talk about feelings and the things that cause different feelings! Name some feelings that youngsters are familiar with—happy, sad, lonely, angry, surprised—add some new feelings, such as anxious and melancholy. Try to think of times you were really feeling emotional! Let the child share those times, too. Try to decide how you can tell if someone is sad, happy, or angry. List as many emotions as the two of you can think of on slips of paper and put them in the coffee can. (You might have to draw smiling or frowning faces or pictures of situations to show the youngster.) Now take turns drawing slips and acting out the feelings without any words. Figure out which feeling it is.

VARIATION   Use pictures or television shows to set up various emotional situations. Line off a piece of paper into large squares. As each situation is presented, ask the child to put a "smile" or "frown" face in the square. When finished, talk about why he felt that way and other ways he could express the same emotion.

ACTIVITY TITLE   ## My Make-Believe Friend

MATERIALS   You need photographs of children, markers, glue, and pictures of kids playing.

PROCEDURE   Start the activity by talking about what makes people friends. Let the child share her ideas. Make sure you share your ideas, too! Make sure you mention that friends share happiness, sadness, thoughts, wishes, feelings, troubles, and trust. Friends also have disagreements and fights, but that doesn't mean you aren't friends any more. Talk about ways friends make up after a fight. Using the photographs (include a boy and a girl), you and the youngster make a mural of what makes a friend and what sorts of things friends do together. Remember that

children don't really know what makes friends until they have experienced friendships themselves. For the child to develop the skills it
takes to make friends, you must treat the child as a true friend.

VARIATION

Do the activity with a group of children. You might help them become
friends!

ACTIVITY TITLE The Grocery Store

MATERIALS

Labels or advertisements of grocery items from newspapers, glue, and
paper are needed.

PROCEDURE

Take the youngster to the supermarket. Ask him to hand you specific
items from the shelves and put them into the grocery cart. After several
trips, the youngster becomes familiar and comfortable at the store. As
he becomes more familiar with the store, start asking him to get certain
items from the shelves. (Make sure the items are on low shelves.)
Children really enjoy these activities. When preparing for the next trip
to the supermarket, let the youngster help make up the shopping list.
As he decides on items, cut out a picture of an actual label from
newspaper advertisements and make up the child's own grocery list.
When you arrive at the store, either go with the child to do his
shopping or send him off on his own. This is a great opportunity to tie
shopping together with the nutritional aspect and the importance of a
balanced diet.

VARIATION

Collect empty cans and cartons of the foods you normally buy at the
supermarket. Set up a play store in the house or classroom using the
same labeling system as found in a store. Let the youngsters make their
own grocery list and shop to their heart's content. With the older
children, you might include a monetary system for purchasing some of
the items.

ACTIVITY TITLE Selling Yourself

MATERIALS

Poster board, markers, mail order catalogs, glue, paint, and paper
scraps are needed.

PROCEDURE

Talk about the advertisements you see all the time on television. Help
the youngster see that the advertisers concentrate on the best parts of
their products and what they can do for you. You and the youngster
each make a poster depicting the best parts of your personalities. Focus
on one or two strengths. Talk about why those strengths are important
and what they can do for you and for other people. Keep a listing of the
strengths the child feels. Help her add to the list.

VARIATION

Pretend you are a radio disc jockey or a television without a picture.
What kinds of things can you say about yourself and your strengths that
would make others want to be like you?

ACTIVITY TITLE	**Sometimes We're All Afraid**
MATERIALS	Paper and pencil are all the objects you need.
PROCEDURE	Use this activity as a game with a group of youngsters (or the family members). Write out a list of incomplete statements that you think will be meaningful to the children. Give them a chance to talk about them without being afraid. The incomplete statements are:

1. I'm most afraid when _____.
2. I'm scared when Mommy _____.
3. I was afraid when _____ got mad about _____.
4. I don't like it when _____.
5. When I grow up I won't be afraid of _____.
6. When I'm alone I _____.
7. At bedtime I'm afraid of _____.
8. The bathroom scares me because _____.
9. I wish I wasn't afraid of _____.

This activity is a chance for the children to express their fears and for you to learn what frightens them. It is *not* a good time to try to rid the child of the fears. Make sure you play the game too! Keep a record of the things that scare them, and try to make them more comfortable when those situations arise.

VARIATION	Take turns telling make-believe stories about things and times that really scare you. Many scary stories are available for reading with children.

ACTIVITY TITLE	**Swapping Roles**
MATERIALS	Dress-up clothes—such as hats, coats, shoes, jewelry—are all you need to make this fun.
PROCEDURE	For a while, trade roles with the youngster. Let him be you and you be him. Let the child know that you are "pretending" to be him by showing some action behaviors that he will identify with. Then ask him to act the way he sees you acting. With more experience, extend the acting to last a half-hour. Wait until the game is over before discussing. Accept the way they depict you while they are pretending. Then talk about how it felt! These points of discussion include:

1. Was it an accurate picture? Why?
2. Are there some times you would really like to change places? Why?
3. Were they fair? Why?

Let two youngsters trade roles. Be sure that they are "fair" to each other. If one is damaging the other, take the opportunity not to reprimand the child but to show what it feels like in this position. Then the child actually takes the other's role.

ACTIVITY TITLE **Finding an Outlet**

MATERIALS You will need a package of pudding and large sheets of paper for this activity—along with *much* sensitivity and patience.

PROCEDURE Begin the activity when the child is feeling good. Talk about what makes her feel good. Then bring up the times when she hasn't felt so good about things. Discuss "what" and "why" she wasn't feeling good. Don't continually repeat these discussions, but talk about them every now and then. The idea is to let the child know that we all have good and "bad" moods. We want children to know that it isn't "bad" to be in a bad mood and that there are ways to channel the bad feelings constructively. The next time the child seems to have "gotten up on the wrong side of the bed" gently remind her of the times you have talked about those feelings. Quite often these low moods are a sign of over-tiredness or perhaps the beginnings of an illness rather than just a "bad" mood.

The first step in finding an outlet for the low feelings is to recognize that you are in a low mood. Give the child opportunity to talk about how she is feeling. Identify some reasons for the feelings. Sometimes there is a simple reason. For example, "Tom broke my new toy! ... Mary pulled my hair! ... The kids won't let me play!" These situations have to be dealt with individually.

Yet at other times there is no apparent reason for the low feelings. On these occasions let the child know it is okay to feel "down!" Accept the feelings she is expressing. Don't try to "snap her out of it" by being overly light and gay. Let her know you understand her feelings by putting the feelings into words. Say, for instance, "I think you are feeling sad, mad, angry, or alone!" Share some of the times you yourself felt that way. Suggest that the child try drawing some pictures that express these feelings. Read or tell some stories. Be with the child when these feelings are discussed.

VARIATION Use the pudding and large paper. Tell the child to use the pudding as fingerpaint and make a painting of the feelings. While she is painting, talk about the feelings she is trying to express. It is OK for her to lick her fingers.

ACTIVITY TITLE **Practice Makes Perfect**

MATERIALS You will need a playground ball (8"), several sheets of graph paper, and a felt tip pen.

PROCEDURE Talk with the youngster about how skills are developed. Use sports figures to show how by practicing specific things people get to be very good at doing them. Include examples such as baseball, tennis, foot-ball, and basketball.

Give the youngster the ball and let him play with it for a while. Now tell him that you are going to teach him a game. Play it every day for a week. Start the game by showing him how to bounce the ball (use one or two hands depending on the age of the child). While you bounce, count the number of times. Let them try it! While bouncing you can count the number of times (each day). This way, they will see that by practicing each day the number of bounces will increase. Use the graph paper to chart each day's number of bounces. Set up the graph so the vertical axis is the number of bounces and the horizontal is the dates of the sessions.

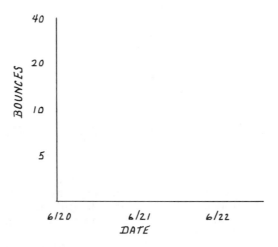

There should be a steady increase in the "line" until it reaches a plateau. If the line doesn't show a continuous increase, discuss the reasons for a low performance on those particular days. Some of the reasons could be fatigue or distraction.

VARIATION

Chart the child's progress on other skills like drawing a straight line, tying shoes, making circles, dancing, and remembering songs.

ACTIVITY TITLE

I'm Feeling ... ?

MATERIALS

You need a large circle of cardboard or borrow a pizza board from your local restaurant. Also gather some felt tip markers, scissors, and a brass fastener.

PROCEDURES

During those times when the youngster seems to show rapid changes in mood, this activity provides a graphic way for her to communicate her current moods.

Use the board as a chart for her emotions, by depicting the moods or feelings youngster is familiar with and by providing a visual means of communication. With the child, decide which emotions should go on the chart: happy, sad, mad, angry, tired, or bored. Help her draw faces to depict those feelings. Use the edges of the board for these faces. Cut an arrow from stiff paper and affix it to the center of the

board with the brass fastener. Now you have an adjustable chart for the child to use in communicating her mood with you. You might set a certain time of day for the child to adjust the chart, and discuss how she is feeling.

Keep a record of the child's feelings. Is there an overall pattern? Note the overall pattern by recording the youngster's moods on a calendar. The pattern may be seen as several "sad" days followed by a mad day. You may see series of happy, sad, happy, and sad, or you might recognize that "bored" always appears in groups of three consecutive days. Use this information to influence "negative cycles."

VARIATION   Have a chart and a special place for it for each member of the family/class. Let everyone set his or her charts to the feeling the first thing in the morning. Let the others talk about and decide on special ways to help each other "work out" of the more negative feelings and to sustain the good ones.

ACTIVITY TITLE   Pets

MATERIALS   You need one pet—a cat, dog, parrot, gerbil—and all the necessary equipment to care for it. Poster paper, markers, and a book on how to take care of it are also necessary.

PROCEDURE   After several weeks of discussing the pet with the family group, surprise the youngsters with it! Either a goldfish, a small turtle, a lizard, or a hamster can be used. Set up a schedule where, for a specific length of time, you will help care for the animal. Make it clear that at the end of the specified time, the responsibility of caring for the pet becomes the

136

youngsters'. Prior to that time, share this responsibility! Help the youngster make a checklist for feeding, cleaning, exercising, and doing the other things that must be done for it. You might want to include a length of time in which you will not do the actual tasks but will remind the youngsters of the things that need to be done.

If you are successful with one pet, you can increase the number and types of them.

VARIATION Build a make-believe pet and pet home. Using pictures of a goldfish bowl, fish, plants, and other necessary items for the pet, put together a scene and list of the things that must be done for it. Work up a schedule of when they should be fed, exercised, and otherwise cared for. Have the youngster actually add pictures and role play the daily chores of caring for the pet(s) before bringing it (them) home.

[3] The acceptance and evaluation of self are other fundamental elements of developing and self and self-esteem. Try the following.

ACTIVITY TITLE You Always Make Me . . . !

MATERIALS You need large sheets of paper or pieces of chart paper and felt tip markers.

PROCEDURE Often you feel like a police officer and children the slaves. This activity will give you, the adult, and the child a chance to look at what things both of you are made to do and what things you make others do.

Begin by asking the youngster, "What do I ask you to do?" List all the responses on the chart. Now on another sheet, make a list of all the things you as the adult feel others ask you to do. Your list is longer than the youngster's because you come into contact with more people than he does.

Give the list to the youngsters and read it over with them. Talk about which of the things you feel you ask him to do and the reasons you feel it is necessary for him to do those things. Discuss how it feels to be asked or made to do things that you don't want to do. How do you feel when you make others do things? From the youngster's list, find some of the things he can do for himself with just some reminders rather than after your constantly asking him to do it. You do the same with your listing.

VARIATION List all the things that others do for you. Have the child do the same. Decide some of the things you can both do or would rather do for yourselves.

ACTIVITY TITLE I Don't Like . . . I Like . . . . !

MATERIALS Use regular notebook paper, along with a pen or pencil for this activity.

PROCEDURE Have a discussion about the people, places, and things that the youngster doesn't like to see, visit, or play with. Be sure to draw her out about the reasons she doesn't like the things listed. Now, on the paper, make a listing of all these things the youngster doesn't like. After reading over the listing, talk again about the reasons. Guide the discussion to find things that are good about that person, place, thing, or situation. Add these positive aspects next to the negative items on the list. When you have finished, you will both be able to see that even in situations that we do not like, we can find something positive and grow from the experience. Save these, pull them out in a month, and see if the youngsters have changed their likes and dislikes.

VARIATION   List all the people that have caused the youngster to feel "bad." Have them explain, "why?" Go back over the list and find some ways that those persons have or could make them feel good rather than bad. Select one or two of the people, get in touch with them, and try to overcome those negative feelings.

ACTIVITY TITLE   ## Things I Do Well!

MATERIALS   You need chart paper, markers, and action pictures for this activity, which deals with things that the child does well—play, sing, draw, talk, sports, cuddle, sleep, take out trash, make beds, cook, and so on.

PROCEDURE   Individually you and the youngster make a listing of things you feel you do the best! Help the youngster think of things and find pictures that will show those strengths. After you have listed at least ten or fifteen, put a star by the ones that were demonstrated in the past day. Put an "X" by the ones that you have done this week, and draw a circle around the ones that you haven't done within the week. With the child, plan times that you can do some of those things together (see Routines and Individual Schedules). Then do some of them. Save these to help keep track of the child's development.

VARIATION   Change the listing to "Things I Most Like to Do!" Follow the same procedures and keep a record of these "likes!"

ACTIVITY TITLE   ## What If They Could Talk?

MATERIALS   You need a collection of common objects (tools, applicance, clothing, chairs, tables, toys), pictures of other objects from home or the school (cars, trucks, trains, houses, stoves, and members of the family), cardboard and markers.

PROCEDURE   Start the activity by telling a story about an object that takes on life-like characteristics: a car that has feelings and can talk, a dog that was lost and felt terrible because no one could tell him how to get home, or the electric razor that was tired of staying in the bathroom and just cutting hairs! Make a poster showing several household objects or an array of objects like a hat, coat, television and radio sets, bike, shoes, bed, bathroom, or baseball bat. Ask the youngsters leading questions, such as: "What would the bed say if it could talk? . . . How would it feel to have someone laying on you all the time? . . . To be left 'unmade' all the time? . . . Pretend you are one of the things in the pictures—how would you feel? . . . What would you say to the person who was using you as the object?"

VARIATION   Using pictures of the family, have the children share what these people would be saying about them! Discuss the accuracy of their perceptions and relate some actual positive statements you have heard them say about them.

ACTIVITY TITLE   WAIT

MATERIALS   No materials are needed for this activity.

PROCEDURE   Try to substitute the word "wait" for the usual word "no" to stop the children from inappropriate behaviors. "Wait" has a much less negative sound. With children, the volume and firmness of voice causes them to stop more than the word used. Later, the word "wait" causes them to stop, and at the same time it leaves you a positive opening to discuss what is not appropriate and other ways to act. Teach them to use the word "wait" before answering questions or telling someone what to do. This practice helps them develop the habit of thinking about what they are saying and doing before doing or saying it!

For the adult there is another important aspect to "wait." After you ask or tell children to "wait," you must model the "wait" for them. You can't expect immediate responses from adults, let alone a youngster. You will find that by using "wait time," the communication and the feelings aroused by the communication are much more positive. Keep a record of how many times you get a response without repeating yourself.

VARIATION   Establish a "password" for each day. Be sure to use it before asking questions or giving directions. Make sure the child models. You can also prompt the youngster for eliciting the "password." The use of the "password" will alert the listener that a question or direction is going to follow.

ACTIVITY TITLE   Being a Bully

MATERIALS   You will need a pencil, paper, and a small container such as a coffee can for this activity.

PROCEDURE   Discuss what types of behavior make a person a "bully!" For instance, some are pushing people around, "bossing," always getting your way, acting rude, and being childish. Write these behaviors on slips of paper and place them into the container. Now take turns drawing slips and role playing the behaviors on the slips. Discuss how it feels to play the "bully" or the person bullied. Which felt better? Ask the children to explain why?

To emphasize the feeling of being "pushed around," match the youngster with a little stronger child and do the following. (Make sure, however, that you begin by matching girls with girls and boys with boys to avoid sex role stereotyping.) Have the youngsters stand face-to-face and about two feet apart. Tell them to put their palms together with a partner that isn't as strong. How did it feel? Write an anecdotal record of the activity. Do the youngsters exhibit a pattern? Here, look for the youngsters who constantly try to "push" others or always submitting.

VARIATION   Make a listing of positive ways to get "your way." Place them into a container and role play them. Try some of them out on an unsuspecting person. How do they compare with being a "bully?"

ACTIVITY TITLE   ## When I'm Angry!

MATERIALS   A pillow case or laundry bag, stuffing (such as rags or a sheet), paper, and pencil are needed for this activity.

PROCEDURE   When youngsters are angry (to the point of tantrums), tell them you know a game that will help them feel better. Stuff the pillow case or bag to make a punching bag. Try to get the children to talk about what has made them angry. Every time the source is mentioned, tell them to punch the bag as hard as possible. If they can't talk about the problem at first, just let them punch the bag as long as they like. Usually after this activity, children can express the problem with much more clarity. This awareness of what has made them angry is the first step to finding acceptable alternatives. After the youngster has "acted out" the anger, you and she can make a listing of possible ways to vent the anger and perhaps even develop some ideas to keep from becoming angry. Keep track of how often these episodes occur. High frequencies may indicate a problem of overreacting to stimulus or lack of ways to vent anger.

VARIATION   Let the youngsters tell you all the things they would like to do when they are angry. You must accept the socially unacceptable ideas like, "I want to run away! . . . I want to smash it . . . I want to kill!" After the child has verbalized these ideas you can go to the punching activity or wait for the anger to subside.

    When the child no longer feels so angry, proceed with the listing of more acceptable ways of showing anger. Use paper and pencil to draw very angry faces. Role play the situations, and let the children act out some of their ideas and some of the ones you suggest.

ACTIVITY TITLE   ## Bleach Bottle Family

MATERIALS   An assortment of household discards are needed for this activity. Save empty bleach and shampoo bottles of different shapes. Make a collection of tinfoil, material, thread, and paper scraps from around the house or classroom.

PROCEDURE   Build a collection of bottle people representing members of the family and significant others in the youngsters' lives. Make anecdotal records of the children playing with the bottle people simply by noting what the children do with the people and which roles each bottle person takes. Take particular notes of the way children use images of

themselves. Join the child's play. Try to show them positive views of themselves, and deal with the negative aspects of the children's views of self.

Discuss the ways they act and the things they do. Make sure you discuss it with them. Be sure to accept the negative view of self from them. We all have some negative views of self and are constantly trying to improve those views through our thoughts and actions.

Dealing with these negative aspects means you let youngsters know you recognize their perceptions of self and that you are willing to talk about them. Manipulate the bottle people to reflect the children's perceptions. Then show more positive actions you have seen from them.

VARIATION   Use the bottle people as props for the youngsters to role play situations you propose. For example, "Sue, do you remember the time that Grandma was very ill? We visited her in the hospital. Here's Grandma [indicating the appropriate bottle person] lying down. Here you are. Show me what you did that time. How did it feel?" Continue to talk about how it felt and what the child did. Sometimes you will pose hypothetical situations to help them deal with unknown experiences.

ACTIVITY TITLE   The Family/Class Council

MATERIALS   A notebook and pen, a small container (such as a coffee can or plastic butter tub), and an object like a small ball, gavel, or any household knick-knack.

PROCEDURE   The Family/Class Council can have many goals. It is basically a set time each week for the family or children in the classroom to get together and be with each other. It doesn't have to be a problem-solving time, although it may be (see Problem Solving). It doesn't have to deal with unpleasant things, but it might. The Council can be whatever the group makes it and can be directed toward whatever the family/class needs. To be effective, the Council must be approached as a time for the

141   family or class members to get together in a *positive light*. The ultimate

goal is for them to be open and trusting. Certain "ground rules" must be established for the Council to be effective. The rules are:

Rule 1: Only one person speaks at a time. Use the "knick-knack" or object and pass it along as the "key to speak."

Rule 2: This is not the time to argue or defend yourself (at least in the beginning). Listening is the first step.

Rule 3: Everyone gets a chance to speak. (Time limits may be necessary.)

Begin your Council session by focusing on positive things, such as the way everyone has been keeping the house, getting to school on time, smiling a lot, or helping each other out. Ask everyone to think of good things to say about each other. As the Council develops, write topics on slips of paper and place them in the container. Have someone draw a topic for the Council's discussion.

VARIATION   Rather than have the adult as a group leader, either draw slips to determine leadership or rotate leadership throughout the group.

ACTIVITY TITLE   ## Problem Solving in the Council

MATERIALS   You will need materials for establishing the Council: a notebook and pen, tape, felt tip marker, and a small object (a ball, gavel, or knick-knack).

PROCEDURE   Since the Council is a positive gathering, problem-solving time must be clearly delineated. When a member has a particular problem with the group or household routine, it can be approached and discussed at the Council.

Prior to the meeting, post a statement of the problem in an obvious place, such as on the refrigerator, dining table, or classroom. Start the meeting, as usual, with the positive aspects of the group. Instead of drawing a slip from the container (see The Family/Class Council), use the problem as the discussion topic. Appoint a secretary to take notes of the proceedings. The object of these sessions is to have the problem *voiced* and *heard*. Often the problem will not be resolved immediately, but inroads to the problem and the feelings caused by the problem are made. The secretary will record pertinent statements and any suggestions made by the group members. If the problem is between two members of the group, the Council may not be an appropriate method of approach. Individual differences need to be resolved between the individuals, with guidance. If the difference involves an adult, it is good to have an uninvolved member as a guide.

VARIATION   Use a three-ring notebook as the log for recording feelings and problems. When anyone has a positive or negative feeling—a problem or whatever—he or she may write about it in the log. (Youngsters may need to draw pictures or ask for help to express their feelings.) Occasionally remind everyone of the log and ask them to initial it when they have read it. Establish a place to keep the log so that it is accessible to everyone. Use the Council occasionally rather than regularly, to discuss the log and approach problems expressed. (Also use the Council to introduce the log idea.)

[4] TIPS

1. Provide opportunities for youngsters to make choices and to experience safe consequences.
2. Clearly define acceptable and unacceptable behaviors.
3. Be consistent in enforcing limits but allow freedom within the limits.
4. Explain and discuss your rules, limits, and demands with children. This will allow children to recognize the possible consequences of their action.
5. Meet youngsters' needs (food, rest, attention, activities) before problems appear.
6. Carefully select models, such as books, movies, television, and people that influence your children.
7. Remember that the development of self-esteem is a *gradual and constant* process involving *all* of the youngsters' experiences.
8. Encourage children to develop verbal skills. Language is a tool that children use to question, label, classify, and communicate thoughts, feelings, and attitudes.
9. Be available when your children ask for help, but be careful not to push yourself on them. Let them solve problems for themselves if possible.
10. You are the most influential model for the youngsters. *Be* the way you want them to be.

Single-Parent Families

CARING IN ACTION

Divorce, separation, or the death of a parent—either of these events causes a structural change in the family, a very frightening and often painful experience. Both adults and children can become confused and have conflicting emotions. For children, the normal childhood fears—abandonment, the loss of love, a fear of the unknown—are amplified and can become a roadblock for development. For adults, also, the old fears are reawakened. Shifting roles and responsibilities become a burden. Self-concepts can suffer severe damage, which can be reflected to the children.

To deal with the new situation, both custodial and noncustodial parents must be actively involved in setting up new lines of communication, in accepting new responsibilities, in recognizing the situation, in establishing new goals, and most of all in working to provide an atmosphere conducive to the positive development of their children.

This chapter provides ideas, activities, and exercises for both "in-house" (custodial) and the "other" (noncustodial or absent) parents. In addition, activities to help children to accept and to adjust to the new situation are provided. But no two people react to new situations in the same way. No two situations are exactly the same. So the following activities should be considered as options for dealing with parents' indecision and guilt and for helping the confused child. They reflect an attempt to answer the common question asked by single parents,

"What *can* I do?" The more particular question of "What *should* I do?" must be answered individually.

In sum, this chapter is a collection of activities designed to offer choices to children and adults. The choices are organized around the areas of:

1. activities for the "in-house" parent and children,
2. activities for the "other" parent and children, and
3. activities to establish and accept new routines.

For these activities to be effective, parents must be aware that their attitudes are directly reflected by children. Your behavior is the most influential aspect of the child's adjustment.

[1] After a change in the family's lifestyle, the child and the "in-house" parent must establish a different relationship. This relationship must help both to accept the new conditions and to consider the needs, expectations, and feelings of the other. Try these activities for the child and the in-house parent to facilitate the necessary growth of the relationship.

ACTIVITY TITLE **Interpreting Divorce**

MATERIALS This activity on explaining your divorce requires paper, pencils, and drawing materials.

PROCEDURES In telling your children about your divorce, you must take their perspective into account. Children have a deep-seated loyalty to both parents, which the divorce strains. So great care must be taken to support this attachment to both parents rather than using the children as weapons or forcing them to take a side with one parent.

The best approach is an open, honest one. You need not share in great detail the things that led to the divorce. Rather tell them something like:

> When we met we fell very much in love and thought we would live together forever. We lived together and had you and were very, very happy. Over the years things have changed. We both changed, and it got to the point that we couldn't work things out together. We just can't seem to be happy together anymore. We've decided that it doesn't make sense for us to live together unhappily. So we are going to live apart and both try to be happy. This is why we are getting a divorce. Divorce means that we are getting unmarried. We will *both* still love you; we just won't be living together.

Try to respond openly to any of the child's questions without placing guilt on anyone. Be sure to accept any comments or feelings of the child.

Write a letter to your children explaining why you are getting "unmarried." Read the letter with the children and talk about the feelings it causes. (It's OK to cry!)

Present the drawing materials and suggest that they draw some pictures about their thoughts and feelings. Let them explain the drawings.

ACTIVITY TITLE ## The Child and Your New Relationships

MATERIALS For this activity on introducing children to your new friends, you will need paper and drawing materials.

PROCEDURES Many single parents are very apprehensive about dating. Dating can fill many needs that single parents have. From dating you get a sense that you are still attractive to someone, a sense of security, companionship, sexual satisfaction, and entertainment. Best of all, you escape that feeling of loneliness.

It is a good idea to let your child know you have these needs. Children cannot fill all of an adult's needs.

To introduce a new friend to your children, plan an activity to do together. Plan this activity to take place outside the home. Focus it on the child's interest, and see that it requires active involvement from everyone. This might be a sporting event, the circus, putt-putt golf, swimming, and the like. The intent is for everyone to have an active and enjoyable time together.

At a later time recall the experience with the child. Present the drawing materials, and the two of you recreate the situation. Without pressing the child, try to elicit his impressions of your friend. To the side of the picture, you and the child list other things you would like to do with the new friend.

Bring new friends into your child's life gradually outside of the home, and then invite them into the home.

VARIATION If your child is displaying negative behaviors to your new relationships, try the following sequence to change the behaviors.

1. Talk to the child about the behaviors before you see the person again. Use a very conversational tone and just describe what the behaviors were. For example, "Last time we saw _____, you shouted and interrupted me a lot."

2. Reflect the feelings or intent you think the child had—"You wanted my attention. You were feeling left out."

3. Ask the child if that sounds right and discuss it.

4. Use "I-Messages" (Chapter 5) to explain how that behavior made you feel. "When you kept interrupting, I felt uncomfortable. I even got a little angry."

5. Explain the behavior that you would like to see and how that would make you feel.

6. Make a contract, verbal or written, about the expected behaviors next time (Contracting, Chapter 5).

7. Reward the child with affection for agreeing to the contract and especially after the contract is successfully completed.

ACTIVITY TITLE **Daily Log**

MATERIALS For this diary activity you will need two diaries or notebooks, some string, and two pens. You may need catalogs, scissors, and tape too.

PROCEDURES We all have experiences and feelings that we do not wish to share with others, especially at times of personal turmoil. During these times we have thoughts and feelings that are not appropriate to share with youngsters. Children also have experiences and feelings that they cannot or will not share. This activity provides an outlet for and a way to keep track of those thoughts and feelings for later reflection.

Present the child the diary (one with a lock is great) or the notebook as a special gift. Show that you also have a similar one for yourself. Use the string to attach the pen to each. Youngsters who do not write can use pictures taped or drawn in to represent their thoughts and feelings. Explain what a diary is and that you thought it would be a good idea for the two of you to keep separate diaries. Leave the option open to share your entries with each other but stress the privacy of the diaries. Offer to share your first few entries to get them started.

You might want to set a daily time for writing or just remind each other often. Some people prefer writing an entry every other day or once a week. Suggest that you periodically (weekly or monthly) read over the log, and write a summary page of how you experienced that period of time.

VARIATION Rather than using a diary, provide a loose-leaf notebook.

During the discussion do not stress the private aspects of the log. Instead, make entries so as to be shared at the end of each day. This will provide a starting place for discussion and a way to see each other's experiences.

ACTIVITY TITLE **Quiet Please**

MATERIALS This activity for the communication of personal needs calls for two large pieces of cardboard, paper, yellow paint or markers, and a black marker.

PROCEDURES There are times when we just do not feel like talking about things, problems, feelings, or anything. In trauma-producing situations this tendency is especially true.

To make it easy to let other people know that you do not feel like talking, do the following: Use the large pieces of cardboard to construct "Quiet Please" signs. Model these after highway yield signs. Turn the squares of cardboard on a corner to made a diamond shape. Using the black marker write "Quiet Please" in large letters. Color the sign yellow. You may want to add a picture of a person with a finger over the mouth saying, "Shhh."

During the construction of these signs, discuss the fact that sometimes people just don't feel like talking. Make the point that open communication between you and the child is vital but also that consideration of each other's feelings is important.

These signs, one for the adult and one for the child, can be used as nonverbal cues for those times that you do not feel like talking.

You might like to add a place for slips of paper that indicate specific topics you do not care to discuss—school, Daddy, money, trips, Mommy, chores, and so on.

Respect these signs and, when you do discuss problematic topics. it will be more productive. You will also be able to see which areas you are both thinking about but not able to discuss.

VARIATION   Make pocket-sized "Quiet Please" signs that you can wear on your shirt of dress. Or make "Green Lights" with the topic that you are ready to discuss. Wait until the other person has a green light with the same topic.

ACTIVITY TITLE   Personal Space

MATERIALS   For this activity on providing personal space you will need to provide poster paper, markers, paper, and possibly a sheet.

PROCEDURE   At a time of death, separation, or divorce, you will find that both the adult and child need both physical and emotional "space." This space is necessary for them to deal with the internal conflicts created by the new situation. While the "Quiet Please" activity can help provide
148   emotional space, this activity can supply the physical space.

Begin this activity by discussing your need for some physical space—a place that is all your own—to keep personal items and to think uninterrupted. The child may or may not express the same need.

The two of you make a tour of the house and decide on a place that you would like to define as your own. When space is limited, choose a part of the bedroom rather than somewhere in the general living areas. Each of you decide how to delineate your space. You might place a chair and table there, make a sign labeling it as your space, or even hang a sheet as a divider. Discuss the ways you think you will use your space—for thinking, working, just to be alone, crying, planning, writing letters, or whatever. Ask the child to brainstorm ways to use the personal space.

Together you will need to set some guidelines for this space. You may leave it open. Or you might set some limits like not interrupting each other, using it only so many times per day or week, staying there for only thirty minutes to one hour, having no friends over while using it, and so on. The rules are up to you and the child.

You might suggest keeping a log of what you do in that personal space.

VARIATION Rather than delineating a physical area, you might prefer setting aside a personal space time of day. Set aside thirty minutes or so every day, or an hour a week, when the personal space guidelines are in effect.

ACTIVITY TITLE ## Sharing the Vacant Roles

MATERIALS For this activity on dealing with new responsibilities, you will need paper and pen.

PROCEDURES If you became a single parent through divorce, separation, or the death of a spouse, I'm sure you have found that your roles as a parent have changed. In a two-parent family, the roles of homemaker, driver, provider, caretaker, finance adviser, bill payer, and bookkeeper are shared. In a new single-parent family the parent may find that he or she tries to assume all of the roles. But such behavior is counter-productive, and it generally means less time for yourself at a time characterized by a need for more time for yourself, by fatigue, and by stress in general. This can create strong resentment about the whole situation, toward the old spouse and even toward the children.

Try this activity to relieve some of the pressure. Make two separate listings. First list all the roles that you filled when you were part of a two-parent family. Next make a list of all the roles that the other parent filled. Read over the two lists. If you find that any are not absolutely necessary, place two X's by them. Now look at the listing for the other parent. Put a circle around all their roles that you now fill.

Write these roles on a separate sheet of paper. This list represents the "overload" that you are now trying to deal with. For each item on this list, brainstorm ways to delete them for your responsibility. You might find a family member or friend to do some, hire someone, decide to do them only occasionally, cook frozen food, skip bed-making, let the kids wash dishes, and so on.

VARIATION Make a list of all the daily things you do that either bother you, that you aren't able to do well, that cause pressure, or that you just can't get to. Rank-order these by placing the number 1 by the most important, 2 by the next most important, and so on. For the least important, design a rotating daily or weekly scheduling so that you skip them sometimes.

You might find that you don't really need to mop, dust, wash clothes, sweep, or do some things every single day.

ACTIVITY TITLE ## What Did You Learn at School Today?

MATERIALS This activity on sharing daily experiences calls for copies of the included questions, pencils, and possibly a tape recorder.

PROCEDURES The title of this activity is a question heard by thousands of children each day. In my experience the usual response is, "Nothing, really." In relation to school this may actually be true. In terms of life, however, this would be a wasted day. This activity is designed to help parents and children share their daily experience.

Make copies of these questions or use the tape recorder to ask and record each participant's response.

1. Today was great / OK / fair / terrible.
2. What made today that way was _____ .
3. The best thing about today was _____ .
4. The worst thing about today was _____ .
5. Today I thought a lot about _____ .
6. If I could do today over I would _____ .

These can be compiled to form a record of your experience for reflection or discussion.

VARIATION Make a chart in the form of a checklist for each person to fill out when they arrive home each day. The items on the chart can be changed or added to at any time. If you cover the chart with clear contact paper and use a washable marker, it can be used repeatedly. Place on the chart sets of faces that reflect different moods. The children might like to make other faces too.

	Tom	Mary	Sue	Mom
1. Today was	_____	_____	_____	_____
2. I felt	_____	_____	_____	_____
3. I wish it was	_____	_____	_____	_____
4. Tonight I will be	_____	_____	_____	_____
5. Tomorrow will be	_____	_____	_____	_____
6.	_____	_____	_____	_____
7.	_____	_____	_____	_____

150 Use the chart for reference and discussion.

ACTIVITY TITLE   A Letter to Sandy (Tom)

MATERIALS   This activity on identifying feelings requires envelopes, paper, and a pen.

PROCEDURE   Explain that this is a pretend activity. Read the following story to the child. Then suggest that the two of you write a letter to tell Sandy or Tom (depending on the sex of your child) everything she or he needs to know about what it is like when one parent is no longer there.

> Sandy (Tom) was _____ (around the age of your child). She lived in _____ (some situation similar to yours). One day she (he) came home and found that her (his) _____ (Mother, Father) was no longer going to be living with her (him). (Here you need to describe why—death, separation, divorce.)
>
> She (he) was very upset by this and didn't know what to do. She (he) went to her (his) room and thought for a long time, and then began to cry. She (he) cried because no matter how hard she (he) thought, she (he) didn't know what to do or think.

Can you help write the child a letter? You might like to try this activity at several points in time. You might also share these with the "other" parent.

VARIATION   You might want to set up a pen pal relationship with this fictional person who is experiencing a similar situation. You can limit the communication to post cards for a more concise expression of ideas and feelings.

ACTIVITY TITLE   What I Miss Most

MATERIALS   For this activity on identifying children's needs, you need paper, pencils, pictures, and scissors.

PROCEDURES   Regardless of how you become a single parent, you miss some aspects of the previous relationship. To deal with your own sense of loss and the child's, you must first identify what you miss, accept this, and then attempt to fill that need.

This activity can help you and the children share that sense of loss and to plan experiences to compensate. Activities of this kind frequently release pent-up emotions, and they should be approached with great care and consideration.

Begin the activity by talking about the absent parent. Both of you participate in recalling what it was like when you were all together. Lead the discussion to talk about how it was when all three of you lived together and what the atmosphere of the home was like then. Suggest that each of you make a listing of the things you miss about the other person.

This list may be very short or very long. As the adult, be sure to
151   include things the child can relate to, like taking trips, doing house and

yard work, sharing the evening meal, and so on. Younger children may need to use pictures to depict what they miss.

When the lists are complete, share them with each other. Share your sense of loss as well as your faith that things have worked out or will work out for the best for all of you.

VARIATION
Rather than entering the activity yourself, make a question and answer sheet for the child. The responses can help you to plan needed experiences or, if the other parent is nearby, help you and the other parent plan activities for the child to do.

ACTIVITY TITLE
Abandonment (No Contact)

MATERIALS
To do this activity on explaining why a parent leaves, you need paper and pen.

PROCEDURES
The fear of abandonment is one of the greatest fears of early childhood. This is as true of two-parent families as it is of single-parent families.

If your spouse has simply left with no explanation, the child and remaining parent likely feel that they somehow caused the parent to leave—that is, they almost feel as though, if they had loved the absent parent more or treated them better, he or she wouldn't have left. In almost all cases such is *not* the case. At any rate, the response to the child should be something like, "I guess Daddy (or Mommy) just didn't think he could be happy living with us. So he left to try to find happiness." While this sort of statement provides some information, you must then reflect the child's feelings, saying something like, "I can tell you miss Daddy. You might be angry some, too! I wonder about him too. Maybe we'll hear from him, but we might not."

Next the child needs repeated reassurance that he or she was not the cause. You may need to take the responsibility for the abandonment just so the child will not suffer the guilt. This reassurance that the child is not a causal factor needs to be repeated whenever discussion about the absent arise.

VARIATION
Follow this format, suggest that writing letters to that parent would be alright even if you aren't able to mail them. This way the child can keep the parent "alive" in the mind; and, if you should ever get in touch, you could mail the letters then.

[2]
As difficult as it is for the "in-house" parent to adapt to changing relationships with children, it may be even more difficult for the "other" parent.

As either the "in-house" or the "other" parent, try these activities. Both parents must be actively involved to foster positive relationships.

ACTIVITY TITLE
Planning Activities for Visitation

MATERIALS
For this activity on visitation, you need paper, pencil, and possibly some literature from the Chamber of Commerce.

PROCEDURES The most important aspect of your visitation as the "other" parent consists not of the activities you plan for your child, but rather of the way in which you share your time and self with the children. So, in planning activities, you must first consider the children's desires and needs. You must also be flexible. Once the plan is made, allow it to flow naturally rather than pressing to fulfill it.

A good way to collect some ideas for activities is to communicate with the in-house parent. Perhaps they either have done the "What I Miss Most" activity or have some suggestions. "What I Miss Most"is also an appropriate activity to do with the absent parent. It is also a good idea to simply ask the children what they would like to do. Often they will want to do quiet things at your home to try reestablishing a relationship.

Collect a listing of ideas, games, crafts, and places the child might like. Spend time with the child discussing which they might like to do today, next week, next month.

Before the end of each visit be sure to discuss any feelings, anxieties, or problems that have become evident.

VARIATION Use the following checklist to determine the causal factors of a not-so-good visit:

1. Was it too painful for you, the parent?
2. Was it too painful for the child?
3. Has the in-house parent created negative expectations of you?
4. Were you or the child ill?
5. Was there a lack of involvement or caring on your part or the child's?
6. Was the child still *very* angry?
7. Did you have difficulty understanding the child's conflicting emotions?
8. Were you overly concerned with being the "nice guy" to compensate?
9. Were you late for the visit?

This checklist represents common problems with visitations. It can be useful in changing your behavior to provide a good visit.

ACTIVITY TITLE Identifying Children's New Emotions

MATERIALS Paper and pencil are needed to do this activity on identifying feelings.

PROCEDURES When the family changes its lifestyle, many new emotions are elicited. Sometimes parents that do not live with their children do not have the opportunity to see these emotions emerge. The children want the visit to be pleasant and good, so they do not always share their feelings.

This activity should be done by both the in-house and the other parent. If at all possible, an opportunity to compare the results is advised.

153

From the following list, choose as many emotions as you think the child has been experiencing and list them on a piece of paper. Remember that having conflicting emotions is normal:

abandonment	disappointment
anger	dismay
anxiety	envy
association with only one parent	encitement
blames one parent	frustration
depression	fantasy of idealized parent
guilt	relief
happiness	rejection
helplessness	responsibility
hurt	sadness
isolation	shame
irritability	tension
loneliness	wish for reconciliation

You may also wish to add other descriptions. Use this listing to create a "picture" of the emotional whirlwind that the child is experiencing.

VARIATION

Many of these feelings are experienced by adults as well as by children. Compile a list of all of your feelings, especially the conflicting ones. Use these lists as discussion starters with the children.

ACTIVITY TITLE

Child Space

MATERIALS

For this activity on helping the child to be comfortable in your new home, you need some of the child's possessions, boxes, and various art supplies.

PROCEDURES

Children are often confused about the different lifestyles in the homes of the two parents. Physical differences in the home and communities, family compositions, and the feelings of displacement are difficult to adjust to. This activity will help to provide a sense of security and to develop familiarity with the parents' new home.

The basic ingredients for the child's new space are physical space, familiar objects from the old home, and some new creative materials for the child. Set aside some space in your new home for the child. A room of his own is great, but a corner, a table and chair, or some space in the kitchen will do. Make arrangements with the child and others to provide some toys, pictures, or favorite items from the other home that can be left with you. Provide either a drawer, some shelf space, or a storage box so that your child will have a place to keep his things. Buy some clay or Play-Dough (or, better yet, make some), crayons, scissors, chalk, yarn, glue, tape, stapler, and other supplies for the child to use. Be careful not to go overboard with buying things for the child. You can't buy the child; it is your attention and affection he needs.

Let the child know that he can use this space almost any way he likes. You can let him know of inappropriate activities for this space, but try not to set many limits.

When the child first begins visiting, take him on a tour of the new place and show him his space. Use this area for sharing activities.

VARIATION

Quite often space is a major problem in the new house. If so, provide a large box that will fit under a bed for storing the child's things. Put up a piece of poster board or bulletin board for displaying the child's letters and artwork. Decide on a place to do sharing and feeling activities, and use it consistently. These areas can be set up for the child's visit and packed away between visits.

ACTIVITY TITLE

When I'm _____, I Feel _____

MATERIALS

For this activity on eliciting feelings, you need paper and pencil.

PROCEDURES

Sometimes it is difficult for the child to share her feelings about the new situation with the other parent. This activity will help you and her to communicate your feelings.

Begin by simply asking the child how she feels. Then suggest that you play a game. The game consists of each of you taking turns asking questions of the format, "When you _____, you feel _____?" Begin the game with very nonthreatening questions: "When you are at the beach, you feel _____? . . . When your friend visits, you feel _____? . . . When your brother hits you, you feel _____? . . . When you really want something, you feel _____?" Once the child is "into" the game and feeling comfortable, ask her some questions that concern the new situation: "When you visit me, you feel _____? . . . When I hug you, you feel _____? . . . Right before you come to visit, you feel _____? . . . When I take you home, you feel _____?" And so on.

Accept any comments without discussion. The intent is to share feelings, not to analyze them. Be sure to answer all the child's questions honestly.

Conclude the activity with a comment like, "That was fun, I sure like knowing how you feel." Then move into a planned activity.

VARIATION

With a young child, do this as a verbal activity with you as record-keeper. Present older children with a listing like the one following and have them fill it out:

I think it's important to:

_____ share feelings with each other.

_____ spend time together.

_____ have friends.

_____ be smart.

_____ be strong.

_____ cry sometimes.

_____ be honest.

_____ sing well.

_____ clean up my own mess.

_____ think about (Mom, Dad, Brother, or someone else).

_____ do my best.

_____ eat well.

_____ go to school.

_____ always have something to do.

_____ like myself.

You can add any areas that you wish to know about. Instruct the child to check the ones he agrees with. Use this listing to plan *future* discussion topics and activities.

ACTIVITY TITLE **What Do You Do Now?**

MATERIALS This activity on sharing how you spend your time requires construction paper, markers, and a calendar.

PROCEDURES A child becomes very curious about what you do now that you live away from her, even though she knows what you did when you were together. This activity will give the child information and provide you both with good opportunities to discuss the reasons you are not living together.

Make fourteen large clock faces, one for each day of the week, for each of you. While you are discussing your activities, draw or write them on the clock faces to create a time record of your week. Help the child to do the same. Share your feelings about doing those things. You can relate what you do now to the things you did at the other home.

VARIATION Make a general schedule of your weekdays and weekends.

Weekday	*Weekend*
7:00—Wake up	9:00—Wake up
8:00—Work	10:00—Eat and read paper
5:00—Cook and eat	12:00—Wash clothes and chores
6:30—Read or TV	1:00—Watch ballgame
8:30—Clean house	3:00—Run errands
10:00—Bed	5:00—Etc.

Ask the child to do the same and discuss each other's activities.

If the child wants to see what you plan to do over a longer period of time, use a calendar to list your plans for the next month.

ACTIVITY TITLE **Consideration of the Other Parent**

MATERIALS For this activity on communication with the other parent, you need paper and pencil.

Often it is difficult if not impossible to empathize with the other parent. This activity is to help you focus on the new responsibilities of the custodial parent and how they affect your children.

Make a list of all the activities, jobs, and roles you filled when you were living together. The list will vary depending on the roles you filled. The following may or may not appear on your list:

disciplinarian	teacher
male/female role model	driver
bookkeeper	child care
fix-it person	lover
cook	nurse
cleaning person	counselor
decision-maker	mediator
friend	others . . .
financial provider	

Read over your list and decide how much support you provided for the family. Did you provide much, moderate, or little support?

Now go over the list and indicate how those roles are being filled now. Place a "P" by those that the other parent does, place an "N" by those that no one does, place an "F" by those someone else in the family does, and an "O" by the ones other people do. Look over the list and determine how much of your role has been filled by the other parent.

Write a short description of how you think that person must feel at the end of the week. If you feel that you could help the children move into some of these roles in some way, make a list and share these thoughts with the other parent.

VARIATION   Set up periodic meetings with the other parent to discuss the situation, the condition, and the development of the children. This meeting can take place over the phone, but a person-to-person meeting is better. If you feel uncomfortable, at first, arrange to have a mutual friend present.

ACTIVITY TITLE   ## Staying in Touch

MATERIALS   This activity on communication with your children requires a notebook, pen, stationery, envelopes, stamps, and postcards.

PROCEDURES   When you are living apart from your children, it is vital that they remain confident of your love and caring. This assurance can be facilitated by the custodial parent, but you must also take an active role. Frequent phone calls will help, but constant phone calls can become an intrusion on the life that the child and the in-house parent are building. Try the following activity as a caring, nonintrusive way to stay in touch.

Before your child's next visit, put together a "stay-in-touch" kit.

Use an attractive folder or notebook. Provide personalized stationery, pens of different colors, stamps, self-addressed envelopes, self-addressed large manila envelopes, addressed postcards, and a selection of rubber stamps.

Let the child know that you really want to share his life but that you understand things aren't the same as before. Suggest that the child write to you, send some artwork, or drop a postcard telling how he is. Of course, for this to work, you must do the same.

VARIATION Set up a schedule of telephone times with the child and the in-house parent. It is important that both agree. Once this schedule is in place, *never miss a call.*

ACTIVITY TITLE ## Loneliness

MATERIALS For this activity on dealing with loneliness, you need paper, pencil, and a phone. It is a good idea to do this activity with other adults.

PROCEDURES Loneliness is a feeling that both the in-house and the other parent must deal with. Loneliness is more than being alone; it is a sense of not having your personal needs fulfilled. Even when surrounded by other people you can sometimes experience a quality of loneliness. This feeling of loneliness can lead to increased anger and resentment toward the other parent, and it sometimes causes a strong emotional attachment to the other parent. Neither of these reactions are conducive to your personal growth or to the positive adjustment of your children.

Make a listing of the times and activities that bring on a strong sense of loneliness. Common ideas are bedtime, TV or reading time, meal time, when you are a single person in a social setting, during crises, and the like.

Next to this listing, indicate the times and activities that you enjoy and that do not cause you to experience loneliness. Compare the two lists. Do you notice any pattern of time or of activities that promote loneliness? Generally the more active you are, the less alone you feel.

VARIATION Single people often need help to overcome this sense of loneliness and other problems. Compile a list of resources available to you for support. Some suggested starters are:

Friends	Parents without Partners groups
Family	Single parent associations
Neighbors	Singles clubs
Local counseling services	Work mates
Church	
Doctor	

Use the phone book and community service listings to help.

ACTIVITY TITLE **Two Houses: Two Sets of Rules**

MATERIALS This activity on understanding rules requires drawing paper, markers, and a pen.

PROCEDURES Often your new home and the other home have different rules. For example, after a visitation, the in-house parent may have to deal with, "But we don't have to do that at Daddy's!" and the absent parent may hear, "I want to live with you; at Mom's we have to make beds, take out trash, and do a lot of things!"

In such cases, several things are important. For one, the rules for the custodial home should not change too radically. The parent living alone, however, will have a very different lifestyle. It is also important that children understand the two sets of rules and the reasons for differences. Otherwise resentment for one parent may grow.

Begin by asking the children to draw pictures of all the chores they have to do in the other house. Ask them to add pictures to any chores they have to do at your house. Help the child make a listing of any rules in the other home and in your home.

Lead a discussion on the needs for rules and the difference in the rules. When children are living in a home, it is necessary for them to have household responsibilities as well as to help the other parent. Stress the fact that the other is fair and tries to do what is best for everyone.

VARIATION Come to an agreement with the other parent on a set of rules that will be in place in both homes. This can include procedures, activities, and chores. Make sure that you also agree on consequences if the rules are broken.

ACTIVITY TITLE **Mom and Dad Are Different People**

MATERIALS For this activity on positive regard for both parents, you will need drawing materials, paper, and pencil.

PROCEDURES Children—especially young ones—tend to view their parents as one person. Sometimes they include the entire family as one entity. This activity is therefore designed to help children see parents as individuals with different needs, aspirations, and personalities, as well as identifying similarities.

Ask the child to make a picture. In the picture have her include Mom, Dad, and herself. Other family members may be included too. You might also make a picture of the family. After she completes the picture, record the child's description of the Mom and Dad. To use as a discussion starter, make a chart similar to the following:

	Looks Like . . .	Things They Do . . .	What They Want . . .
Mom			
Dad			

159

Point out the things that are alike and different. Stress the facts that you are two different people and expect to be treated differently, that you are both good people and, above all, that both of you love the child.

VARIATION   Ask the child to list all of the best things about the other parent. Be sure that you also have some things to add. Discuss the other parent in a positive manner. Reinforce the idea that both of you are trying to do what is best for everyone in the family. Point out the differences between the two parents, and stress that both of you need to be considered.

[3]   The change from a two-parent to a single-parent family means much adjustment for children and adults. Not only are the lines of communication and personal roles changed, but the routines and responsibilities are different. Try the following activities to help with this difficult transition period.

ACTIVITY TITLE   Parents' Responses to Children

MATERIALS   To complete this activity on responding to children's behaviors, you need paper and pencil.

PROCEDURES   During such a time of turmoil, children will probably say and do many things that really "get" you. Typically parents respond to these acts defensively and impulsively—considering their own needs.

This activity presents some of the common acts of children that cause consternation for the parent. Our reaction to these acts is very influential in the child's adjustment to the new situation. Although there are no "right" ways to react, thinking about them from the children's perspective is the first step to helping them.

Read the following descriptions. After reading each one, write what you think your initial reaction would be. After you have responded to each of them, read through them all again. Code each one with the letter "C" if you responded with the child in mind, and an "A" if you responded with the adult in mind. By each write why you think the child did that.

Try to imagine or recall other child actions that initiated a negative response from you. Ask yourself questions like: Do you get defensive or angry? Do you react to the children's feelings? Do you try to protect the children from their own feelings or help confront them? Do your own feelings get in the way?

Sample situations:

1. An eight-year-old returns from school. His face is bruised, and his shirt is torn. He says, "The kids always pick on me! I never start fights; the teacher picks on me, too."

2. Your ten-year-old used to go out to play with friends every day

after school. Since your divorce, he stays inside doing nothing or watching TV. His response to your questioning is, "I don't know, I just don't want to do anything anymore."

3. Your six-year-old returns from a visit with the other parent and says, "I don't want to live here anymore. I have to do all the work around here, and you're mean to me."

4. Your eleven-year-old tells you that if you don't let her go to the dance on Saturday, she will tell the other parent that you are mistreating her and using the child support money to buy yourself clothes.

5. Your five-year-old comes to you crying with a very red face and says, "I hate you! You made Daddy go away."

VARIATION   Plan similar situations that might occur between the child and the other parent. You play the part of the other parent and let the child play his or her role. Make sure that the child knows these are fictional situations.

ACTIVITY TITLE   ## All Families Are Not the Same

MATERIALS   This activity on understanding and accepting the family's situation requires paper, pen, drawing materials, scissors, pictures of adults and children, and glue.

PROCEDURES   Many children are uncomfortable dealing with their family's new situation. They have a stereotyped image of a family consisting of a Mother, Father, and children. This stereotyped image makes it difficult for them to accept the new situation. This activity is to help children realize that many types of families and a large number are in their situation.

Begin the activity by asking the child to draw or cut and paste a picture of everyone that lives in her house. Help her label each person depicted. Make sure that everyone is included. If the child includes the absent parent, comment that that person doesn't live with you but that now you have a picture of the family. If the other parent is not included, suggest that you turn it into a picture of the family by adding the other parent. (Omit this part if the other parent is completely out of touch.)

Next ask the child to describe as many different families as she can. If she has difficulty, bring to mind some friends who have different family compositions. Be sure to include the traditional two-parent families: (1) with children, (2) without children, (3) with a single mother, (4) with a single father, and (5) an extended family with grandparents.

Together you and the child make pictures to represent all the family types. Discuss the different roles, feelings, and activities that each family style must experience. Relate this to your own family. Stress that all the families are OK and that they share the common bonds of love, care, and consideration for each other.

VARIATION   With older children it might be better to report statistics of family types
to help them feel less different. These can be found at the public library
or in the U.S. Census. Here are some starters:

1. In 1970 there were 3.5 million single-parent families; in 1975, 5.2
   million.

2. In 1975, there were more than a million single-father families.

3. By 1978, more than a million divorces were recorded.

4. Today approximately one out of every six children lives in a one-
   parent family.

5. The major causes of single-parent families are:
   a. divorce, desertion, or separation,
   b. death,
   c. unmarried parenting, and
   d. single parent adoption.

Typical Reactions

For this activity on understanding the child's behavior, you need paper and pen.

Everyone experiences confusion and conflicting emotions when dealing with becoming a single-parent family. A large number of people need professional help to come to terms with the situation. This activity explores the typical reactions of children, and it can help parents determine if they should seek professional help for the children.

Keep in mind that these are typical reactions. You can expect children to exhibit some of them. However, if the reaction is severe, if it endures more than ten months, or if the child exhibits a series of them, you should consider consulting a professional.

1. *Anger*—Anger is a normal reaction. Children's anger may be directed toward either or both parents, or toward themselves and the world in general.

2. *Aggression*—Aggression takes verbal or physical form. It may be directed toward peers, adults, or objects. Children often show this aggression in play.

3. *Body ills*—This can take the form of a stomach ache, constipation, diarrhea, a loss of appetite, sleeping trouble, headaches, aches and pains, and so on. Any constant or reoccuring physical problems should be checked out by a physician.

4. *Crying*—Crying is a normal way of dealing with painful emotions. Extreme or uncontrolled crying may not be normal.

5. *Concern*—Where will I live? Will you love me? What will become of me? Concern is normal; obsession is not.

6. *Denial*—Some children will not admit to others or to themselves that their parents are not together. In one case, the reason may be embarrassment; in the other, it might be a lack of acceptance. Acceptance takes time.

7. *Helplessness*—They lose the "I'd-rather-do-it-myself" attitude. This is an attempt by children to have you prove your love and care for them.

8. *Leave me alone!*—This withdrawal from one or both parents or from everyone may be necessary for the child to deal with internal conflicts.

9. *Regression*—Children may exhibit behaviors typical of an earlier age, such as baby talk, thumbsucking, and the like.

10. *Overactivity*—This behavior is also common to adults. They feel if they are constantly on the go, they will not have to deal with the problems.

Keep anecdotal records of your child's behavior. Choosing a different time and situation every day, record exactly what your child did. After

writing a very behavioral description, add your own impressions of why he or she acted that way. Use these records to keep track of the child's behavior and for reflection. For example:

> *Actions:* Shawn, four years old, shares a sandbox with a four-year-old girl. Shawn is sitting in the corner playing alone with two trucks. About every two minutes he looks at the girl. He throws a truck out of the box and gets sand in his eye. He rubs it hard and starts to cry. He jumps up, runs to the girl, and throws sand on her.

> *Impressions:* I think he was angry with himself and took it out on the girl. He may have thought it would get the sand out of his eye if he put it into the girl's.

ACTIVITY TITLE ## It's Not Just Me!

MATERIALS For this activity on recognizing that your feelings are shared by others, you need library resources, a pencil, paper, and drawing materials.

PROCEDURES Children should realize that their conflicting feelings are understood by others. This understanding *must* be shown by parents, but knowing that others understand is also vital.

Chapter 10 of this book will provide you with resources to use for this activity. Select a number of these resources and acquire them from your local library. You and the child read some of them together. Approach this activity when you feel ready to discuss the topics covered in the book. It is necessary for you to preview the books to select the appropriate ones. To set the stage for this activity, choose a quiet time when you will not be interrupted, as well as a comfortable place where you can sit close together. Introduce it by telling the child you are going to look at books about people that are experiencing a situation like yours. Be totally accepting of the feelings your child expresses. The time to deal with problems is later.

VARIATION You and your child make your own book to express the feelings and problems you are having. Use one of the listed resources, like *Talking About Divorce*, as a model.

ACTIVITY TITLE ## Providing Choices

MATERIALS This activity on decision-making requires paper and pen.

PROCEDURES The most important aspect of developing independence is giving the child opportunities to make decisions: the more opportunities a child has to make choices, the more self-confident he becomes and the more his trust for you will grow. He will see that you have confidence in his ability and trust in his decisions. This does not mean, however, that the child can decide to do or not to do homework, but rather that she can decide when or where to do it.

This activity is to help you design times when you can offer a child choices. The responsibility for the child's development and the outcomes of his decision is still yours.

Make a list of all of the requirements, rules, and limits you place on the child. This list includes:

1. chores (cleaning the room, taking out the trash, washing the car, and so on),
2. rules (play area boundaries, locking the bicycle, no running inside, no playing in street, being home on time, and so forth),
3. meal times,
4. foods,
5. bed times, and
6. whatever else you consider important.

Make this listing as complete as possible. Read it over and decide which ones you could offer options for. For rules, options might be rewards for compliance or consequences for noncompliance, choices of play areas, times to be home, times for meals, for menu planning, for bedtimes, and so on.

Make a list of the choices you have come up with. Through discussion, help your child to consider the alternatives and consequences of various decisions. Let her choose the option she prefers:

VARIATION Involve the child in planning all aspects of the household function— including the tasks, the times, and the methods. Involving the child in the planning stages will help her to feel included and help to alleviate the you-make-me-do-everything attitude.

ACTIVITY TITLE ## Socialization and the Peer Group

MATERIALS For this activity on providing social contacts, you need paper, pen, telephone, a telephone book, and transportation.

PROCEDURES Living in a single-parent family can have a notable effect on children's peer relations. In the middle childhood years (school age), the socialization process is greatly affected by the influence of peer relations. During these years children are in the process of mastering a variety of physical and social skills. The development in later years depends on the development of these skills.

This activity is to help you consider important aspects of the child's social development, peer influence, and resources for children's social involvement. Begin by considering these points:

1. During these years children learn more and more to care for their physical needs. The parents' role shifts to providing psychological support and guidance.
2. The peer group becomes a major influence in the child's social development.
3. Parents are learning to let children go, that is, to make more independent decisions.
4. School is a major source of social interaction.

5. Personal habits and patterns of relating to people are being established.

Think about the social interactions that you provide for your child. Divide them into separate categories, indicating times when children are with:

1. parents,
2. other familiar adults,
3. new adults,
4. individual familiar children,
5. individual new children,
6. no one, and
7. groups of children.

If you find that provisions are not made for a variety of social contacts, discuss this need with the child and plan some enjoyable experiences involving each of these situations.

VARIATION Make a listing of all peer groups that your child could be involved with: Boys' and Girls' Clubs, 4-H, Campfire Girls, Brownies, Cub and Boy Scouts, Church, YMCA, YWCA, single-parent groups, crafts classes, sports leagues, art/music/dance clubs, and the like. This list can be supplemented through the *Yellow Pages*, recreation centers, the Chamber of Commerce, and the schools.

Provide a description of the activities and objectives of each group to present to the youngsters. Help them select several that they might like to participate with. Visit the groups with the children and help them to evaluate their interests and goals. Be careful not to let them overload their lives as an escape.

ACTIVITY TITLE I'd Rather Do It Myself!

MATERIALS This activity to encourage children to accept household responsibilities requires paper, pens, a straightedge, and chart paper.

PROCEDURES Review this activity on Task Analysis in Chapter 5 before doing this activity. To facilitate the growth of independence and the smooth functioning of the household, children must take responsibility for themselves and household tasks. Besides the usual keep-your-room-straight/take-out-the-garbage chores, children in single-parent families can be helped to take a more active role in maintaining the house.

This section contains some sample ideas, but you will be able to think of many more, depending on the developmental level of the child. As you do, however, you must bear certain points in mind. First, you must remember that they are still children; they should not be pushed to take more responsibility than they can successfully handle. You need to have reasonable expectations for them and for yourself!

Also, as you decide on tasks to turn over to the youngsters, teach them how to do them. Approach the activities as a *game*, a big help to you and a sign of their maturity. Use the task analysis method to break the task into step-by-step procedures. Discuss this "cook book" with the children and help them work through it several times. When you feel they are able to perform the task alone, make a chart to record a star for each time it is done. This serves as additional positive reinforcement.

Laundry: Older children could actually take over the entire task with a little training. Middle children could collect and pack the laundry. Younger children can be provided two boxes for dirty clothes—one for white, one for color. A fun game can be designed for stripping the beds.

The Kitchen: An ongoing food inventory or shopping list can be made to hang on the icebox. Even young children can plan and prepare breakfast (see Fun with Food Groups, Chapter 6)—cereal, fruit and juice, English muffins, cheese, and so forth. Some children enjoy cooking eggs and hot cereal so they can watch the physical change. Frozen and prepackaged meals are also available.

Menu planning and shopping can be a family affair, and so can filling the dishwasher, stacking the dishes, setting and clearing the table, and other kitchen duties.

Weekly car washing, cleaning the bathroom, dusting, vacuuming, beating rugs, yard work, and other tasks can all be fun activities.

Be careful not to overload the children. The main intent is to help them accept responsibility. Helping you is secondary; the major responsibility for the functioning of the home is yours.

VARIATION Make a large checklist of all the daily and weekly tasks, and hang it in a convenient place. Ask each person to sign up to do some of the tasks each week. When they have done the task, instruct them to check it off. This kind of chart not only lets children choose responsibilities but lets everyone see who does what. You will need to provide tasks at different skill levels to match the developmental levels of the children.

		M	T	W	Th	F	S	Sun
	Garbage	K	K	K	K	K	K	
Daily	Beds	CK	CK	CK	CK			
	Dishes	K	K	C	C	C	C	
	Cooking	C	C	C	C	C	K	C
	Laundry	K				C		
Bi-Weekly	Bathrooms		C		C			C
	Car		K					

C=Craig
K=Keef

TV Time

For this activity, you need a TV, paper, a pencil, a program guide, and an electric timer.

You will probably agree that, even in two-parent households, children spend a lot of time at the TV. In the early mornings and while the parent is doing household tasks, children are likely to watch TV, just as they are whenever you are watching TV and they are in the room with you. But when children live in a single-parent family, they become more independent, and so they have more time to fill by themselves— usually with TV watching.

You as a parent have to make your own judgment about the appropriate times and length of time for TV viewing. Accordingly, this activity is intended to give you some ideas of ways to turn TV time into a shared experience. The variation presents some ways of setting the guidelines you have decided on.

With children, especially young children, it is good to discuss the passive observer aspect of *watching* TV. Build the idea that TV isn't bad but that activities requiring active participation are better.

When you and the child are watching together, discuss the shows. Try to follow these suggestions:

1. Make sure that the children understand their fictional nature. Point out times that you can tell there was special camera work.

2. When situations that do not occur in real life are depicted, ask the child if that could really happen. Use the "if _____, then _____" activity in Chapter 5 to show what would happen in real life.

3. Help children focus on the emotions and communication skills that different characters use. Analyze motives behind their actions.

4. Point out the stereotypes presented and work at showing how untrue they are.

5. Give children plenty of opportunities to talk and share their ideas.

6. Don't ignore the commercials. These often reflect stereotypes, as well as providing a chance to discuss the child's consumer role. Besides, young children prefer the commercials to many shows.

To establish viewing guidelines, set a maximum number of TV hours, either per day, per week, or both. Use a TV program directory to help the child plan which shows to watch. You can also use it to select educational programs to watch with the child. You can get listings of shows in the mail from your local Public Broadcasting System.

When a special show is to be seen, help the child to decide on what usual show he will give up. Keep the program directory with the child's selections circled or your own day-by-day listing near the TV.

It is a good idea to limit your own viewing time too. This helps to cut down the you're-not-fair feelings. It will also cut down the time the children are watching your shows.

Since turning the TV off is often a time of tension and sometimes anger, try a timer for the set. These are inexpensive and can be set so that the set will turn itself on and off.

ACTIVITY TITLE	Be Home on Time! Or Latch Key Kids
MATERIALS	For this activity on helping the children be responsible, you will need paper, pencil, a bulletin board, and a watch for the child.
PROCEDURES	For the single parent with children old enough to be out in the neighborhood, one of the ongoing problems is getting the child home on time. With children in the upper elementary grades, it is impractical to hire a babysitter for the time between when school gets out and when the parent gets home. This situation has created a group of children often described as "Latch Key Kids." This label, although unnecessary, does not have to be a derogatory one. It can indicate that you have a responsible, independent, reliable child.

Try this activity to facilitate the smooth functioning of this kind of arrangement. To first establish the system, discuss the plan with the child stressing the responsibility she will have and the confidence you have in her. If the child does not feel confident with the arrangement, then arrange for supervision through sitters, day care, friends, or relatives. Once both of you are satisfied with the idea, make a specific set of plans and some guidelines.

1. Plan a specific route to travel to and from school. Walk the route with the child.
2. Set specific boundaries within the neighborhood where the child is allowed to play.
3. Present the child with a home key. Provide a necklace or key chain that will attach to belt, pocket, purse, or some other article. Insist that the key be kept attached to her person.
4. But ask a nearby friend, relative, neighbor, or building to keep a key, just in case. Another possibility is to hide the key away from the house.
5. Make a message center in a convenient place. Include telephone numbers for emergencies, for friends and relatives, your work, and any other possible situations.
6. Set a time for the child to call you at work, or insist on a note at the message center telling what time she left the house, where she is, and when she will return.
7. Make sure the child has a watch. Digital is best.

VARIATION	If you find that this plan is not working, design a behavioral contract for the child (Chapter 5).

ACTIVITY TITLE	Roles of Siblings
MATERIALS	For this activity on sibling relations, you need sheets of paper, pencils, and drawing materials.
PROCEDURES	In the single-parent family, siblings play a very important role in the psychosocial development of all the children. Reactions among families differ radically, ranging from a total dependence among siblings to a total lack of consideration or involvement.

For younger children, the older siblings who are of the same sex as the absent parent usually become the primary role model for development. Older children learn to use authoritarian social tactics with younger siblings. You can see this pattern through bossing, threatening, and using physical force. It may cause younger children to become submitting, nonassertive children, or they may react with teasing, tattling, aggressiveness, or sulking. These experiences with siblings are a basic training ground for children's social relations with peers and with adults outside of the family.

Observe and keep records of your children's interactions (see the Variation of Typical Reactions in Chapter 8). Take note of the relationships and attitudes exhibited. Do you see the children operating in stereotypical roles? Can you see yourself or the other parent reflected in their interaction? Are the children considerate of each other?

After you have collected a group of observations in various circumstances, find a time to discuss them with each child individually. Try describing what you saw and let the children describe their feelings and the other children's feelings.

With the older children, stress that they are not responsible for or able to fill parental roles.

VARIATION   Make copies of a questionnaire to be filled out by each child individually. Young children's responses can be dictated, or they can use pictures. Ask questions like:

A good (brother/sister) is one that _____.

A bad (brother/sister) is one that _____.

It makes me feel (good/bad) when my (brother/sister) _____.

I wish (name) would stop _____.

Have the children also complete another one for each of the siblings. Distribute these without comment or discussion to the older children. Discuss them with the younger ones. Observe any changes in behavior.

[4] TIPS

1. Above all other concerns, you must help your child retain self-worth and a positive self-concept!

2. Adjustment to new situations takes time for children and adults. Don't push!

3. View your new "single-hood" as a chance for personal growth. It is a beginning rather than an end.

4. Parents have needs too. To fill your child's needs, your basic needs must also be satisfied.

5. Parents' attitudes toward themselves, the situation, and the other parent are the most influential aspect of your children's adjustment. Take care!

6. Children need love and respect of both parents. Promote the caring of the other parent.

7. Visits with the other parent are times to establish a new relationship. Sharing with each other is more important than planning activities or giving gifts.

8. Inappropriate behaviors may be a way that children make things "OK" for themselves. Be sensitive to intent.

9. Everyone needs support from others. Seek help when needed.

10. Divorce is a grown-ups' problem. Do not let children share the blame.

The Handicapped

CARING WITH SPECIAL FRIENDS

Public Law 94–142 is a federal mandate that requires mildly handicapped children to be placed in the least restrictive environments possible in public schools that already provide services to the handicapped. So school districts that already service the handicapped need also to integrate (or *mainstream*) mildly handicapped youngsters with normal children in regular classrooms. Such integration helps mildly handicapped youngsters to grow, mature, learn, and develop with normal children. Enhancing this development is *normalization*, a process first used sometime ago by Maria Montessori and also required by Public Law 94–142. Hence this law seeks to enhance mildly handicapped youngsters to function as closely as possible to "mainstream" or "normal" children.

In a fashion similar to mainstreaming, *reverse mainstreaming* provides opportunities for "normal" children to work with handicapped ones—rather than for handicapped to work with normal children—in regular home or classroom settings. The goal of integrating and having the nonhandicapped work with the handicapped is also a form of *normalization*.

The concepts of integrating normal with handicapped youngsters and of having them work with those that are handicapped are also ideal for nurturing caring in both handicapped and nonhandicapped children—for a number of reasons:

1. The nonhandicapped youngsters get the opportunity of practicing caring actions with the handicapped—their special friends. The nonhandicapped realize that no individual is exactly alike another.

2. The nonhandicapped realize that their special friends have similar caring needs such as friendship, happiness, success, decision-making, responsibility, and others. By helping the handicapped, the "normal" youngsters become more aware of their friends' needs and problems, show more willingness to help them and others, and better understand their own feelings.

3. Handicapped children benefit from working and playing with regular youngsters because they learn to communicate their wants and needs to their peers and others.

4. The handicapped learn self-help skills effectively and efficiently from nonhandicapped on a peer-to-peer basis.

5. The handicapped can model and be helped in manipulative and and gross motor skills by the nonhandicapped. By receiving assistance from other children, the handicapped especially grow in social awareness. From this interaction, the handicapped are more aware of their peers and look forward to working and playing with them.

When helping the nonhandicapped work effectively with the handicapped, a slow rather than a fast pace is recommended, so that the nonhandicapped youngsters better understand their special friends and how to care for them in a systematic way. Pushing them too quickly into helping roles, without step-by-step procedures, may make them anxious, fearful, and insecure with regard to the handicapped, and none of these feelings facilitate the growth of caring. These step-by-step procedures are:

1. preparing the nonhandicapped to work with the handicapped,
2. performing simple caring and helping routines, and
3. completing more advanced ones.

Initial Preparation

Step one obliges "normal" youngsters to see the handicapped in work and play and to become sensitized to them and their various handicaps. This preparatory sensitizing step is important because it makes the nonhandicapped accustomed to handicapped youngsters' physical and mental behaviors and actions, thus making their peer-to-peer interactions more meaningful and relevant. From this preparatory experience, "normal" youngsters should understand that the handicapped are special friends who do not need pity but who do need help in certain ways to develop caring and helping skills. In addition, "normal" youngsters will recognize that the handicapped learn at a generally slower rate and have shorter attention spans than they do. Further, in some respects, they will learn to communicate in special ways with some of the, to become aware that they may have behavior problems, and to show consistency in working with them. Through preparation, the nonhandicapped will recognize that all people are different and that these differences make them individuals and special friends.

Simple Routines

In step two, the nonhandicapped perform simple helping and caring routines with handicapped youngsters. These simple caring routines may include activities such as opening doors for the handicapped, teaching their special friends some new caring actions, and helping them while playing indoors and outdoors. These simple routines help to stimulate interest in helping and caring for the handicapped. They also help the children better understand the individual differences among people at a level that does not overtax, overburden, and over-commit them. It is important to remember that the nonhandicapped are also learning caring and caring routines themselves. Requiring too much responsibility all at once may lead to frustration and guilt if they are not able to help effectively. As "normal" children become better acquainted with handicapped youngsters in these small and simple ways, they will also come to understand their own uniqueness and special traits.

Advanced Routines

The final step consists of performing more advanced helping and caring routines with the handicapped children. After completing steps one and two, the youngsters are better able to understand the importance of individuality, of helping and caring for others, and of using systematic procedures. Caring and helping routines at this level include activities such as dressing, eating, drinking, grasping, stringing beads, matching, sorting, and others. At this level, they can better conceptualize the importance of individuality, as well as the benefits of helping and caring for others.

Caring for special friends—the handicapped—is caring and helping in action. The outcome of such sharing is the learning that occurs between the handicapped and nonhandicapped on a peer-to-peer basis.

The following section offers many activities in which "normal" youngsters may work with handicapped children to learn, practice, and use caring with their special friends and themselves. These activities are presented in a format that arms you with the tools of actively nurturing caring actions with the nonhandicapped for the handicapped and for themselves.

[1]   At the preparatory level, the nonhandicapped become sensitized to the handicapped for them to understand their individuality and to prepare them to work and play with their special friends. Some of the following activities are characteristic of this preparatory step.

ACTIVITY TITLE	## Using the Communication Board
MATERIALS	In showing youngsters the importance of communication, as well as some of the problems that handicapped children encounter in daily living, you need a thin board about 2'x8"x2" and several pictures showing various needs such as eating, dressing, toileting, caring, loving, or helping. The pictures are tacked or glued to the board with two inches between each of them.
PROCEDURES	To communicate his basic needs and desires, the youngster pretends that he cannot speak or orally express himself. Instead, he is guided to communicate his needs by pointing to pictures of them on the communication board. The youngster carries the board with him, and he points to these pictures to communicate his needs as they arise.
VARIATION	As a variation, different pictures are placed on the board. These pictures should be objects the youngster will use throughout the day. For another variation, the child can visit a center or school classroom. There he can actually observe handicapped children in action and watch how they communicate their needs to the adult and to their peers.
ACTIVITY TITLE	## Gesturing to Communicate
MATERIALS	This activity shows how the gesturing of some handicapped youngsters is used to communicate their needs and desires to others. No specific materials are used.
PROCEDURES	The youngster cannot speak in this activity. She is guided to use her body or specific parts to communicate her needs, desires, and wishes. For example, the youngster uses her arm and wrist to signify "Come here," her hand and arm held upright to mean "Stop," or her hand, pointing finger, and open mouth to show "Eat."
VARIATION	As a variation, the youngster can be shown gestures using simple sign language. These simple gestures make extensive use of the hands, wrists, and arms to describe specific objects, wants, needs, and desires. For instance, the youngster might use her hands to communicate the object "ball" by showing roundness with hand gestures. As another variation, older children can spell out words using their fingers, which is characteristic of the communication routines of deaf youngsters.
ACTIVITY TITLE	## Learning to Walk
MATERIALS	For this activity in sensitizing normal children to those with walking handicaps, child-sized crutches and a wheelchair are needed.
PROCEDURES	The youngster learns to walk using the crutches. Guide him to walk forward. After practicing walking forward, the child learns to walk

backward and sideways with the crutches. Body movements to the left and right can be attempted and practiced.

VARIATION   As a variation, have the child hold one leg behind his body. In a "hopping" fashion, he learns to balance and hop forward and backward, move sideways, and turn. Another variation requires the youngster to learn to walk using the wheelchair.

ACTIVITY TITLE   ## Using the Senses

MATERIALS   In sensitizing youngsters to various handicaps and to the problems of handicapped youngsters, you use a mask, a blindfold, or a handkerchief to cover the eyes, along with cotton for the ears.

PROCEDURES   Guide the youngsters in reaching a better understanding of handicaps by having them cover their eyes with a mask, blindfold, or handkerchief. You will need to tie it around their heads. Without being able to see, they can walk and perform simple activities such as coloring, cutting paper, finding and sitting in a chair, and so forth. They can also be taught to guide the blind by placing one of their hands on the children's elbows to lead them. At the end of these activities, ask the youngsters to discuss the frustrations they encountered in completing them.

VARIATION   In this variation, cotton is placed into the child's ears to simulate a hearing handicap. The child is guided to perform actions and activities that require hearing such as listening to directions, records, tapes, and television. As another variation, the hearing and seeing handicaps can be combined. Guide the youngsters to complete various activities and actions. With the end of both of these variations, the children should discuss the frustrations they encountered in completing them.

ACTIVITY TITLE   ## Applying Social Reinforcers

MATERIALS   For this activity of sensitizing children to the learning needs of the handicapped, no special materials are necessary.

PROCEDURES   In showing the youngster that handicapped children need a great amount of social reinforcement to learn effectively, model the use of reinforcers. Reinforcers also show that one individual cares about the other, and they also call attention to how well the handicapped are learning appropriate behaviors. As examples of social reinforcers, give the youngster a hug and a smile, while she is successfully completing an activity or immediately after finishing it; or you can pat her on the head or arm. Give the child time to practice these social reinforcement methods, and correct her if she is using the reinforcers inappropriately.

VARIATION   As a variation, use other social reinforcers that are verbal rather than physical: "Nice job! . . . Good work! . . . Excellent!" These reinforcers are

applied under the same conditions as other forms of social reinforcement. The child should also practice this type of reinforcement. Depending on the difficulty of the task, she should be able to use these
rewards occasionally instead of on constantly. You can also take a trip
with the youngster to a classroom or center where teachers use social
reinforcers with handicapped children.

ACTIVITY TITLE ## Reinforcing Selectively

MATERIALS For this activity to help regular children selectively reinforce the
actions of the handicapped, no materials are needed.

PROCEDURES Helping children to become sensitive to the attention-seeking behaviors of the handicapped enables them to work more effectively with
them. The basic principle is understanding that special attention for
inappropriate actions and behaviors can do handicapped youngsters
more harm than good. When special attention is shown for inappropriate behaviors, the handicapped may learn to show these actions
as a means of making themselves the center of events. For this activity,
the children might visit a center and observe the teacher's actions
when handicapped youngsters have accidents such as spilling or drop-
ping a plastic glass filled with milk or knocking an object on the floor.
They can also see how the adult handles behavior problems, such as
temper tantrums, self-abuse, or striking out. While observing how
these behaviors are handled, you need to guide the children to understand that the teacher selectively reinforces the actions of the handicapped and that special attention for wrong or inappropriate actions
might teach them to learn these unwanted ones.

VARIATION As a variation, you might show slides of handicapped children ex-
hibiting unwanted behaviors and of teachers handling them. Each of
the slides can be discussed. After you show them again, you might ask
the children to identify inappropriate behaviors of the handicapped
youngsters and to tell them how the teacher minimized attention to
their inappropriate actions.

ACTIVITY TITLE ## Having a Handicap for a Day

MATERIALS In having the youngster take on a handicap for a day, no special
materials are needed.

PROCEDURES The child decides which handicap he wants to assume for a day:
deafness, muteness, blindness, paraplegia, and so on. For one day the
youngster role plays an individual with that handicap. At the conclusion of the experience, he talks about his experiences and the
frustrations of this handicap.

VARIATION As a variation, ask the child to think about some of the problems he
would encounter if he had a particular handicap. After he is given
some time to think about the problem, discuss his ideas with him. His

insightful answers may surprise you. Prompt where necessary and give situations such as, "When you want to play with this toy, how would you find and get it!"

ACTIVITY TITLE ## Recognizing Individuality

MATERIALS For this activity on recognizing individuality, no materials are used.

PROCEDURES The youngsters need to recognize that all people are individuals and that no two of them are exactly alike. Guide the youngster to compare two or more children, and then try the same comparisons using adults. Even though identical twins are not alike in personality and personal likes and dislikes, they should not be chosen for this activity of recognizing individuality. The individuals can be compared on the basis of hair and eye color, height, body shape, likes and dislikes, and other characteristics. By comparing them, they realize that each individual is unique—no other is exactly the same.

VARIATION As a variation, you and the child might identify the many characteristics that distinguish individuals from each other. Talk about such characteristics as eye, hair, and skin color, as well as speech, temperament, and behavior. All such distinguishing characteristics of children and adults show their individuality.

ACTIVITY TITLE ## Talking About Differences in Intelligence

MATERIALS This activity, focusing on differences in intelligence among people, requires no special materials.

PROCEDURES	Ask the children to list some of the things that can be repaired. This list might include dolls and other familiar objects, as well as cars that we drive and ride in. In addition, ask them to identify some of the things that can't be repaired. In this listing, they might include glass containers and others. Finally, include the human brain as another thing that can't be fully repaired when it is damaged. Guide the youngsters to talk about the fact that handicapped children must be helped by others due to their low functional intelligence.
VARIATION	As a variation, visit a school or center for handicapped children and have the youngsters observe them to see the types of help they receive. Guide them to identify those youngsters who seem to need the most help. These handicapped children also have lower functional intelligence than those who need less help. In addition, talk about the differences in the type and the kinds of help offered the handicapped youngsters.
ACTIVITY TITLE	Learning to Write
MATERIALS	For this activity, which shows youngsters the difficulties encountered by the handicapped in writing, you need one crayon and 8½x12″ drawing paper.
PROCEDURES	Have the youngster draw a favorite object or person on his paper, but guide him to hold the crayon in the hand opposite his usual writing hand. Talk with the youngster about the problems and frustrations he felt as he drew his pictures. Not being fully able to control motor movements and thus to draw specific objects is a recognizable frustration of some handicapped children.
VARIATION	As a variation, child can also practice learning to write by holding the crayon between the toes of his feet. Use the same procedure.
[2]	At the more advanced level (step 2), the nonhandicapped perform simple helping and caring routines with the handicapped in short, small, and simple ways. Try some of the activities at this step in helping these youngsters learn to show caring with handicapped children.
ACTIVITY TITLE	Caring in Outdoor and Indoor Settings
MATERIALS	For this activity in caring, no materials are used.
PROCEDURES	Caring in this activity means showing and practicing helping skills with the handicapped. Use short activities that focus on showing caring with handicapped children such as "opening doors" for them. Afterward the youngster should use these same caring routines with the handicapped.
VARIATION	Other simple caring routines can be used, such as helping the handicapped youngsters to get objects they want to play with, taking them

out of the play yard, walking and running with them, and other ways of showing caring.

ACTIVITY TITLE **Helping with Eating Routines**

MATERIALS In showing caring with the handicapped in simple eating routines, no materials are required.

PROCEDURES When the handicapped are eating, there are plenty of ways to show caring and helping. For example, nonhandicapped children can pour a small amount of water into the handicapped's nontippable cup. After the handicapped child takes a sip and replaces the cup, the non-handicapped can reinforce this skill by saying, "Good job" or by using other comparable social rewards. Social reinforcement can also be used as youngsters properly use their utensils and show other appropriate eating routines.

VARIATION As a variation, the youngsters can become more directly involved with caring for the handicapped during eating routines at breakfast, lunch, dinner, and snack times. These routines include helping to set the table for the handicapped, calling them to eat, and reinforcing proper eating habits. If accidents occur, the helpers should recall and use the preparatory activity, "Reinforcing Selectively" by not giving undue attention to them.

ACTIVITY TITLE **Helping to Dress**

MATERIALS In the activity of helping handicapped children dress themselves, no specific materials are needed.

PROCEDURES In helping the handicapped to dress, children can perform numerous small and simple activities. Initially, model the procedure for helping putting on the handicapped's hats, loose-fitting coats, and sweaters. The nonhandicapped should help them put one arm into the coat or sweater at a time and praise them for showing their successes.

VARIATION As a variation, the nonhandicapped can help with more difficult clothing items such as boots, shirts, blouses, and belts, and they can assist with zippering and buttoning coats and sweaters.

ACTIVITY TITLE **Playing Ball**

MATERIALS For helping the nonhandicapped play ball (with the handicapped youngster), a volley ball or one of similar size and quality is required.

PROCEDURES In this free activity, the children sit on the floor a short distance apart. The nonhandicapped youngster gently rolls the ball along the floor to the handicapped, and as the ball approaches he uses the command "Push." At that command, the handicapped should push the ball away from and toward his friend. Help where needed.

VARIATION	As a variation, the handicapped, on the command of "Push," rolls the ball toward the helping child. The handicapped youngster in this variation initiates the activity. As other variations, several different activities can be used with the ball and practiced with the handi-capped child. The command "Push" and social reinforcement should also be used in these variations.

ACTIVITY TITLE **Running**

MATERIALS	For this activity of running, no materials are needed.
PROCEDURES	The children start from the same point in running for distance. The nonhandicapped child is appropriately guided to use the command "Start," and she and the handicapped youngster run to a designated point. Also show her how to use the command "Stop" to end their activity.
VARIATION	This free play activity can also be completed by running around the perimeter of a circle. In addition, make sure that the nonhandicapped youngster uses and practices the commands "start" and "stop" with the handicapped child. As another variation of running as a free activity, relays can be used. With this variation more children should be used.

ACTIVITY TITLE **Understanding Body Movement**

MATERIALS	In practicing body movements with the nonhandicapped helping the handicapped, no special materials are needed.
PROCEDURES	Guide the nonhandicapped to use various commands with the handi-capped such as "Turn your head," "Hold up your arm," and "Roll over." This activity can be practiced over and over until the handicapped child has associated these new commands with his body movement. The helping child will need to use social reinforcement when the youngster successfully shows these appropriate actions.
VARIATION	As a variation of understanding body movement, directional cues can be added. For example, guide the helping child to emphasize, "Hold up your left (or right) arm," "Turn your head to the right (or left)," and "Roll over to your left (or right) side." The variations should also be used with appropriate commands. If handicapped children have difficulty in recognizing their right and left hands, they can wear one color glove on the right and another color on the left.

ACTIVITY TITLE **Doing Puzzles**

MATERIALS	A simple two- or three-piece form board puzzle could be used in this activity.
PROCEDURES	In a free play activity, the handicapped are guided by the youngster to put a very simple form board puzzle together. The nonhandicapped

youngster helps the handicapped one complete the puzzle. The helping child socially reinforces the handicapped youngster as she correctly inserts one or more pieces in the form board.

VARIATION

Different puzzles of similar difficulty can be tried. As long as the handicapped enjoy doing the activity, the variation can be continued.

ACTIVITY TITLE

Practicing Nonbalance Movements

MATERIALS

In helping the nonhandicapped work with the handicapped to practice nonlocomotor movements, no materials are needed.

PROCEDURES

The helping child models and practices the nonlocomotor movement of twisting with the handicapped youngster. Standing in one location, the youngsters move their bodies from left to right and from right to left positions. To begin these movements, the command "Twist" should be used, and the nonhandicapped should help the handicapped perform these actions.

VARIATION

There are a number of additional variations of nonlocomotor movements. For example, the youngster can guide the handicapped to show swaying, stretching, bending, and stooping movements. Like twisting, commands for these other nonlocomotor movements should be used. In addition, social reinforcement should also be used when the handicapped youngster successfully completes the actions.

ACTIVITY TITLE

Walking

MATERIALS

For youngsters helping handicapped children walk from one place to another, five or six large (12x18") swatches of a rug are needed.

PROCEDURES

For this activity, the swatches should be two inches from each other. Holding each other's hand, the youngsters walk from one rug to the other using them as steppingstones. The command "Walk" is used to begin the activity, and the handicapped child is praised when he successfully completes each of these actions.

VARIATION

As variations, the distances between the swatches can be increased from two to four and then to six or more inches. The same procedure is repeated with each of these variations. As an extension of walking, try hopping from rug to rug.

ACTIVITY TITLE

Stepping Over Objects

MATERIALS

Gather four or five small objects that can easily be stepped over, such as small blocks, broomstick handles, stuffed dolls, and others. Records of marching songs are also used.

PROCEDURES

Place the objects in a line, with each one about four or five inches apart. The helping youngsters are guided to use the command "Step" every time they want the handicapped to raise and move their feet over the objects. The youngsters praise their special friends when they successfully follow the commands and step over each of the objects.

VARIATION As a variation, marching music can be played. The nonhandicapped should guide the handicapped in stepping over objects using the command "Step." As another variation, the pace can be speeded up or records requiring faster movements can be used.

[3] For the most advanced level (step 3), the nonhandicapped perform more complex caring and helping activities with the handicapped. For caring and helping at this level, try some of the following more advanced activities.

ACTIVITY TITLE ## Positioning of Objects

MATERIALS In helping the nonhandicapped work with handicapped youngsters in positioning, four small light wooden blocks are required.

PROCEDURES The children guide the handicapped by using the command "Put on," and they place one block on top of the other with help until all are stacked in vertical fashion. After each one is successfully "put on," the handicapped should be praised for showing their appropriate actions.

VARIATION As a variation, the handicapped youngsters can be guided to disassemble each of the stacked blocks with the command, "Take off." As a second variation, the command "put under" can be modeled and practiced, and the children will place one block beneath the other to complete this activity. Again, the handicapped youngsters are prompted and praised for those actions that are successfully completed.

ACTIVITY TITLE ## Looking at My Shadow

MATERIALS This activity requires three children—one to guide and lead the other two youngsters to perform the actions.

PROCEDURES Each youngster sits on the floor, and the helping child guides them in performing the activity. The helping child calls out movements such as "Back to back" or "Feet to feet." The other children respond by putting their backs or their feet together. Other commands that could be used include "Head to head ... Hands to feet ... Elbows to elbows ... Elbows to feet." As each command is correctly completed, the youngsters are immediately praised for their successes.

VARIATION As a variation, directional terms can be added to each of the actions and where appropriate. Examples include, "Left hand to left foot ... Right leg to left hand" and so forth. Again, the helping child prompts and praises the youngsters after they successfully complete each of the movements.

Stringing Beads

For this activity, large waxed shoelaces and brightly colored beads, with holes bored through them, should be used.

The nonhandicapped helps the handicapped string beads by modeling and practicing the simple movements required in putting the points of the shoelaces through the beads. As the handicapped child strings each of the beads, guide the helper to praise him for his successful attempts.

The helping child puts on three beads in a specific order by color—for example, first red, then blue, and then yellow. The handicapped youngster practices and completes this pattern. As another variation, the beads with different shapes are used, such as all circles, squares, or rectangles. Or the shapes can be sequenced; for example, the square, then the circle, and then the rectangle are repeated in that order. Again, the helper praises each proper placement of the bead on the string.

Developing the Senses

Pictures of foods and objects are required in helping nonhandicapped children work with the handicapped to develop the use of their senses.

The handicapped children's eyes, ears, nose, tongue, and fingers are used in this activity. The helping youngster holds up a picture of a food, for example, an ice cream cone. The handicapped youngster is guided to point to the sense that she uses the most with that food or object. In this case, the handicapped child would point to her tongue. Other pictures of foods and objects used in this activity could be popcorn (tongue), lemon (tongue), cut finger (finger), barking dog (ears), radio (ears), flower (nose), clouds (eyes), and soft fur (fingers).

As a variation, the helping youngster can call out the name of a favorite food or familiar object, and the handicapped child points to the sense most involved (by touching one of her five main senses). In addition, other pictures and/or names can be used. The helper praises the handicapped child when she correctly points to the appropriate sense.

Copying Actions

In having handicapped children copy the actions of nonhandicapped ones, no specific materials are needed.

The youngsters stand about three to four feet apart—facing one another. The helping child initiates actions and movements, and the nonhandicapped child copies these same movements. Other movements used could be jumping up and down, running in place, bending the head forward, and so forth. These and other movements are completed very slowly and deliberately.

VARIATION As a variation, the same movements are used, but they are performed faster. In addition and after the handicapped child understands and practices the procedures, she can lead; the helping youngster then becomes the "mirror." These variations can also lead to singing games such as, "Simon Says." As in the initial activity, the nonhandicapped should praise the handicapped child when the movements are made correctly.

ACTIVITY TITLE **Touching and Striking**

MATERIALS Several brightly colored balls, varying in size from small to large, are the objects used in this activity.

PROCEDURES Guide the helping youngster to roll the balls, one at a time, toward the handicapped child who is sitting on the floor. The handicapped child touches or strikes the ball on the command of "Touch" or "Strike."

VARIATION The balls can be hung from the ceiling with cord. For this variation, place masking tape around lightweight beach balls, tie cord around

their centers, and suspend them from the ceiling. The handicapped child then touches and strikes them. As another variation, additional motor actions should be used with the balls, such as hugging and patting.

ACTIVITY TITLE **Moving Body Parts**

MATERIALS No actual materials are used in this activity of moving body parts.

PROCEDURES The helping child guides the handicapped youngster to investigate the many movements that her body parts can make. For example, the nonhandicapped youngster models several distinct movements of her "pointing" finger. She should move her "pointer" up, down, sideways, and in circular patterns. As each movement is done separately, the youngster models or copies the movements and is praised after each correct one.

VARIATION As a variation, other body parts should be used, such as elbow, wrist, arm, neck, leg, and ankles. In addition, the helper should guide the handicapped child to explore the movement potential of her entire body through stretching, curling, bending, and twisting. As before, modeling and praising are used with the handicapped.

ACTIVITY TITLE **Hiding the Cord**

MATERIALS For this activity the nonhandicapped help the handicapped hide a piece of three-foot cord with their bodies.

PROCEDURES Guide the helper to make a design with the cord. The design could be a circle, a straight line, a ninety-degree angle, and so forth. The helping child models hiding the cord by placing his body over the cord to form the particular design. As the handicapped child copies these body actions, his successful moves are praised. This youngster may need to be assisted to hide all of the cord.

VARIATION In this variation, two pieces of cord are used, and two additional youngsters are also needed. The two pieces of cord one of which is bent and touches the other, are used. This variation requires the two youngsters to work together to hide the cords with their bodies.

ACTIVITY TITLE **Kicking the Ball**

MATERIALS Several large balls that are soft and easily kicked are required for this activity.

PROCEDURES The helper models kicking these balls in stationary positions for the handicapped youngster, who then attempts and practices kicking stationary balls. The helping youngster should praise her for her successful kicking movements.

VARIATION For one variation, the nonhandicapped child gently and slowly rolls the ball as he guides the handicapped youngster to kick it. Kicking a moving ball (from a stationary position) becomes more difficult with this variation. For another variation, the handicapped youngster can be shown the procedures for running and kicking a slowly moving ball. With each of these variations, a target may be used; for example, the youngsters can kick the ball into a large box.

ACTIVITY TITLE ## A Moving Object

MATERIALS For this activity a tennis ball with a hole drilled through it, a long piece of strong cord, and an "eye" screw are needed.

PROCEDURES Before the activity begins, you will need to insert the cord through the hole in the tennis ball and tie it. Also, put the "eye" screw into the ceiling and hang the tennis ball with the cord from it so the ball is three feet from the floor. By modeling, the helper guides the handicapped youngster to lie on his back beneath the ball with his body straight and his arms at his sides. The helping child moves the ball in a vertical fashion and asks his friend to follow the moving ball with his eyes without moving his head. The helper praises the child as he successfully completes this activity. As a prompt, the nonhandicapped youngster may need to hold his friend's head still if it moves with the ball.

VARIATION As a variation, the handicapped youngster is guided to raise his left hand as the ball moves to his left side and to raise his right one as it travels to his right side. This same variation can be used with his feet and then with both his hands and his feet. The handicapped youngster will need to be praised immediately after he successfully accomplishes each of these actions.

[4] TIPS

1. When the helping and handicapped children are in competitive games, such as races, you need to explain to the nonhandicapped children that their special friends should also be able to win the game. Success provides for more success.

2. When you and the nonhandicapped child work with the handicapped youngster, make sure the materials and objects used in these activities are brightly colored and large enough for them to grasp or hold.

3. Praise handicapped children during or immediately after they successfully complete an activity that enhances learning. Praising constantly should be changed to praising occasionally only after the handicapped have mastered the skill.

4. As the helping child works and plays with the handicapped, make

sure that you also take an active part in these activities whenever possible. These youngsters enjoy adult participation in their activities and are greatly influenced by it.

5. As you help to set up these activities with the nonhandicapped child, make sure that the number of possible distractions are removed or reduced. The handicapped youngster's mind easily wanders, and distractions—such as too many other objects in the area or interruptions with other children—reduce their attention and the effectiveness of the learning activity.

6. Take safety precautions and watch for possible dangers or hazards as the handicapped child plays and works at these activities. The handicapped tend to be more accident-prone than nonhandicapped youngsters because they do not recognize potential dangers as quickly.

7. The attention span of the handicapped child is relatively short. So the activities should not be conducted for more than ten minutes unless he or she shows attending behaviors and enjoys doing them.

8. You will need to set a slow and deliberate pace, so the helping children can model your movements with the handicapped as they work with them.

9. Much of the learning of the handicapped children is accomplished through imitation. You need to work with nonhandicapped children and show them that they need to model the activities for the handicapped and that these demonstrations must be specific, exact, and repeated often in order for their special friends to learn successfully.

10. When behavior problems occur with the handicapped, you will need to tell the helping children to ignore their aggressive, inappropriate, and uncooperative behaviors and/or to quietly come and let you know when they occur.

Caring

USEFUL RESOURCES

Teaching young children to care for themselves and others in school and in home setting is fundamental to their positive social, emotional, and cognitive growth. In each of the chapters, you have learned how to provide opportunities to develop, practice, and enhance caring, nurturing, consideration, expectations, self-esteem, and role-taking abilities for caring. Then too, you have learned to provide experiences in creativity that encourage caring in action in single-parent families and with special children in home and school settings.

In addition, and after you have used some or all of these activities, you might want to extend further your expertise in teaching youngsters about caring and caring for others. To help you do so, we have listed some books and articles that we have found useful. These resources are grouped under the chapter titles in this book. You will find that these resources complement and extend the content covered in each chapter.

You should be able to find them easily in your community or school library by using the author's index in the card catalog listings. If they are not available, you might ask your librarian to give you the addresses of the publishing companies that put out the textbooks and journals. You can write to the publishers directly for the ones that you want to order.

Through your efforts, the youngster's growth in caring for self and others will continue to blossom. As a famous radio and TV commentator, Paul Harvey, would say, "And, you are the rest of the story!"

Caring

Books and Articles

Bax, M. and Bernal, Jr. *Your child's first five years*. New York: St. Martin's Press, Inc., 1975.

Berman, L. M. and Roderick, J. A. (eds.). *Feeling, valuing, and the art of growing: Insights into the affective*. Washington, D.C.: Association for Supervision and Curriculum Development, 1977.

Berman, L. M. and Roderick, J. A. *Curriculum: Teaching the what, how, and why of living*. Columbus, Ohio: Charles E. Merrill Publishing Company, 1977.

Bernhardt, D. K. (ed.) *Being a parent: Unchanging values in a changing world*. Toronto, Can.: University of Toronto Press, 1970.

Calhou, J. A. Developing a family perspective. *Children Today*, 1980, 9 2–8.

Carro, G. Teaching kids to be kind in a tough world. *Ladies Home Journal*, 1979, 96, 144.

Denmakr, L. D. *Every child should have a chance*. New York: Vantage Press, 1971.

D'Evelyn K. E. *Meeting children's emotional needs*. Englewood Cliffs, N.J.: Prentice-Hall, Inc. 1957.

Diskin, E. *Yoga for children*. New York: Arco Publishing Company, Inc., 1976.

Elkind, D. *A sympathetic understanding of the child*. Boston: Allyn & Bacon, Inc., 1978.

Feeney, S. and Christensen, D. *Who am I in the lives of children?* Columbus, Ohio: Charles E. Merrill Publishing Company, 1979.

Guerney, B. Filial therapy: Description and rationale. *Journal of Counseling Psychology*, 1964, 28, 304–310.

Hendrick, J. *The whole child: New trends in early education*. St. Louis, Mo.: The C. V. Mosby Company, 1975.

Hobbs, N. Families, schools, and communities: An ecosystem for children. *Teacher College Record*, 1978, 79, 756–766.

Ilg, F. L. and Ames, L. B. *Child behavior*. New York: Harper & Row, Publishers, Inc., 1955.

Kawin, E. *Parenthood in a free nation*. New York: Macmillan, Inc., 1963.

McDiarmid, N. J., Peterson, M. A., and Sutherland, J. R. *Loving and learning: Interacting with your child from birth to three*. New York: Harcourt Brace Jovanovich, Inc., 1975.

Monahan, R. *Free and inexpensive materials for preschool and early childhood*. Belmont, Cal.: Fearon-Pitman Publishers, Inc., 1975.

Mussen, P. H., and Eisenberg-Berg, W. *Roots of caring, shaping, and helping: The development of prosocial behavior in children*. San Francisco: W. H. Freeman & Company Publishers, 1977.

Read, D. A. and Simon, S. B. (eds.). *Humanistic education sourcebook*. Columbus, Ohio: Charles E. Merrill Publishing Company, 1975.

Read, K. and Patterson, J. *The nursery school and kindergarten*. New York: Holt, Rinehart, & Winston, 1980.

Ross, H. *Fears of children*. Chicago, Ill.: Science Research Associates, 1951.

Rowen, B., Byrne, J., and Winter, L. *The learning match*. Englewood Cliffs, N.J.: Prentice-Hall, Inc., 1980.

Rubin T. I. Mothers and daughters who can't get along. *Ladies Home Journal*. 1981, 98, 54.

Simons, S. *I am lovable and capable*. Niles, Ill.: Argus Communication Publishers, 1974.

Slavson, S. R. *Child-centered group guidance of parents*. New York: International Universities Press, 1958.

Spock, B. *Baby and childcare*. New York: Pocket Books, Inc., 1977.

Tarrow, N. B. and Lundsteen, S. W. *Activities and resources for guiding young children's learning*. New York: McGraw-Hill Book Company, 1978.

Thatcher, D.A. *Teaching, loving, and self-directed learning*. Pacific Palisades, Cal.: Goodyear Publishing Co., Inc., 1973.

Nurtured and Nurturing

Books and
Articles

Almy, M. *The early childhood educator at work*. New York: McGraw-Hill Book Company, 1975.

Ames, L. B. and Ilg, F. L. *Your five-year-old: Sunny and serene*. New York: Delacorte Publishers, 1979.

Ames, L. B. and Ilg, F. L. *Your six-year-old: Defiant but loving*. New York: Delacorte Publishers, 1979.

Andrews, J. D. (ed.). *One child indivisible*. Washington, D.C.: National Association for Education of Young Children, 1975.

Brim, O. *Education for child rearing*. New York: The Free Press, 1965.

Brown, G. *Human teaching for human learning*. New York: The Viking Press, 1971.

Burns, M. *I am not a short adult: Getting good at being a kid*. Boston: Little, Brown & Company, 1977.

Buscaglia, L. *Love*. Thorofare, N.J.: Charles Black Publishers, 1972.

Callard, E. D. Developing socially valued behavior in young children. *Education Digest*, 1979, *44*, 8–11.

Clausen, J. A. American research on the family and socialization. *Children Today*, 1978, 7, 7–10.

Cooper, J. How does your toddler grow? *Parents*, 1979, 54, 29–33.

Cummings, P. *I'm telling you for the last time*. New York: Schuman Publishers, 1951.

Dinkmeyer, D. C. and McKay, G. D. *Raising a responsible child: Some practical steps*. New York: Simon & Schuster, Inc., 1973.

Dobson, J. *Dare to discipline*. Glendale, Cal.: Regal Books, Inc., 1972.

Dobson, F. *How to discipline with love: From crib to college*. New York: Rawson Associates, Inc. 1977.

Dobson, F. *How to parent*. Bergenfield, N.J.: The New American Library Publishers, 1971.

Dreikurs, R. *Children: the challenge*. New York: Hawthorn Books, Inc., 1964.

Dreikurs, R. and Soltz, V. *Children: The challenge*. New York: Hawthorn Books, Inc., 1964.

Evans, G. *The family circle guide to self-help*. New York: Ballantine Books, Inc., 1979.

Fontana, V. C. When your child doesn't feel well. *Parents*, 1979, *54*, 80–81.

Gazda, G. *Human relations development: A manual for educators*. Boston: Allyn & Bacon, Inc. 1977.

Gordon, T. *Parent effectiveness training*. New York: P. H. Wyden Publishers, 1974.

Greene, C. C. *Getting nowhere*. New York: The Viking Press, 1977.

Just, W. S. *A family trust: A novel.* Boston: Little, Brown & Company, 1978.

Lane, H. *Talks to parents and teachers.* New York: Schocken Books, Inc., 1969.

Marcus, R. F. and Leiserson, M. Encouraging helping behavior. *Young children,* 1978, *33,* 24–34.

May, R. *The courage to create.* New York: W. W. Norton & Co., Inc., 1978.

Rogers, C. R. *Freedom to Learn.* Columbus, Ohio: Charles E. Merrill Publishing Company, 1969.

Suzuki, S. *Nurtured by love.* New York: Exposition Publishers, 1969.

Role of the Child in Caring: Roletaking

Books and Articles

Abt, C. *Serious games.* New York: The Viking Press, 1973.

Ambron, S. R. and Irwin, D. M. Role taking and moral judgment in five-year and seven-year olds. *Developmental Psychology,* 1975, *11,* 102–114.

Batchhelder, M. *Puppets and plays.* New York: Harper & Row, Publishers, Inc., 1956.

Baylor, B. *Sometimes I dance mountains.* New York: Charles Scribner's Sons, 1973.

Biddle, B. and Thomas E. (eds.). *Role theory: Concepts and research.* New York: John Wiley & Sons, Inc., 1966.

Burton, E. C. *Physical activities for the developing child.* Springfield, Ill.: Charles C. Thomas, Publisher, 1980.

Chambers, D. *Storytelling and creative drama.* Dubuque, Iowa: William C. Brown Co., Publishers, 1970.

Cherry, C. *Creative movements for the developing child.* Palo Alto, California: Fearon-Pitman Publishers, Inc., 1972.

Chesler, M. and Fox, R. *Role-playing methods in the classroom.* Chicago: Science Research Associates, 1966.

Cohen, D. H. Growing in humanness. *Children Today,* 1978, *7,* 26–29.

DeMille, R. *Put your mother on the ceiling: Children's imaginative games.* New York: The Viking Press, 1973.

Dubos, R. *Beast or angel: Choices that make us human.* New York: Charles Scribner's Sons, 1974.

Edwards, C. *Creative dramatics.* Dansville, N.Y.: The Instructor Publishers, 1972.

Elardo, P. and Cooper, M. *AWARE: Activities for social development.* Menlo Park, Cal.: Addison-Wesley Publishing Co., Inc., 1977.

Flavell, J. H. *The development of role-taking and communication skills in children.* New York: John Wiley & Sons, Inc., 1968.

Flavell, J. H. *The development of role-taking and communication skills in children.* New York: John Wiley & Sons, Inc., 1968.

Furness, P. *Role play in the elementary school: A handbook for teachers.* New York: Hart Publishers, 1976.

Gartner, A., Kohler, M. and Reissman, F. *Children teach children: Learning by teaching.* New York: Harper & Row, Publishers, Inc., 1971.

Gillies, E. *Creative dramatics for all children.* Washington, D.C.: Association for Childhood Education International, 1971.

Hanford, R. *Puppets and puppeteering.* New York: Drake Publishers, 1976.

Kings, S. and Katsman, C. *Imagine that: Illustrated poems and creative learning experiences.* Pacific Palisades, Cal.: Goodyear Publishing Co., Inc., 1976.

King, K. You can prepare for good behavior—and get it! *Parents Magazine*, 1975, *50*, 40–42.

Latchaw, M. and Egstrom, G. *Human movement with concepts applied to children's movement activities.* Englewood Cliffs, N.J.: Prentice Hall, Inc., 1969.

Lipson, G. B. Folk play: A new technique. *Clearing House*, 1977, *50*, 354–357.

Moustakes, C. *Creative life.* New York: Van Nostrand Reinhold Company, 1977.

Sarason, I. and Sarason, B. *Constructive classroom behavior: A teacher's guide to modelling and roletaking techniques.* New York: Behavior Publications, 1974.

Siks, G. B. *Drama with children.* New York: Harper & Row, Publishers, Inc., 1977.

Spivack, G. and Skune, M. B. *Social adjustment of young children.* San Francisco: Jossey-Bass, Inc., Publishers, 1974.

Taylor, L. *Pantomime and pantomime games.* Minneapolis, Minn.: Burgess Publishing Co., 1965.

Ward, W. *Play making with children.* New York: Appleton-Century-Crofts, 1957.

Wilcox, H. G. Organized child. *Human Behavior*, 1978, *7*, 49–51.

Consideration

Books and Articles

Arnstein, H. S. *The roots of love: Helping your child learn to love in the first three years of life.* New York: Bobbs Merrill Co., Inc., 1975.

Beck, J. *Effective parenting: A practical and loving guide to making child care easier and happier for today's parents.* New York: Simon & Schuster, Inc., 1976.

Bee, H. L. *The developing child.* New York: Harper & Row, Publishers, Inc., 1978.

Browne, R. B. and English, J. W. *Love my children: An autobiography.* New York: Meredith Publishers, 1969.

Byrne S. How to raise courteous well-mannered children in your own home. *Redbook*, 1978, *152*, 61–62.

Cohen, D. R. Who's who: Children see it differently. *Psychology Today*, 1978, *12*, 36–37.

Dinkmeyer, D. *Manual for developing understanding of self and others.* Circle Pines, Minn.: American Guidance Services, 1970.

Ford, E. E. *For the love of children: A realistic approach to raising your child.* New York: Anchor Press, 1977.

Gaylin, W. *Caring.* New York: Alfred A. Knopf, Inc., 1976.

Katz, L. Authorities and priorities: Preschoolers. *Parents Magazine*, 1979, *53*, 102–103.

Kellerman, J. *Helping the fearful child: A parent's guide to everyday and problem anxieties.* New York: W. W. Norton & Co., Inc., 1981.

Light, P. *The development of social sensitivity.* Cambridge, N.Y.: Cambridge University Press, 1979.

Martin, R. J. *Teaching through encouragement: Techniques to help students learn.* Englewood Cliffs, N.J.: Prentice-Hall, Inc., 1980.

Piers, M. W. *Growing up with children.* New York: Quadrangle/The New York Times Book Co., Inc., 1966.

Roedell, W. C., Slaby, R. B., and Robinson, H. B. *Social development in children.* Monterey, Cal.: Brooks/Cole Publishing Co., 1977.

Rubin, Z. *Children's friendships.* Baltimore: Harvard University Press, 1980.

Sanderson, J. D. *How to stop worrying about your kids.* New York: W. W. Norton & Co., Inc., 1978.

Selman, R. L. and Selman, A. P. Children's ideas about friendship. *Psychology Today*, 1979, *13*, 70–72.

Steel, D. *Loving.* New York: C. K. Hall, 1981.

Tough, J. *Talking, thinking, growing: Language with the young child.* New York: Schocken Publishers, 1974.

Warner, S. L. *Your child learns naturally.* New York: Doubleday & Co., Inc., 1976.

Warren, R. *Caring: Supporting children's growth.* Washington, D.C.: National Association for the Education of Young Children, 1977.

Expectations

Books and Articles

Acherman, P. *Signals: What your child is really telling you.* New York: The Dial Press, 1978.

Almy, M. *Ways of studying children: An observation manual for early childood teachers.* New York: Teachers College Press—Columbia University, 1979.

Babcock, D. E. and Keepers, T. D. *Raising kids O.K.: Transactional analysis in human growth and development.* New York: Grove Publishers, 1976.

Bigner, J. J. *Parent–child relations: An introduction to parenting.* New York: Macmillan, Inc., 1979.

Brooks-Gunn, J, and Mathews, W. S. *He and she: how children develop their sex role identity.* Englewood Cliffs, N.J.: Prentice-Hall, Inc., 1979.

Callahan, S. C. *Parenting: Principles, and politics of parenthood.* Garden City, New York: Doubleday & Co., Inc., 1973.

Dunn, R. S. and Dunn, K. P. *How to raise independent and professionally successful daughters.* Englewood Cliffs, N.J.: Prentice-Hall, Inc., 1977.

Dreikurs, R. *Logical consequences.* New York: Hawthorn Books, Inc., 1968.

Dreikurs, R. and Grey, L. *A new approach to discipline: Logical consequences.* New York: Hawthorn Books, Inc., 1968.

Elkind, D. What young children need most in changing society. *Parents Magazine*, 1977, *52*, 40–42.

Ellis, A. and Harper, R. A. *A new guide to rational living.* Los Angeles: Wilshire Publishers, Inc., 1975.

Entwisle, D. R. and Haydok, L. A. *Too great expectations: The academic outlook of young children.* Baltimore: John Hopkins University Press, 1978.

Feinberg, G. *Consequences of growth.* New York: Seabury Publishers, 1977.

Ginot, H. *Between parent and child.* New York: Macmillan, Inc., 1965.

Govid, S. *How to raise an independent child.* New York: St. Martin's Press, Inc., 1979.

Hill, P. H. *Decision making.* Reading, Mass.: Addison-Wesley Publishing Co., Inc., 1977.

Levine, J. A. Real kids versus the average family. *Psychology Today*, 1978, *12*, 14–15.

McNett, I. Social development in young children. *American Education*, 1975, *12*, 35–36.

Patterson, G. R. and Gullion, M. E. *Living with children*. Champaign, Ill.: Research Press Publishers, 1968.

Pogrebin, L. C. *Growing up free: Raising your child in the 80's*. New York: McGraw-Hill Book Company, 1980.

Raffini, J. P. *Discipline: Negotiating conflicts with today's kids*. Englewood Cliffs, N.J.: Prentice-Hall, Inc., 1981.

Ramos, S. *Teaching your child to cope with crisis*. David McKay Co., Inc., 1975.

Rutter, M. *Helping troubled children*. New York: Plenum Publishing Corporation, 1976.

Schaefer, C. E. Raising children by old-fashioned parent sense. *Children Today*, 1978, *7*, 7–9.

Senn, M. J. and Solnit, A. J. *Problems in child behavior and development*. Philadelphia: Len and Febiger Publishers, 1970.

Segal, J. *A child's journey: Forces that shape the lives of our young*. New York: McGraw-Hill Book Company, 1978.

Smith, M. J. *When I say no, I feel guilty*. New York: Bantam Books, Inc., 1975.

Steiner, C. *Scripts people live*. New York: Bantam Books, Inc., 1974.

Tomlinson-Keasey, C. *Child's eye view: A new way of understanding the development and behavior of children*. New York: St. Martin's Press, Inc., 1980.

White, B. L. and Kaban, B. Effective parent, competent child. *Parents Magazine*, 1976, *51*, 38–40.

Self and Self-Esteem

Books and
Articles

Alexander, T. Conditions of personal change. *Intellect*, 1975, *104*, 232–234.

Auila, D. L., Combs, A. W., and Purkey, W. W. *The helping relationship source book*. Boston: Allyn & Bacon, Inc., 1971.

Axline, V. M. *Dibs: In search of self*. New York: Ballantine Publishing Co., 1967.

Briggs, D. C. *Your child's self-esteem*. Garden City, N.Y.: Doubleday & Co., Inc., 1970.

Coopersmith, S. *The Antecedents of self-esteem*. San Francisco: W. H. Freeman & Company Publishers, 1967.

DeFranco, E. B. For parents only: Strengthening the child's self image. *PTA Magazine*, 1974, *68*, 10–12.

Despert, J. L. *Children of divorce*. Garden City, N.Y.: Doubleday & Co., Inc., 1953.

Dobson, J. *Hide or seek*. Old Tappan, N.J.: Fleming H. Revell Publishers, 1971.

Dreikurs, R. and Cassel, P. *Discipline without tears*. New York: Hawthorn Books, Inc., 1974.

Felker, D. W. *Building positive self-concepts*. Minneapolis, Minn.: Burgess Publishing Co., 1974.

Fitts, W. H. and Adams, J. L. *The self concept and self actualization*. Nashville, Tenn.: Dede Wallace Center, Inc., 1971.

Fluegelman, A. *The new games book.* New York: Doubleday & Co., Inc., 1976.

Gardner, R. A. *The boys and girls book about divorce.* New York: Bantam Books, Inc., 1970.

Ginott, H. G. *Between parent and child.* New York: Macmillan, Inc., 1969.

Glickman, B. M. and Springer, W. B. *Who cares for the baby?: Choices in child care.* New York: Schocken Publishers, 1978.

Gordon, I. *Children's views of themselves.* Washington, D.C.: Association for Childhood Education International, 1972.

Gordon, I. The beginnings of the self: The problem of the nurturing environment. *Phi Delta Kappan,* 1969, *1,* 7.

Gordon, T. *Parent effectiveness training.* New York: P. H. Wyden Publishers, 1974.

Hamachek, D. E. *Encounter with the self.* New York: Holt, Rinehart, & Winston, 1971.

Moore, S. and Kilmer, P. *Contemporary preschool programs.* New York: John Wiley & Sons, Inc., 1972.

Orlick, T. *The cooperative sports and games book.* New York: Pantheon Books, Inc., 1978.

Raths, L. E. *Meeting the needs of children: Creating trust and security.* Columbus, Ohio: Charles E. Merrill Publishing Company, 1972.

Rosenberg, M. *Conceiving the self.* New York: Basic Books, Inc., Publishers, 1979.

Rubin, Z. *Children's friendships.* Cambridge, Mass.: Harvard University Press, 1980.

Samuels, S. C. *Enhancing self-concept in early childhood.* New York: Human Sciences Press, 1977.

Satir, V. *Peoplemaking.* Palto Alo, Cal.: Science and Behavior Publishers, 1972.

Sears, P. S. and Sherman, V. S. *In pursuit of self-esteem.* Belmont, Cal.: Wadsworth Publishing Co., Inc., 1964.

Survant, A. Building positive self-concepts. *Instructor,* 1971, *81,* 94–95.

Tocco, T. S. and Bridges, C. M. The relationship between the self-concept of mothers and their children. *Child Study Journal,* 1973, *3,* 61–79.

Yamanoto, K. (ed.). *The child and his image.* Boston: Houghton-Mifflin Publishers, 1972.

Yawkey, T. D. (Ed.) *Young child's self concept.* Provo, Utah: The Brigham Young University Press, 1980.

"Caring" in Action: Single Parent Families

Books and Articles

Arnstein, H. S. *What to tell your child about birth, death, divorce, illness, and other family crises.* New York: The Bobbs Merrill Co., Inc., 1962.

Axline, V. M. *Play therapy.* New York: Ballantine Books, Inc., 1969.

Barber, D. (ed.). *One parent families.* London, England: David Poynter Publishers, 1975.

Berman, E. *The cooperating family.* Englewood Cliffs, N.J.: Prentice-Hall, Inc., 1977.

Bernstein, J. (ed.). *Books to help children cope with separation and loss.* Ann Arbor, Mich.: R. R. Bowker Company, 1977.

Brammer, L. M. *The helping relationship: Process and skills.* Englewood Cliffs, N.J.: Prentice-Hall, Inc., 1979.

Brazelton, T. B. Mother alone. *Redbook*, 1975, *145*, 56–58.

Croft, D. J. *Parents and teachers.* Belmont, Cal.: Wadsworth Publishing Co., Inc., 1979.

Daniel, G. But what of girls without fathers. *PTA Magazine*, 1974, *68*, 13.

Despert, J. C. *Children of divorce.* Garden City, N.Y.: Doubleday & Co., Inc., 1962.

Dreikurs, R. and Grey, L. *A parent's guide to child discipline.* New York: Hawthorn Books, Inc., 1970.

Fraiberg, S. *The magic years: Handling the problems of early childhood.* New York: Charles Scribner's Sons, 1959.

Galdston, R. Coping with behavior problems: One-parent household. *Parents Magazine*, 1977, *52*, 97.

Gardner, R. A. *The boys' and girls' book about divorce.* New York: Bantam Books, Inc., 1970.

Gardner, R. A. *The parent's book about divorce.* New York: Doubleday & Co., Inc., 1977.

Gaylin, J. Family: It is changing, not breaking up. *Psychology Today*, 1977, *11*, 36–40.

Grollman, E. A. *Talking about divorce: A dialogue between parent and child.* Boston, Mass.: Beacon Press, 1975.

Horner, C. T. *The single-parent family in children's books.* Metuchen, N.J.: Scarecrow Press, Inc., 1978.

Jones, C. *Learning about separation for little kids.* Boston: Houghton Mifflin Publishers, 1979.

Jones, S. *Learning for little kids: A parent's sourcebook for the years 3 to 8.* Boston: Houghton Mifflin Publishers, 1979.

Keniston, K. *All our children: The American family under pressure.* New York: Harcourt Brace Jovanovich, Inc., 1977.

Kelin, C. *The single parent experience.* New York: Walker Publishers, 1973.

Levine, J. A. *Who will raise the children?: New options for fathers (and mothers).* Philadelphia: J. B. Lippincott Company, 1976.

Maddox, B. *The half-parent.* New York: Signet Books, 1976.

Rowlands, P. *Children apart: How parents can help young children cope with being away from the family.* New York: Pantheon Books, Inc. 1974.

Salk, L. Guilt and the single parent. *Harper's Bazaar*, 1976, *109*, 89–91.

Salk, L. *What every child would like parents to know about divorce.* New York: Harper & Row, Publishers, Inc., 1978.

Schlesinger, B. *The one-parent family: Perspectives and annotated bibliography.* Toronto, Canada: The University of Toronto Press, 1978.

Spilke, F. S. *What about children?: A divorced parent's handbook.* New York: Crown Publishers, 1979.

Steinzor, B. *When parents divorce: A new approach to new relationships.* New York: Pantheon Books, Inc., 1969.

Stuart, I. and Abt, L. E. *Children of separation and divorce.* New York: Grossman Publishers, 1972.

Wollerstein, J. S. and Kelly, J. B. *Surviving the breakup: How children and parents cope with divorce.* New York: Basic Books, Inc., 1980.

Weiss, R. S. *Going it alone: The family life and social situation of a single parent.* New York: Basic Books, Inc., 1979.

Wertheimer, B. M. *We were there: The story of working women in America.* New York: Pantheon Books, Inc., 1977.

Caring With Special Friends—The Handicapped

Books and Articles

Abel, G. L. (ed.). *Concerning the education of blind children.* New York: American Foundation for the Blind, 1959.

Allen, K. E. *Mainstreaming in early childhood education.* Albany, N.Y.: Delmar Publishers, 1980.

Apgar, V. and Beck, J. *Is my baby all right?* New York: Pocket Books, 1974.

Barraga, N. *Visual handicaps and learning: A developmental approach.* Belmont, Cal.: Wadsworth Publishing Co., Inc., 1976.

Best, G. A. *Individuals with physical disabilities: An introduction for educators.* St. Louis, Miss.: The C. V. Mosby Company, 1978.

Cartwright, G. P., Cartwright, C. A., and Ward, M. E. *Educating special learners.* Belmont, Cal.: Wadsworth Publishing Co., Inc., 1981.

Complo, J. *Fun tactics: Movement and speech activities for special children.* Belmont, Cal.: Fearon-Pitman Publishers, Inc., 1979.

Corbin, C. B. *A textbook for motor development.* Dubuque, Iowa: William C. Brown Co., Publishers, 1973.

Cratty, B. J. *Active learning games to enhance academic abilities.* Englewood Cliff, N.J.: Prentice Hall, Inc., 1971.

Cratty, B. J. *Perceptual and motor development of infants and children.* New York: Macmillan, Inc., 1970.

Fraiberg, S. *Insights from the blind.* New York: Basic Books, Inc., 1977.

Gallagher, J. J. *Teaching the gifted child.* Boston: Allyn & Bacon, Inc., 1975.

Gardner, W. I. *Children with learning and behavior problems: A behavior management approach.* Boston: Allyn & Bacon, Inc., 1974.

Gearheart, B. and Weishahn, M. *The handicapped student in the regular classroom.* St. Louis, Mo.: The C. V. Mosby Company, 1980.

Geddes, D. *Physical activities for individuals with handicapped conditions.* St. Louis, Mo.: The C. V. Mosby Company, 1974.

Ginglend, D. and Stiles, W. *Learning activities for the learning disabled.* Belmont, Cal.: Fearon-Pitman Publishers, Inc., 1977.

Guralnick, M. J. (ed.). *Early intervention and the integration of handicapped children.* Baltimore: University Park Press, 1978.

Humphrey, J. H. and Sullivan, D. *Teaching slow learners through activity games.* Springfield, Ill.: Charles C. Thomas, Publisher, 1970.

Kephart, N. C. *The slow learner in the classroom.* Columbus, Ohio: Charles E. Merrill Publishing Company, 1965.

Kirchner, S. L. *Play it by sign: Games in sign language.* Northridge, Cal.: Joyce Media Publishers, Inc., 1980.

Levine, H. Bowling as an activity for the educationally mentally retarded. *Training School Bulletin,* 1961, *65,* 135–137.

Moran, J. and Kalakian, L. *Movement experiences for the mentally retarded or emotionally disturbed child.* Minneapolis, Minn.: Burgess Publishing Co., 1974.

Morris, R. H. Evaluation of a play environment for blind children. *Therapeutic Recreation Journal*, 1974, *8*, 151–155.

Morris, R. J. and Dolker, M. Developing cooperative play in socially withdrawn retarded children. *Mental Retardation*, 1974, *12*, 24–27.

Neisworth, J. T. and Smith, R. M. (eds.). *Retardation: Issues, assessment, and intervention.* New York: McGraw-Hill Book Company, 1978.

Payne, J. S., Kauffman, J. M., Brown, G. B., and De Mott, R. M. *Exceptional children in focus.* Columbus, Ohio: Charles E. Merrill Publishing Company, 1979.

Perlmutter, R. Papercrafts and mobiles. *Teaching Exceptional Children*, 1972, *4*, 134–141.

Sobol, H. L. *My brother Steven is retarded.* New York: Macmillan, Inc., 1977.

Stein, S. B. *About handicaps: An open family book for parents and children together.* New York: Walker Publishers, 1974.

Strain, P. S. Increasing social play of severely retarded preschoolers through sociodramatic activities. *Mental Retardation*, 1975, *13*, 7–9.

Van Witsen, B. *Perceptual training activities handbook.* New York: Teachers College Press—Columbia University, 1979.

Vodola, T. *Individualized physical education programs for the handicapped child.* Englewood Cliffs, N.J.: Prentice Hall, Inc., 1973.

Wedemeyer, A. and Cejka, J. *Creative ideas for teaching exceptional children.* Denver, Col.: Love Publishers, 1981.

Weintraub, F. J., Abeson, A., Ballard, J., and La Bor, M. L. (eds.). *Public policy and the education of exceptional children.* Reston, Va.: Council for Exceptional Children, 1976.

Index